"What a marvelo  distinguished schol er.

... Murray Harris has a knack for ...ung crystal clear the meaning of notoriously difficult and misunderstood texts, and for shedding new light on both familiar and overlooked texts that leads to deeper insights. The engaging style makes this book accessible for everyone, but it definitely should be in every minister's and Bible teacher's toolbox to consult when confronted by the questions concerning the meaning of New Testament Scripture."

—DAVID E. GARLAND, professor of Christian Scriptures,
George W. Truett Theological Seminary,
Baylor University, Waco, Texas

"Murray Harris's *Navigating Tough Texts* is a crisp but clear look at many problem texts in the New Testament. In a few pages each, he describes the issue and works through it with the exceptional skill of someone who has taught Scripture for many years. Most texts people wrestle with will be found here, and with solutions that consistently make sense."

—DARRELL BOCK, senior research professor of
New Testament studies, Dallas Theological Seminary

"Murray Harris was my exegesis teacher, and was the finest teacher I ever had. His gentle voice, his probing questions, his expectation of careful scrutiny of the Greek text, and his leading us to compelling answers set for me a model of education I shall never myself achieve. But I know I'm a better reader of the Greek text because of time spent with him. This book is but a taste of his brilliant classroom teaching. You, the reader, are privileged to listen to one of the great Greek minds of our day."

—SCOT MCKNIGHT, Julius R. Mantey Chair of New Testament,
Northern Seminary, Lisle, Illinois

"Nuanced. Concise. And from a veteran teacher. Harris adeptly deals with a host of problem passages in the New Testament. This is a book that will serve pastors for years to come and should be a first stop for a brief solution to some of the most troubling or debated passages in the New Testament."

—PATRICK SCHREINER, associate professor of New Testament language and literature, Western Seminary, Portland, Oregon

"Murray Harris is one of God's wondrous gifts to the whole church—Protestant, Catholic and Orthodox alike. With brilliant insight, remarkable clarity, and theological wisdom, he leads readers through the interpretive alternatives of significant texts in the New Testament. Topics include judging others, the unpardonable sin, anger, the perpetual virginity of Mary, and others that are relevant to church history, theology, evangelism, Christology, and Christian living—all in just a few pages per topic. In short, this is a user-friendly resource that interprets problematic texts for every thinking Christian."

—BRADLEY NASSIF, professor of biblical and theological studies, North Park University, Chicago

"Murray Harris brings his immense expertise in New Testament Greek and his lifetime of study and research to bear on those tough New Testament texts that perplex or confuse us. Packed full of understanding and insight, this volume gives clear, accessible, and wonderfully helpful discussions of these challenging passages. This is a veritable treasure trove of wisdom, inspiration, and spiritual nourishment."

—PAUL TREBILCO, professor of New Testament studies, University of Otago, Dunedin, New Zealand

NAVIGATING TOUGH TEXTS

A Guide to Problem Passages in the New Testament

MURRAY J. HARRIS

NAVIGATING TOUGH TEXTS

**A Guide to Problem Passages
in the New Testament**

LEXHAM PRESS

Navigating Tough Texts: A Guide to Problem Passages in the New Testament
Copyright 2020 Murray James Harris

Lexham Press, 1313 Commercial St., Bellingham, WA 98225
LexhamPress.com

Print ISBN: 9781683593959
Digital ISBN: 9781683593966
Library of Congress Control Number: 2020935381

Unless otherwise noted, Scripture quotations are the author's translation.

See pages 225–26 for copyright information regarding the sources of Scripture quotations.

Lexham Editorial: Derek Brown, Elliot Ritzema, Matthew Boffey, David Bomar
Cover Design: Joshua Hunt
Typesetting: Danielle Thevenaz

CONTENTS

ACTS

PART 2: EPISTLES AND REVELATION

ROMANS

1 CORINTHIANS

PREFACE

I have had the inestimable privilege of reading and teaching the Greek New Testament for over fifty years and of being involved in the translation of the New International Version (NIV) for twenty-five years. The present work is the product of these enriching experiences and includes insights already found in the various books I have written in the field of New Testament studies.

The studies found in this volume have not arisen from reading the New Testament in the many splendid English translations available today, but from an analysis of the text as it was originally written in Greek. Not surprisingly, many of the studies are grammatical in nature. Some relate to word meaning and usage, while others stem from a careful consideration of immediate contexts or background data. As one might expect from any treatment of material from the New Testament, most of the insights are of theological significance, focusing on the person and work of Jesus Christ, and have practical relevance for Christian living.

The studies are designed for pastors, theological students, and thinking Christians who are not afraid to reflect deeply about their faith or to be exposed to some of the intricacies of the Greek language.

All the verses and passages treated in these studies could be classified as either "problem texts" or "key verses," but, as it happens, one could also classify most of them as falling into one of the following categories:

1. Verses that have been significant in church history (e.g., Matt 1:25; 16:18; 28:19–20; Rom 9:5; 2 Pet 1:4; 1 John 5:16–17).

2. Theologically important verses (e.g., Matt 10:29; Mark 10:45; 15:34; Rom 3:25; 10:4; 1 Thess 4:13–15).

3. Evangelistically significant verses (e.g., Luke 14:26; John 3:16, 36; 2 Cor 5:16; Col 2:14; Phlm 17–19a).

4. Verses that contain apparent contradictions (e.g., Acts 21:4; Col 1:24) or special difficulties (e.g., Matt 6:13; 1 Cor 6:18; 15:29) that can be eased or resolved by grammatical considerations.

5. Issues relating to the Christian life (e.g., Matt 7:6; Luke 7:47; Acts 8:16; Rom 1:1; 1 Cor 16:2; Heb 11:34, 37).

6. Key passages that are illuminating for understanding the person of Christ (e.g., John 1:14, 18; 1 Cor 15:20, 23; Rev 7:17) or his claims (e.g., Luke 17:21) or his teaching (e.g., Matt 16:19; John 6:53).

7. Crucial passages about the Holy Spirit (e.g., Mark 3:29; John 3:5; Eph 1:13–14; 5:18–21).

It is my hope and prayer that the insights offered here may prompt in the reader a deeper love of the biblical text, a richer appreciation of its principal themes, and an enhanced devotion to its ultimate Author—and perhaps even a desire to learn Greek!

ACKNOWLEDGMENTS

As indicated in the preface, my teaching and writing career has spanned more than fifty years. It is little surprise, therefore, that in these studies I have sometimes made use of material already published in the following works to which I own the copyright, and which the publishers have kindly given permission for me to use: *From Grave to Glory: Resurrection in the New Testament* (Zondervan, 1990); *The Expositor's Bible Commentary: 1 & 2 Corinthians* (Zondervan, 1995); *The Expositor's Bible Commentary: 2 Corinthians* (Zondervan, 2008); *Prepositions and Theology in the Greek New Testament* (Zondervan, 2012); *Raised Immortal: Resurrection and Immortality in the New Testament* (Eerdmans, 1985); *Colossians and Philemon* (Eerdmans, 1991; Broadman & Holman, 2010); *John* (Broadman & Holman, 2015); *Slave of Christ: A New Testament Metaphor for Total Devotion to Christ* (InterVarsity Press, 1999); *Jesus as God: The New Testament Use of Theos in Reference to Jesus* (Baker, 1992; Wipf & Stock, 2008); *Three Crucial Questions about Jesus* (Baker, 1994; Wipf & Stock, 2008); *John 3:16: What's It All About?* (Wipf & Stock, 2015); *The Seven Sayings of Jesus on the Cross: Their Circumstances and Meaning* (Wipf & Stock, 2016).

Permission has also been granted to use material first published in a multi-authored series where the publisher holds the copyright: *The Second Epistle to the Corinthians: A Commentary on the Greek Text,* The New International Greek Testament Commentary (W. B. Eerdmans Publishing Company, 2005).

Warm thanks are due to Dr. Derek Brown, academic editor at Lexham Press, for his kind acceptance of my manuscript for publication. Also I wish to express my warm gratitude to Elliot Ritzema, one of the editors at Lexham Press, for his professional expertise, patience, and care in preparing the manuscript for publication.

I am privileged to dedicate this volume to my wife, Jennifer, who, in the midst of coping with multiple sclerosis (MS) for over thirty years, has given me her unfailing support in all my teaching and writing.

ABBREVIATIONS

Barclay	*The New Testament: A New Translation. Vol. 1: The Gospels and the Acts of the Apostles* (1968); *Vol 2: The Letters and the Revelation* (1969)
Cassirer	H. W. Cassirer, *God's New Covenant: A New Testament Translation* (1989)
cf.	*confer* (Latin), compare
CSB	Christian Standard Bible (2017)
ESV	English Standard Version Bible (2001)
EVV	English versions of the New Testament
GNT	Good News Translation (1992)
Goodspeed	E. J. Goodspeed, *The New Testament: An American Translation* (1923)
HCSB	Holman Christian Standard Bible (2003)
JB	The Jerusalem Bible (1966)
LXX	Septuagint (Greek version of the OT)
Moffatt	J. Moffatt, *The Moffatt Translation of the Bible* (1935)

NAB	New American Bible: Revised New Testament (1986)
NASB	New American Standard Bible (1977)
NEB	New English Bible (1970)
NIV	New International Version (2011)
NJB	New Jerusalem Bible (1985)
NLT	New Living Translation of the Bible (2013)
NRSV	New Revised Standard Version Bible (1989)
NT	New Testament
OT	Old Testament
REB	Revised English Bible (1990)
RSV	Revised Standard Version of the Bible (1952)
RV	Revised Version (New Testament) (1881)
TCNT	Twentieth Century New Testament (1904)
Weymouth	R. F. Weymouth, *The New Testament in Modern Speech* (1909)

PART 1
GOSPELS AND ACTS

MATTHEW

1: MARY'S PERPETUAL VIRGINITY?
(Matt 1:25)

The doctrine of the perpetual virginity of Mary became official teaching of the Roman Catholic and Greek Orthodox churches at the Council of Chalcedon in AD 451. In the liturgies of these churches Mary is referred to as *aeiparthenos*, "the ever-virgin" or "the perpetual virgin"; that is, she was a virgin before and after the birth of Jesus Christ. But is this view in keeping with Matthew 1:25a: "But he (Joseph) had no sexual relations with her (Mary) until she had given birth to a son"? Does the word "until" imply that sexual relations began after the birth?

After establishing the Davidic ancestry of Joseph, the foster father of Jesus, by tracing the genealogy of Jesus (Matt 1:1–17), Matthew proceeds in 1:18–25 to describe the circumstances of Jesus' birth. Verse 25a states the one qualification (introduced by "But") to the statement "he took Mary home as his wife" (v. 24b): "But he did not know her." "Know" is a euphemism for sexual intercourse. There was an unbroken period of sexual abstinence.

The prepositional phrase *heōs hou* ("until") is a shortened form of "until the time when." When it is preceded by a negated action ("did not know"), there is sometimes an implication that the negated action continued after the point of time indicated. For example, when we read in Genesis 28:15 (in the LXX) "I will certainly *not* leave you *until* I have done everything I have promised you," we may assume that God did not desert Jacob after the fulfillment of his promises.

But far more often we may assume that the *opposite* of the negated action occurs. In Genesis 8:7 (again in the LXX) we read, "The raven went out and did *not* return *until* the water had dried up from the earth." Like the dove subsequently (Gen 8:8–11), the raven apparently did return to the ark. Similarly, in John 13:38, "The rooster will *not* crow *until* (*heōs hou*) you have disowned me three times"; and Matthew 17:9, "Tell *no one* what you have seen *until* (*heōs hou*) the Son of Man has been raised from the dead." In such cases, the negated activity ends at the point of time indicated by the "until" clause, and the implication is that the opposite then occurs.

If Matthew believed in the perpetual virginity of Mary, he would be unlikely to express himself in a way that linguistically leaves open the possibility that Joseph began to have sexual intimacy with Mary after Jesus was born. If he had wished explicitly to assert Mary's permanent virginity, he could have simply added "or from that time on" (*ē apo tote*) after "she had given birth to a son."

Five renderings of the verse, while paraphrastic, highlight its clear implication:

- "while yet refraining from being on terms of intimacy with her until after she had given birth to her son" (Cassirer)

- "but kept her a virgin until she gave birth to a Son" (NASB)

- "but did not know her intimately until she gave birth to a son" (HCSB; similarly CSB)

- "But he did not have sexual relations with her until her son was born" (NLT)

- "But he did not consummate their marriage until she gave birth to a son" (NIV)

See also part 1, ch. 16: "Mary's Perpetual Virginity? (Mark 6:3)."

2: GOD AND SATAN ACTING TOGETHER?
(Matt 4:1; 2 Cor 12:7)

It might sound blasphemous to suggest that God and the devil could act in unison on some project. But there are two noteworthy scriptural passages (among several others, such as Job 1:6–2:7) where it appears that these two persons are acting together, in the sense that they are working at the same time in the experience of the same person, although for completely different purposes.

The first is found in Matthew 4:1. "Then Jesus was led *by* the Spirit into the wilderness in order to be tempted (*peirasthēnai*, an infinitive that expresses purpose) *by* the devil." The "then" looks back to Jesus' baptism by John the Baptist, when the Holy Spirit witnessed the Father's confirmation of Jesus as the Son whom he loves and who brings him consummate pleasure (Matt 3:16–17). One and the same preposition (*hypo*, "by") is used in reference to the two agents, the Spirit and the devil, who were acting on the same person, Jesus. But one is "leading," the other "tempting." It is characteristic of the Spirit to guide, superintend, and direct, always for the person's benefit. It is characteristic of the devil to entice people to sin, always to their detriment (1 Cor 7:5; 1 Thess 3:5).

The Spirit's aim in guiding Jesus into the wilderness was apparently to confront him with the taunts of the devil (Matt 4:3, 5–6, 8–9), so that in rejecting the devil's temptations Jesus would be confirmed in his understanding of his true mission as the Suffering Servant of Yahweh. He would not be satisfying people's desire for physical satisfaction, nor dazzling them by the misuse of his divine prerogatives, nor abandoning his exclusive worship of God in exchange for worldly splendor. We may assume the devil was seeking to deflect Jesus from his "messianic cross-purpose" (in H. E. W. Turner's phrasing). This was to be Satan's aim throughout Jesus' ministry, as when he used Peter to rebuke Jesus for his intention to suffer and die (Matt 16:21–23; see part 1, ch. 18), and later used the passersby at the crucifixion, together with the Jewish hierarchy, to encourage Jesus to come down from the cross and so terminate his messianic suffering (Matt 27:29–43).

The second relevant passage is 2 Corinthians 12:7. In the context of Paul's boasting about the things that showed his weakness (2 Cor 11:30; 12:5), he says, "Because of the extraordinary nature of the revelations (see 2 Cor 12:1–4), then, so that I might not become over-elated, there was given me a thorn in the flesh, a messenger of Satan sent to pummel me so that I might not become over-elated." In Classical Greek, *skolops* often means "stake," but in the regulative Greek OT (the LXX) the term never means "stake," but always "thorn" or "splinter." In all probability, some painful physical ailment is indicated. "A thorn in the flesh was given (*edothē*)" is a theological passive, with God as the implied agent, as is the case with the preceding passive, "caught up," in 12:2 and 4. Yet this God-given thorn was simultaneously "a messenger of Satan," a messenger belonging to Satan or, better, a messenger sent by Satan (a subjective genitive). It is not that God is here working through Satan, but that Satan is active at the same time as God and by his permission (compare Job 1:12; 2:6).

As Paul experienced his "thorn," he discovered it to be both a gift from God and a tool of Satan. It was God's gift because it had the effect of deflating Paul's elation in having been caught up to the third heaven and hearing inexpressible things (2 Cor 12:2–4). Twice in verse 7 Paul notes the divine purpose of the "thorn": "so that I might not become over-elated." The deflation of pride is God's distinctive work (Prov 16:5; Isa 13:11; Matt 23:12; Luke 1:51). The "thorn" was Satan's tool because it inflicted suffering: "to pummel/harass me." The infliction of suffering is Satan's distinctive work (Job 1:8–19; 2:3–7; Luke 13:16; 1 Cor 5:5). Also, if the "thorn" was a recurrent physical malady, it may have sometimes been a hindrance to the spread of the gospel, either by arousing the contempt of Paul's hearers (compare Gal 4:13–14) or by so incapacitating him that travel plans were frustrated (see 1 Thess 2:18). See further part 2, ch. 31.

We can therefore conclude that sometimes, by God's permission, the devil's actions promote or fulfill God's purposes. Since Satan is not omniscient, he will be unaware of God's overarching aims when he, unwittingly, by his machinations serves those aims.

3: HEADING FOR HELLFIRE
(Matt 5:22)

In Matthew 5:21–48 we find six sections, each of which begins with Jesus using some variation of the antithesis, "You have heard that it was said ... but I tell you." In the first part of each antithesis Jesus cites some commandment or well-known saying that was given "to the people long ago" (Matt 5:21, 33). Then, on the basis of his authority as the One who fulfills the Law and the Prophets (= the Scriptures of the OT) (Matt 5:17), Jesus proceeds to point his hearers to the real and ultimate meaning of those earlier commandments or sayings. In all six antitheses, Jesus begins his redefinition with the emphatic "I" (*egō*, "I myself"), "But *I* tell you." Verses 28–41 exemplify the new righteousness of the kingdom of heaven that outstrips the righteousness of the Pharisees and teachers of the law (Matt 5:20) in both quality and quantity.

> You have heard that it was said to those of ancient times, "You shall not murder, and whoever commits murder will be guilty before the court." But I tell you that everyone who is angry with his brother or sister will be guilty before the court. Again, whoever says to his brother or sister, "Raka," will be answerable to the Sanhedrin. And whoever says, "You rebel!" will be guilty enough to go into the hell of fire. (Matt 5:21–22)

Here, in Jesus' redefinition of the nature of murder, there is a gradation in the nature of the offense committed:

- Angry thoughts directed against one's brother or sister that remain unchecked and consequently grow with time lead to murderous acts (this is assumed), acts that are culpable before any court. Anger that is unchecked gives the devil a foothold and leads to sin (see Eph 4:26–27). To reduce the impact of this hard saying of Jesus, some scribes later added the qualifying phrase "without a cause" to "everyone who is angry." This reading is reflected in the KJV but is missing from the original Greek text.

- "Raka" was apparently an Aramaic term of dangerous and provocative abuse, a put-down denoting a lack of intelligence—comparable to the English terms "imbecile," "empty-head," "blockhead," or "numskull."

- To Greek ears, the insult *mōre* would mean "You fool!" But for Jews the term would have meant "You rebel," someone guilty of open rebellion against God, for the similar-sounding Hebrew word *mōreh* denotes willful disobedience (Num 20:10; Ps 78:8; Jer 5:23). In his frustration and anger at the rebellion of the Israelites in the Wilderness of Zin, Moses chided them with the words, "Listen now, *you rebels*, must we bring you water out of this rock?" (Num 20:10). Because of these damning words and his own disobedient action in twice striking the rock, Moses was excluded from entering the promised land (Num 20:11–12).

There is also a gradation in the tribunal that assesses and carries out judgment on the offense. In the first case, the "court" referred to could be the local courts established for each tribe (Deut 16:18), but more probably it is a general reference to legal processes—the judiciary. In the second case, the reference is to the supreme court of Judaism, the Sanhedrin. Finally, Jesus identifies the last and ultimate tribunal as (literally) "the Gehenna of fire," or "hellfire" (KJV). Gehenna was a ravine on the south side of Jerusalem that in the first century was the city's rubbish dump and permanent incinerator. It symbolized the eternal punishment of hell.

In his redefinition of the nature of murder, Jesus teaches that murderous action begins with unchecked anger (see Gen 4:5–8) that may spiral into provocative insult and devilish accusation.

4: "LEAD US NOT INTO TEMPTATION" (Matt 6:13)

Although the Greek of this sixth petition of the Lord's Prayer is unambiguous, its meaning is certainly elusive and has exercised the minds of Christians for centuries. The key word is *peirasmos*, which may mean "temptation" in the sense of "enticement to do wrong." But against this possible meaning, James 1:13 states a truth that admits of no exceptions: "When tempted, no one should say, 'I am being tempted by God.' For God cannot be tempted by evil, and he himself tempts no one." Consequently, it is impossible for God actively to lead people into wrongdoing; he cannot contradict his nature.

This prompts the interpreter to consider the other, more common meaning of *peirasmos*—"trial," "test," or "testing." Thus the NAB translates the verse, "Do not subject us to the final test," the trials or tribulations destined to occur at the end of the age (compare Rev 3:10). But the difficulty here is that the noun *peirasmos* lacks the definite article, which would be expected if the meaning were "the (well-known) final test."

Attention is therefore sometimes given to the preceding verb, "bring/lead into," which is sometimes given a permissive force: "Do not allow us to be brought into trial," or "Don't let us yield to temptation" (NLT). But it is linguistically doubtful that "Do not bring us" can be construed as meaning "Do not let us be brought/yield."

The testing of faith can be beneficial, as Peter makes clear in his first letter. In the midst of various kinds of trials, the proven genuineness of his readers' faith would result in praise, glory, and honor when Jesus Christ was revealed (1 Pet 1:6–7). On the other hand, tested faith can result in the loss of faith, whether temporarily or permanently. Jesus says to Peter, "Simon, Simon, Satan has asked to sift you (plural) as wheat. But I have prayed for you (singular) that your faith may not fail" (Luke 22:31–32a). In Peter's case, this failing of faith was to prove temporary, for Jesus added, "And when you have turned back, strengthen your brothers" (Luke 22:32b). As Peter himself later said, "The Lord knows how to rescue the godly (such as Noah and Lot) from trials" (2 Pet 2:9)—not from the trials themselves, but from the hazards that accompany trials, such as the danger of losing faith.

There is reason to believe that 1 Corinthians 10:13 is Paul's commentary on this sixth petition in the Lord's Prayer. He writes to the Corinthian believers, "No testing has overtaken you except what is common to humankind. But God is faithful, and he will not allow you to be tested beyond what you can bear. But when you are tested, he will also provide a way out so that you may be able to endure it." That is, Paul is saying that God will not bring us into testing that we cannot endure. But then we might ask, "Why make the petition, if we trust God's judgment about the intensity of the testing?" Perhaps the petition is prompted by a humble and commendable self-distrust, since we are fully aware of the possibility of losing faith when immersed in severe testing (see Luke 22:31–32, cited above). Peter showed the opposite of this self-distrust after Jesus predicted that all his disciples would fall away. "For it is written, 'I will strike the shepherd, and the sheep will be scattered'" (Mark 14:27, citing Zech 13:7). Peter's brazen and prideful response was, "Even if all become deserters, I will not. ... Even if I must die with you, I will never disown you"(Mark 14:29, 31).

This use of 1 Corinthians 10:13 to understand the petition is reflected in the fifth-century Eastern *Liturgy of St. James* (cited by F. F. Bruce). After the celebrant recites the Lord's Prayer, he continues, "Yes, O Lord our God, lead us not into temptation which we are not able to bear, but with the temptation grant also the way out, so that we may be able to remain steadfast."

In the second part of the sixth petition we are encouraged to pray, "but deliver us from the evil one." The "but" introduces a contrast between divine testing (v. 13a) and divine deliverance (v. 13b). If *apo tou ponērou* meant simply "from evil," we might have expected "from *every kind of* evil" (as in 2 Tim 4:18). And *ho ponēros* refers to "the evil one" in Matthew 13:19, 38, and probably 5:37, as also in John 17:15. Satan is particularly active when Christians are being tested, using his wiles and stratagems in an effort to bring about their downfall.

We conclude that this sixth petition in the Lord's Prayer is a request for the avoidance of severe testing that would result in the failing of faith and dishonor to the name of God. It should be translated not simply "Do not bring us to hard testing" (GNT), but rather "Do not lead us into unbearable testing."

5: FORGIVE AND FORGET?
(Matt 6:14)

"Just forgive and forget! Let bygones be bygones." Such is the all-too-common advice given to someone struggling with the hurt inflicted by another person's heartless action. But is this always—or ever—the right advice to give to such a person?

To discover the real nature of human forgiveness, it is helpful to consider carefully the characteristics of divine forgiveness.

First, the aim of forgiveness is the restoration of harmonious relations between the offending party and the aggrieved party. Anything short of such a reconciliation is less than the full-orbed sense of forgiveness. Enmity must be removed. "Once you were estranged from God and enemies in your minds because of your evil deeds. But now he has reconciled you ..." (Col 1:21–22).

Second, on both sides there must be an appropriate attitude toward the other. For the offended person, there must be a willingness to forgive. "God our Savior ... wants all people to be saved" (1 Tim 2:3–4; cf. 2 Pet 3:9), that is, to receive the forgiveness of sins. On the part of the person who has committed the wrong, there needs to be an acknowledgment of wrongdoing (= confession), and a turning away from their wrongful attitude and action (= repentance) (Luke 24:47; Acts 2:38; 3:19; 1 John 1:9). In the Bible, forgiveness is never portrayed as automatic. Christ died for all (2 Cor 5:15), but not everyone is forgiven. Confession and repentance are required.

It is clear that when God forgives our sins, he does not "forget" them, for he is omniscient and cannot forget anything. On the contrary, all things—past, present, and future, real and potential—are simultaneously and permanently present to his consciousness. When he forgives our sins, he chooses not to remember them in the sense that in his divine accounting he no longer reckons them to our account. So we read in 2 Corinthians 5:19, "God was in Christ reconciling the world to himself, not holding people's transgressions against them." And centuries earlier the psalmist restated the divine blessing on the person whose transgressions were forgiven by saying, "Blessed is the one whose sin the LORD does not count against them" (Ps 32:1–2 NIV; cf. Isa 43:25; Jer 31:34).

From this analysis of God's forgiveness, we may infer some principles that can guide Christians seeking to know the proper way to deal with wrongs done to them. To pretend that the wrong did not happen or to try to erase it from the memory (= to "forget" it) is pointless, if not impossible. We must aim at reconciliation with the wrongdoer, encouraging them to acknowledge the wrong and repudiate the attitude that prompted the action, and assuring them that we are eager for harmony to be restored—for forgiveness in its full sense.

But forgiveness offered does not always guarantee forgiveness received. When repentance is not present (see Luke 17:3), we must maintain a willingness to forgive and transfer to God responsibility for forgiveness, as Jesus did when he was confronted by unrepentant soldiers who were simply doing their duty but were unaware of the significance of their actions: "Father, forgive them, for they do not realize what they are doing" (Luke 23:34; see part 1, ch. 27).

6: NO PEARLS TO THE PIGS!
(Matt 7:6)

Our English word "judge," like the Greek verb *krinō*, has two totally different senses. It can refer to passing a negative verdict on a person or thing (= "condemn"), or it may refer to exercising careful evaluation over persons or things (= "discern"). For example, we judge laziness to be wrong, but we judge one solution to a problem to be more appropriate than another. We find both types of judgment discussed within one paragraph of the Sermon on the Mount (Matt 7:1–6).

In Matthew 7:1 Jesus states the general principle: "Do not judge, so that you may not be judged." He is not forbidding all "judging," for he himself shortly demands that his followers identify and reject "false prophets" (Matt 7:15–20). Rather, he is requiring his people not to be *judgmental*, quickly coming to a negative verdict without proper, careful analysis. To be constantly judgmental is in reality a misguided effort to assume God's distinctive role as Judge of all people, and such folly exposes oneself to God's infallible and final judgment.

Verses 2–5 provide two applications of the general principle: "For in the same way you judge others, you will be judged, and with the measure you use, it will be measured to you" (Matt 7:2). If we judge harshly, we will be judged harshly. If we judge generously, we will be judged generously. Indirectly, this is a call to be generous in our attitude to others. Then in verses 3–5 Jesus gives an example of misguided judgment. How can a person ever succeed in removing a speck of sawdust from his neighbor's eye (a commendable task in itself) if his own eyesight is impaired by a whole plank? Such hypocrisy is laughable!

But when we resolutely refuse to be censorious, there is sometimes the danger that we will lack the necessary discernment regarding people and things (v. 6):

> Do not give dogs what is sacred;
> do not throw your pearls before pigs.
> If you do, they will trample them under their feet,
> And turn and tear you to pieces.

"Dogs" in Scripture are generally not household pets but scavenging hounds capable of inflicting a severe mauling on humans who frustrate them. "Pigs" represent what is unclean and despised, animals preoccupied with eating whatever is thrown to them. Our initial instinct with verse 6 is to relate the first and third lines, and the second and fourth lines (thus ABAB). But dogs don't trample things underfoot, and pigs don't tear people to pieces. Here we have an instance of the literary technique called "chiasmus" (or "chiasm" in its shortened form), from the Greek word *chiasmos* (reflecting the Greek letter X, *chi*). This is the "placing crosswise" of clauses in an ABBA pattern, so that the first corresponds to the fourth, and the second to the third.

If dogs are given "what is sacred"—perhaps the "holy flesh" of sacrificed animals—they will not recognize its difference from regular scraps of flesh. Having greedily devoured all the meager flesh given them, they will turn on the giver in their frustration or disgust and begin to maul them. Similarly, pigs will fail to see the value of pearls, mistaking them for food, and in their haste to get actual food will scornfully trample the pearls underfoot.

Jesus is calling for discernment and discrimination in giving. Not all people recognize and are ready for "what is sacred," the exquisite value of the gospel of God's kingdom, the "pearl of great value" (Matt 13:45–46). Sometimes silence is called for. Even when Herod Antipas "plied him with many questions," Jesus remained silent (Luke 23:9).

So in addition to avoiding a censorious and condemning attitude toward others, the followers of Jesus must also be perceptive and discriminating in their giving to others. They are, simply, to "judge rightly" (John 7:24).

7: A FATHER WHO KNOWS AND SUPERINTENDS EVERYTHING (Matt 10:29)

A young child is trying valiantly to climb a tree on her own. Her father says, "Without me you won't be able to do that." Instinctively, the child understands "without me" to mean "without my help." All languages have examples of this type of gap (or ellipsis) in sense. The immediate context fills in the gap. So in John 15:5 when Jesus affirms, "Apart from me you can do nothing at all," his disciples will understand him to be saying "Unless you remain in me as the vine, you will be unproductive as branches."

This helps us to understand Jesus' statement in Matthew 10:29. Three times in Matthew 10:26–31 Jesus admonishes the Twelve to refrain from fear, although their persecution is certain (verses 16–25): "Do not be afraid" (vv. 26, 28, 31); "Rather, hold in awe the One who has power to destroy soul and body in hell" (v. 28). Then, to illustrate further the Father's limitless power throughout creation, Jesus asks, "Are not two sparrows sold for a penny?" and affirms, "Yet not one of them will fall to the ground without your Father" (v. 29).

How are we to fill in the elliptical "without your Father" (RV) or "apart from your Father" (ESV, NRSV)? From what we know of God's character, it would not be appropriate in this context to complete the ellipsis with "without your Father's help" or "without your Father's command." Instead, there are three possibilities:

1. "Without your Father's knowledge" (REB) or "without your Father knowing it" (NLT). The next verse (Matt 10:30) speaks of God's complete knowledge, and the parallel passage in Luke 12:6 reads, "Yet not one of these sparrows has escaped God's notice."

2. "Without your Father's consent" (GNT, HCSB, CSB).

3. "Without the knowledge and consent (of your Father)" (BDAG 78a). Interestingly, two papyri, using the same word for "without" (*aneu*), support this double completion of the ellipsis. In one, "the associates (do) nothing without the knowledge and wish of the secretaries." In the other papyrus, "nothing happens without the cognizance and permission of the gods."

Option three, the combination of the first two, fits best. The train of thought in Matthew 10:29–31 is this: if God as Creator knows about and consents to the death of one of his apparently insignificant creatures (the sparrow), how much more is God as an all-knowing Father concerned about his infinitely more valuable children, especially when they face death by martyrdom (see v. 28)? The assumption is that if God knows and consents, he also protects from ultimate harm. Every aspect of the lives of God's children, including the trauma of persecution, is known to him and is included within his providential consent and sovereign care.

8: MISGUIDED EXPECTATIONS
(Matt 11:2–6)

John the Baptist's message was a clarion call to his hearers to repent and produce behavior in keeping with that repentance (Matt 3:6). This would prepare for the arrival of the Messiah, who would bring the blessing of the purifying Holy Spirit but also judgment on the unrighteous (Matt 3:7–12). John likened this judgment to the farmer's role after the harvest when he uses his winnowing fork to toss the grain and chaff into the air so that the heavier grain falls to the ground and then is stored in the granary, while the lighter chaff is scattered by the wind, swept up, and consigned to the fire (Matt 3:12).

When Jesus the Messiah finally arrived, John identified him as the Lamb of God who would take away the sin of the world (John 1:29). This announcement looked forward to what Jesus would accomplish by dying without reference to what he would be doing during his public ministry before his death.

John's own public ministry ended when he was imprisoned by Herod Antipas, tetrarch of Galilee and Perea, because he had confronted Herod about his unlawful act of marrying Herodias, his brother Philip's wife (Mark 6:17–18). As John languished alone in his prison cell—a stark contrast with his earlier life in the freedom of the desert—and heard about Jesus acting mercifully but apparently not enacting judgment, he entertained doubts about Jesus' identity.

So he sent some of his disciples to Jesus with the crucial question, "Are you the Coming One or should we expect someone else?" (Matt 11:2–3). Jesus wisely detained John's deputies long enough for them to witness what Jesus was actually doing as Messiah—healing the blind, the lame, the deaf, and those with leprosy, and proclaiming the good news to the poor (Matt 11:5; cf. Isa 35:5–6; 61:1). John's disciples reported to him all they had seen and heard, along with Jesus' disconcerting final comment, which was a gentle and indirect reproof of John's understanding: "A blessing on anyone who takes no offense at me." Nevertheless, as John's disciples were leaving, Jesus spoke to the crowd in glowing terms about the unparalleled greatness of John (see part 1, ch. 9).

Sadly, John had felt let down by Jesus' actions of mercy; he had taken offense at Jesus. He had expected the Messiah to exercise ruthless judgment, but in fact Jesus had shown gracious kindness. John's expectations were misguided because they had been formed by contemporary hopes rather than by the OT predictions about the signs of the new age: "Then the eyes of the blind will be opened, and the ears of the deaf unstopped. Then the lame will leap like a deer, and the mute tongue shout for joy" (Isa 35:5–6). Also there was Isaiah's prediction about the messianic year of the Lord's favor: "The Spirit of the LORD God is on me, because the LORD has anointed me to proclaim good news to the poor" (Isa 61:1).

This is a salutary warning for us to let our hopes for the future be guided by Scripture rather than by contemporary hopes and expectations.

9: BEING GREATER THAN THE FORERUNNER OF THE MESSIAH (Matt 11:11)

How could any person possibly be greater than the man chosen to announce the imminent arrival of God's long-expected Messiah?

We can begin to answer this question by observing that there are basically two types of greatness. Some, like Prince Charles, heir to the British throne, are "great" owing to their elevated status by birth and privilege. Others, like Mahatma Gandhi, are great or become great because of their exceptional character and service. Greatness in character or service, and greatness in status or privilege.

This distinction is relevant to the interpretation of Jesus' enigmatic saying, "I solemnly tell you: Among those born of women no one greater than John has ever appeared; yet the least in the kingdom of heaven is greater than he" (Matt 11:11). In Luke's version of this saying (7:28), "kingdom of God" replaces "kingdom of heaven." The two expressions are identical in meaning; "heaven" was a common synonym for "God" among Jews.

After issuing John the Baptist a gentle and indirect rebuke in Matthew 11:6 ("A blessing on anyone who takes no offense at me"; see part 1, ch. 8), Jesus immediately addresses the crowd with a series of penetrating questions, all designed to show the unique and superlative character and service of John as the Messiah's forerunner and messenger (Matt 11:7–10). Then follows the enigmatic saying cited above. In this saying, "the person who holds the lowest place" fills out the expression "the lowest/least." But given John's uniqueness as the greatest human being ever, how could "the least" be greater than John?

John's place in God's plan of salvation was like that of Moses, who climbed up to the top of Mount Pisgah and surveyed the promised land across the Jordan River but himself never entered the land (Deut 3:27). Similarly, John the Baptist was at the turning point of two eras—he was at the end of the prophetic line (Matt 11:13) and stood on the threshold of the kingdom of heaven without actually entering it.

The most insignificant person in the kingdom that Jesus was announcing surpasses John in two regards. First, coming after the ministry, death, and resurrection of Jesus, "the least" can witness to Jesus the Messiah more fully and clearly than John ever could. Second, "the least" in the kingdom now enjoys a status and privileges that were foreign to John's experience. For example, we have been adopted into God's family as redeemed individuals; we have received the gift of God's Spirit as a permanent resident in our lives; we have eternal life as a present possession, not only as a future acquisition; and when we pray to God we can invoke the powerful name of his Son as our heavenly advocate and intercessor.

10: VIOLENCE AND THE KINGDOM
(Matt 11:12)

If we needed evidence that the second part of this verse is difficult to understand, we need only read the translations of the verse found in two successive versions of the NIV:

> From the days of John the Baptist until now, the kingdom of heaven has been forcefully advancing, and forceful men lay hold of it. (1984)

> From the days of John the Baptist until now, the kingdom of heaven has been subjected to violence, and violent people have been raiding it. (2011)

We can gain a greater understanding of this verse by paying attention to the voice of the verb *biazō*, "inflict violence/force on." There are three "voices" in ancient Greek: active ("I grasp"), passive ("I am grasped"), and middle ("I grasp for myself"). Sometimes the middle bears an intransitive sense, with no object implied. If here the verb (in the form *biazetai*) is passive in meaning, the sense will be "the kingdom of heaven is being subjected to violence" (= "From ... until now ... has been subjected to violence"). But the verb is normally middle and intransitive; thus "force a way in," "advance forcefully," "make a path with victorious force." Jesus was saying that the kingdom of heaven was now making dramatic inroads into the realm of Satan, with the new age he inaugurated advancing irresistibly on the present age. Crucial in that advance was his proclamation of the good news (Luke 16:16) and his performance of miracles (Matt 12:28).

We find another use of *biazetai* as an intransitive middle in the parallel passage in Luke 16:16. Since the time of the Law, the

Prophets, and John the Baptist, "the good news of the kingdom of
God is being preached, and everyone is forcing their way into it"
(NIV), or "everyone tries to enter it by force" (NRSV). Here the "force"
presumably refers to the determined, energetic, and enthusiastic
action of all those seeking to enter the kingdom ("everyone is eager
to get in," NLT). Compare Luke 13:24, "Make every effort to enter
through the narrow door."

But whereas this verb *biazetai* as an intransitive middle bears a
positive sense, its cognate noun *biastai*, used later in the verse, has
strongly negative connotations: "predatory men," "violent people."
The precise identity of these "violent people" is unclear, but various
proposals have been made:

- Jewish antagonists, especially the Pharisees, about whom
  Jesus said, "You shut the door of the kingdom of heaven
  in people's faces. You do not go in yourselves, nor will
  you let those enter who are trying to do so" (Matt 23:13)

- Herod Antipas, who had earlier imprisoned John the
  Baptist (Matt 14:3; Mark 6:17)

- Spiritual powers hostile to God, working through human
  agents

- The Zealots, who wanted to eradicate Roman rule from
  Judea. In AD 6 the revolt of one such "violent man," Judas
  the Galilean, was crushed by the Romans (Acts 5:37)

Regardless of who these people were, their aim was to create
devastating hindrances to the advance of the kingdom. They were
trying (*harpazousin*) to plunder the kingdom, to claim it for themselves. I therefore suggest that Matthew 11:12 should be rendered,
"From the days of John the Baptist until now, the kingdom of heaven
has been forcefully advancing, and violent people have been trying
to raid it."

11: PETER AND THE ROCK
(Matt 16:18)

When Peter confesses that Jesus is "the Messiah, the Son of the living God," Jesus assures him that this confession did not result from some natural insight but came to him as a revelation from God (Matt 16:16–17). To this divine revelation about his person, Jesus in turn adds a second revelation, this time about his work. He himself would build his own community of believers that would withstand the power of death and evil (Matt 16:18).

Jesus prefaces this second revelation with an address to Peter: "I also say to you, 'You are Peter (Greek *petros*), and on this rock (Greek *petra*) I will build my church." Some point out that if Jesus was speaking in his native Aramaic, the same word *kepa'* would have stood in both places in the wordplay, since that word can mean both "stone" and "rock." But we must work with the verse as it stands in Greek, not with any supposed Aramaic original. In Greek, *petros* refers to a piece of rock, a stone (a *petrotomos* is a "stonecutter"). *Petra*, on the other hand, means "rock," "crag," or "bedrock" (of some massive rock formation, as in the city of Petra), with the adjective *petraios* meaning "rocky." It would seem, therefore, that there is an intended wordplay on the root *petr-* and a contrast between a stone and a rock.

But what is the "bedrock" or firm foundation on which Jesus would build his church? There are two main suggestions.

First, there is *Peter himself* as (1) the leader and representative of all the apostles ("first among equals"), or (2) as a representative of the church to be formed by Jesus, or (3) as the first confessor of Jesus as Messiah, the Son of God. (On this last view, Peter was first in time, but not in status.) However, we should observe that Jesus does not say "on you" or "on you as a rock," and it could be questioned whether so stately an edifice as a messianic community, erected by the Messiah himself, would be built on such an insecure foundation as a mere mortal. Moreover, Peter himself later spoke of Christ as the "cornerstone" of the church, and all believers, including himself, as "living stones" that form a "spiritual temple," the church (1 Pet 2:4–6).

The second and better option is *the messianic confession of Peter* recorded in verse 16. The difference in meaning between *petros* and *petra* described above suggests that the two words probably refer to different things. And the use of "this" with "rock" (*petra*) is a shift from a personal statement ("you") to an impersonal statement ("this rock"). Note, too, in favor of this option, that the earliest and foundational confession made by Christians was in fact "Jesus is the Messiah" (see Acts 18:5, 28; cf. Acts 2:36; 9:22; 17:3).

12: "BINDING" AND "LOOSING" (Matt 16:19; 18:18)

As the first confessor of the messiahship of Jesus (Matt 16:16), Peter was entrusted with "the keys of the kingdom of heaven" (Matt 16:19a), that is, the privilege and responsibility of "proclaiming the good news of the kingdom" (Matt 4:23). In fulfilling this role, he was to use these "keys" to unlock the kingdom for certain people ("loosing") and shut it up against others ("binding").

Among the Jewish rabbis, "binding" and "loosing" were idiomatic terms to denote certain types of conduct that were either prohibited ("bound") or permitted ("loosed"), forbidden or authorized. Jesus used these two categories when he explained to Peter what was involved in using the "keys." "Whatever you bind on earth is already bound in heaven, and whatever you loose on earth is already loosed in heaven" (Matt 16:19 HCSB; similarly CSB). The same guarantee is repeated in Matthew 18:18 in reference to all Jesus' disciples (see Matt 18:1), for the singular "you" in 16:19 (three times) becomes the plural "you" in 18:18 (three times).

Whenever evangelists affirm that all those who repent and believe in Jesus Christ have their sins forgiven, they are declaring that such people are "loosed" and have entered the kingdom. In this declaration, they are dramatizing on earth the standing verdict that heaven (= God) has already made. Similarly, those who remain unrepentant unbelievers are "bound," and the kingdom is shut against them.

Heaven has already affirmed this truth, for "salvation is found in no one else" than Jesus the Cornerstone (Acts 4:11–12).

If this interpretation seems to stumble over the "whatever" (the neuter relatives *ho ean* in 16:19 and *hosa ean* in 18:18), it should be noted that the neuter often refers to a class of people, not things or in this case earthly declarations.

It is strong motivation to know that when we assure people that all who surrender themselves to Jesus Christ as Savior and Lord gain eternal life, that assurance already has divine approval. We are declaring on earth a fixed heavenly decree.

However, it is certainly possible that both these verses should be rendered "Whatever you bind on earth will be bound in heaven, and whatever you loose on earth will be loosed in heaven" (NIV, NRSV; similarly KJV, NASB, GNT, NAB, ESV). That is, God will confirm or ratify the earthly "binding" or "loosing."

There are two clear examples of this divine ratification in the NT. When Peter recognized the carefully planned deception of Ananias and Sapphira in pretending that their gift was the whole of the proceeds of the sale of their property, he accused them of lying to God under the influence of Satan (Acts 5:1–4). Their sudden deaths amounted to God's dramatic confirmation of Peter's rebuke (Acts 5:5–10). With news of sexual immorality in the Corinthian church, Paul directed the assembled congregation to hand the man guilty of incest over to Satan "for the destruction of the flesh" (1 Cor 5:1–5). In this case, God's ratification of Paul's and the church's judgment would come through the agency of Satan.

But it is not the case that all decisions made by church leaders, whatever their nature, will automatically gain divine approval. The direction of the Holy Spirit must be sought and received. For example, the verdict of the apostles and elders in Jerusalem concerning the conditions under which Gentile believers could be received as fellow believers was issued as a decision that "seemed good to the Holy Spirit and to us" (Acts 15:28). Similarly, in 1 Corinthians 5:4,

"When you are assembled and I am with you in spirit, and the power of our Lord Jesus is present ..."

13: FORGIVENESS MAY PREVENT DIVORCE
(Matt 19:9)

One party in an established Christian marriage has just discovered that their spouse has been involved in prolonged unfaithfulness. After the initial mutual shock of discovery, the innocent party begins to investigate their options. Their thoughts will turn instinctively to the Scriptures for guidance, and especially Jesus' words in the Sermon on the Mount: "Anyone who divorces his wife, except for sexual immorality, causes her to commit adultery, and anyone who marries the divorced woman commits adultery" (Matt 5:32).

Does "except for sexual immorality" (NIV) give the innocent party the right to initiate divorce proceedings with spiritual impunity? Further, the longer treatment of divorce in Matthew 19:1–19 seems to add another right for the innocent party: "Anyone who divorces his wife, except for sexual immorality (NIV, HCSB), and marries another woman commits adultery" (Matt 19:9). Does "except for sexual immorality" give the innocent party the right to remarry with spiritual impunity?

Although the Greek behind the phrase "except for sexual immorality" differs in these two passages, the meaning is the same: "except on the basis of (sexual) immorality." The difference is in form, not substance. Most commentators (rightly) agree that the immorality referred to is adultery.

But in this situation, should we be discussing rights or investigating preferred remedies?

When Jesus' disciples asked him, "Why did Moses command that a man give his wife a certificate of divorce and send her away?" he replies, "Moses permitted you to divorce your wives because your hearts were hard. But it was not this way from the beginning" (Matt 19:7–8). The implication is clear. Divorce proceedings are not necessary where hearts are not hard. That is, where there is a willingness to forgive on the part of the "innocent party," there is an alternative to the endless pain of divorce.

Once more (see part 1, ch. 5), we are brought back to the nature of Christian forgiveness. It is not a case of turning a blind eye to the sin committed as if it never occurred and endeavoring to forget it. Rather, it involves, first of all, the open acknowledgment of the sin and of the seriousness of the offense in light of marital vows of purity and all the persons affected. This will lead to a full confession of guilt before God and to one's spouse. Evidence of genuine repentance is seen in a frank discussion between husband and wife of remedies to be put in place to reinvigorate mutual affection and love and to prevent any recurrence of the wrongdoing. Only then can the offended party say with wholehearted commitment to the other, "I forgive you!" See further part 2, ch. 13.

14: "GO AND MAKE DISCIPLES"
(Matt 28:19–20)

Misinformation is rife about the Greek grammar of these two crucial verses containing Jesus' Great Commission. We are told, first, that there is no command to "go," only a participle that means "as you go." But in the Greek language, when someone wants to express two commands in succession, such as "Go and see," they usually decide which is the main command and express that by the imperative (= command) mood, while using a participle to express the subsidiary command. Thus, literally, "Having gone, see" = "Go and see." We actually see this twice in Matthew 28:

Go (*poreutheisai*, aorist participle) and tell (*eipate*, aorist imperative) (Matt 28:7)

Go (*poreuthentes*, aorist participle) and make disciples (*mathēteusate*, aorist imperative) (Matt 28:19)

We can infer that the command to "make disciples," being in the imperative mood, is more important than the "going," which is of secondary significance. Also, we should note that if the sense had been "as you go," the present participle, not the aorist participle, would have been used, to express action coincident with the making of disciples.

It is also sometimes claimed that because "make disciples" is in the aorist tense, it implies a single action. Not so. All the aorist signifies here is that the whole process of making disciples is being considered as a unit.

This one Greek sentence (vv. 19–20) continues with two present participles—"baptizing" (*baptizontes*) and "teaching" (*didaskontes*)—that are grammatically dependent on the main verb, "make disciples." They do not specify two results of the formation of disciples, but at a minimum they describe two simultaneous actions that accompany disciple-making. More probably, they depict the two primary but separate means, but not necessarily the only means, by which obedient disciples will fulfil Jesus' basic command to make disciples.

It is precisely as Jesus' disciples carry out his command that they can claim his perpetual empowering presence: "And remember, I am right with you all the time, right up to the end of the present age" (v. 20).

MARK

15: THE UNPARDONABLE SIN
(Mark 3:29; Luke 12:10)

Our English word "blaspheme" derives from two Greek words—*blaptō* ("harm," "damage") and *phēmē* ("reputation"). To blaspheme is to injure the reputation of God by slanderous speech about him, or by misusing his name (Exod 20:7; Deut 5:11). Originally blasphemy also involved the repudiation of the political and social order that God commanded and upheld. But today in the Western world, "blasphemy" has been watered down to the offense of religious hatred, and in particular "hate speech."

Jesus' teaching about the unforgivable sin may well have been given on more than one occasion. In Mark's Gospel the setting was the arrival in Galilee of experts in the Jewish law from Jerusalem who were investigating Jesus' work of exorcism, the expelling of demons from demon-possessed sufferers. Their bizarre conclusion was that Jesus himself had "an impure spirit" and was under the control of Beelzebul, the prince of demons (Mark 3:22, 30)! After pointing out the absurdity of this conclusion (Mark 3:23–26), Jesus speaks of sins and slanderous utterances that God could forgive, and one sin that was impossible to forgive—the attributing of the works of Jesus to the activity of Satan: "Truly I tell you, people can be forgiven all their sins and whatever blasphemies they utter. But whoever blasphemes against the Holy Spirit will never have forgiveness; they are guilty of an eternal sin" (Mark 3:28–29). In reality, it was by the Spirit of God that Jesus was expelling demons (Matt 12:28), but these visitors from headquarters in Jerusalem were so perverted and hardened in their

25

spiritual outlook that they saw only darkness where there was light, and evil where there was only good.

The context of Jesus' saying is different in Luke. Jesus has been warning his disciples against hypocrisy, reminding them that everything purportedly concealed will ultimately be revealed (Luke 12:1–3). He then admonishes them to fear God, not their adversaries (Luke 12:4–7), before continuing, "Whoever disowns me before others will be disowned before the angels of God. And everyone who speaks a word against the Son of Man will be forgiven, but the person who blasphemes against the Holy Spirit will not be forgiven" (Luke 12:9–10). That is, to deny on earth that one belongs to Jesus, the Son of Man (v. 10a), has eternal consequences before the heavenly tribunal. If verse 10b looks back to verse 9, to disown Jesus—to become apostate—is to blaspheme against the Holy Spirit.

In recording the words of Jesus about the unpardonable sin, Mark and Luke are complementing, not contradicting, each other. To have an attitude implacably opposed to God (Mark) or to commit apostasy (Luke) are simply two expressions of the permanent and irremediable rejection either of God himself (Mark) or of a faith in God once held (Luke), in spite of the gracious overtures of the Holy Spirit.

Did Peter commit the unforgivable sin when he disowned Jesus three times (Luke 22:54–62)? No, because he "turned back" and strengthened his brothers (Luke 22:32). What of Ananias and Sapphira, apparently believers, who lied to the Holy Spirit and conspired to test the Spirit of the Lord (Acts 5:3,9)? All we know for certain is that there was immediate divine judgment on them both for their conspiracy of deceit (Acts 5:5, 10), but we cannot know their eternal destiny. It is said of Simon the sorcerer the he "believed and was baptized" (Acts 8:13). But when he tried to bribe Peter and John so that he could (magically?) convey the gift of the Holy Spirit, Peter responded with the rebuke, "May your money perish with you! ... your heart is not right before God" (Acts 8:20-2). Simon's feeble response to Peter's directive to repent (Acts 8:22, 24) suggests he remained "captive to sin" (Acts 8:23) as a hardened unbeliever who lacked God's forgiveness.

Finally, was Paul guilty of the "eternal sin" because of his systematic persecution of Christians (Acts 9:1) that even involved efforts to make them blaspheme (Acts 26:11)? No, because he "acted in ignorance and unbelief" (1 Tim 1:13) and embraced the light of the gospel when it confronted him (Acts 9:3–9; 2 Cor 4:6).

In sum, blasphemy against the Holy Spirit is unforgivable, not because God is unwilling to forgive, but because the repentance that is the necessary precondition for God's forgiveness is absent. The heart has become so hardened that no need for repentance is recognized, and so no request for forgiveness is offered. Strangely, to have a fear that you have committed the unpardonable sin is evidence that you have not done so, for those who have are unaware of their sin or unconcerned about it.

16: MARY'S PERPETUAL VIRGINITY?
(Mark 6:3)

In part 1, ch. 1, we saw a slight degree of ambiguity in Matthew 1:25 regarding the question of the "perpetual virginity" of Mary, the mother of Jesus. But all ambiguity disappears if it can be shown that Jesus had siblings.

After Jesus had taught in the synagogue at Nazareth, his hometown, many expressed amazement at his learning, wisdom, and miracles (Mark 6:1–2). They asked, "Isn't this the carpenter? Isn't this Mary's son and the brother of James, Joses, Judas, and Simon? And aren't his sisters here with us?" (Mark 6:3).

During church history there have been three main interpretations of the NT references to the "brothers" of Jesus:

1. They were the children of Joseph by a previous marriage, Mary being his second wife. This is called the "Epiphanian view" after Epiphanius, bishop of Salamis. They were Jesus' stepbrothers, having no common biological parent, but became the "relatives" of Jesus through Joseph's second marriage.

2. They were cousins of Jesus. This is called the "Hieronymian" view after Jerome, the biblical scholar and translator.

3. They were half-brothers of Jesus, having one common biological parent (Mary), and Jesus was the eldest son in the family. This is called the "Helvidian view" after Helvidius, a fourth-century contemporary of Jerome.

The issue relates to the meaning of the Greek word *adelphos*. In the OT, it can on occasion refer to male "relatives" of various degrees of genealogical closeness (e.g., Gen 13:8; 29:12). But in the NT, it has three main uses in the singular or plural:

1. A member of the Christian community, a "brother" in Christ (e.g., Rom 16:23; 1 Cor 1:1).

2. Those with a close spiritual affinity with Jesus (e.g., Matt 12:49–50; 25:40; Mark 3:33–35; Luke 8:21; Heb 2:11–12), especially his disciples (e.g., Matt 28:10; John 20:17).

3. Males from the same womb of a particular woman (Matt 12:46–47; 13:55; Mark 3:31–32; 6:3; Luke 8:19–20; John 2:12; 7:3, 5, 10; Acts 1:14; 1 Cor 9:5; Gal 1:19).

If the brothers of Jesus were simply his male relatives, there was a Greek word to convey this—*syngenēs*, meaning "relative," "someone belonging to the same family," "kinsman" (used in Mark 6:4). If the brothers were simply cousins, again a special word was available—*anepsios*, "cousin" (used in Col 4:10 in reference to Mark, the cousin of Barnabas).

Perhaps the strongest argument for believing that Jesus' brothers were in fact his blood brothers is that this is the most natural way to understand the term "brother" when there are associated references to a named mother, her son, and his sisters, as in Mark 6:3 (see also Acts 1:14). Even when references to literal motherhood or sisterhood are absent in the immediate context, the initial assumption must be that "brother(s)" refers to a physical relationship, as when the text speaks of "his brothers" (John 7:5) or "the Lord's brother(s)" (1 Cor 9:5; Gal 1:19).

17: FEED THE CHILDREN FIRST!
(Mark 7:27)

According to Mark 7:24–30, Jesus left Jewish territory and entered Syrian Phoenicia, a Gentile region to the northwest of Galilee, probably to withdraw from public gaze and recuperate. This temporary withdrawal was interrupted by the urgent request of a woman from the area who pleaded with Jesus to deliver her daughter from a demonic spirit.

In order to stimulate the woman's faith, and perhaps with a twinkle in his eye (as at least one commentator has suggested), Jesus responds provocatively with a remark that at first sight is racist and offensive: "You must first of all allow the children to be fed, for it is not right to take the children's food and toss it to their dogs." In this stunning metaphor that reflects the prevailing Jewish outlook on Gentiles, the children of the household represent the Jews and the "dogs" represent the Gentiles. This sentiment of "children first!" is similar to Romans 1:16, where Paul affirms that the gospel is to be offered "first to the Jew, then to the Gentile." If "salvation is from the Jews" (John 4:22), it is appropriate that it is offered to them first.

The woman's quick-witted reaction was swift and incisive, yet respectful. "True, good sir, but even the dogs under the table feed on the children's leftovers."

There are two Greek words for "dog" used in the New Testament. *Kyōn* is an unclean dog, often a detestable wild scavenger found on the street, such as the dogs that licked Lazarus's sores in the parable recorded in Luke 16:19–31. The other word, twice used in our story, is *kynarion*, a smaller domesticated dog that children could play with and that would eat the meal scraps tossed to them from the household table.

For this woman, the "later" time, implied by Jesus' "first of all," had already arrived. Gentiles also could now receive God's mercies. Jesus agrees with the woman's insight ("Because of your reply ..."). He saw in her response evidence of a real and deep faith that asks for mercy, which he immediately rewarded by healing her daughter—at a distance (see v. 28 in the parallel passage, Matt 15:21–28). Remarkably, here we have Jesus, a Jewish man, helping a Gentile woman in Gentile territory! Whenever persistent faith is present, Jesus invariably responds with warm acceptance, sometimes intervening miraculously.

In his missionary strategy, Paul regularly proclaimed the gospel to the Jew first, as he moved from one synagogue to another, but in the response to the gospel it was often the Gentile first and then the Jew. And he foresaw a time when Gentile response would trigger a major Jewish turning to God (Rom 11:25–27).

18: "GET AWAY BEHIND ME, SATAN!"
(Mark 8:33)

Mark records three predictions made by Jesus of his forthcoming suffering, death, and resurrection: 8:31; 9:30–32; and 10:32–34. The first follows immediately after Peter's declaration at Caesarea Philippi of Jesus' messiahship (Mark 8:27–30).

After the second prediction, we read that the disciples "did not understand what he meant and were afraid to ask him about it" (Mark 9:32). Apparently they did grasp the general import of the prediction, ignoring the promise of the resurrection, for it prompted their spokesman, Peter, to offer some advice to Jesus. Gently taking Jesus' arm, Peter took him aside, perhaps out of earshot of the other disciples. The colorful verb *proslambanomai* ("take aside") is also used in Acts 18:26 when Priscilla and Aquila quietly took Apollos aside (the NIV has the paraphrase "invited him to their home") and explained the way of God to him more accurately (see part 1, ch. 54).

Said Peter to Jesus, "Mercy on you, Lord! This will never happen to you" (Matt 16:22). The expression *hileōs soi* literally means "Mercy on you," an abbreviation of "May God be merciful to you!" = "May God mercifully spare you from this!" Some English versions render it as "God forbid it!" (GNT) or "Far be it from you!" (ESV) or "Oh no, Lord!" (HCSB, CSB).

Jesus' response to Peter was even more drastic. "Get away behind me, Satan!" Whereas Peter's rebuke of Jesus was given privately, Jesus' rebuke of Peter was delivered in front of all the disciples: "Turning (to confront Peter face-to-face) and looking at his disciples, Jesus rebuked Peter" (Mark 8:33). It was a message relevant to them all, a message they all needed to hear, since Peter had simply been their spokesman (as so often).

The term "Satan" (*ho satanas*) was originally a common noun meaning "adversary," but it became a proper name or title for "the accuser/slanderer" (*ho diabolos*) in the heavenly court, and more generally the archenemy of God and his people (2 Cor 11:14–15; 1 Thess 2:18) who incites humans to sin. In the present case, Satan uses Peter's natural human instincts—abhorrence at the prospect of a friend dying a cruel and premature death—to tempt Jesus to abandon his God-given task as the Suffering Servant destined to die for his people (Isa 42:1–4; 52:13–53:12). As Jesus said, Peter was viewing matters from a purely human and popular perspective, not from God's perspective (Mark 8:33b). Peter the "rock" (*petros*) had become a "stumbling block" (*skandalon*) to Jesus (Matt 16:18, 23).

This temptation of Jesus to relinquish his divine vocation revived his wilderness temptation to embrace alternative ways of pleasing God and winning human praise (Matt 4:1–10). At that time he dismissed Satan with similar words, "Away from me, Satan!" (Matt 4:10). It was a temptation that would recur in different ways throughout his public ministry, only to resurface during his final hours: "Let him come down now from the cross, and we will believe in him" (Matt 27:42; see part 1, ch. 2).

It is sadly possible for any one of Jesus' followers to be God's mouthpiece one moment (Mark 8:29) and Satan's mouthpiece the next (Mark 8:32–33).

19: A SUBSTITUTIONARY RANSOM
(Mark 10:45)

On one occasion, ten of Jesus' inner circle of disciples were jealously indignant with the brothers James and John because they had requested prime positions in Jesus' coming glory. This prompted Jesus to call all the Twelve together and teach them that true greatness consists of slave-like service to all (Mark 10:35–44). Then he added, "For even the Son of Man did not come to be served, but to serve, and to give his life a ransom for many (*lytron anti pollōn*)" (Mark 10:45).

"Son of Man" was Jesus' favorite self-designation. With its background in Daniel 7:9–14, it was Jesus' indirect way of declaring his messiahship without fostering false messianic hopes that involved the overthrow of the Roman overlords and their Jewish collaborators.

Everyone in the first century AD would have known about the emancipation of a slave or the freeing of a prisoner by the payment of a *lytron*, "the purchase price for release." The slave or prisoner was set free because a substitutionary payment had been made. The preposition *anti*, as usual, means "for" in the sense of "in the place of" or "instead of." What the word *lytron* already implies, *anti* simply reinforces—the idea of substitution or vicariousness.

A close parallel to the expression *lytron anti* ("a ransom for") is found in the Jewish historian Josephus (*Antiquities* 14.107–8). Eleazar the priest gave the Roman general Crassus a gold bar "as a ransom for all (*lytron anti pantōn*)" the ornaments of the temple in the hope that Crassus would keep his oath and not remove anything else out of the temple. That is, the gold bar was offered "instead of" the ornaments.

Psalm 49:7–9 throws further light on the ransom concept. "No one can redeem the life of another or give to God a ransom for them—the ransom for a life is costly, no payment is ever enough—that they should live on forever and not see decay." What a person cannot do for anyone else—redeem someone's life by paying God a costly ransom—the Son of Man, Jesus, did for "many" when he redeemed their forfeited lives through the sacrifice of his own. Their impotence was matched by his competence. The "many" in Mark 10:45 are not opposed to the "few," but are "all" as opposed to "one" (compare Mark 14:24; Rom 5:15, 19).

Paul clearly had in mind Jesus' ransom saying in Mark when he referred to "the man Christ Jesus, who gave himself a ransom for all people (*antilytron hyper pantōn*)" (1 Tim 2:6). The apostle seems to have coined the word *antilytron*, "vicarious ransom," to stress the substitutionary nature of Christ's self-surrender. The preposition *hyper* ("for") is wider than *anti*, expressing both representation ("on behalf of") and substitution ("instead of"). The "many" is rightly understood as "all." Christ acted on behalf of everyone when he took their place.

Thus, the general meaning of the ransom saying may be expressed this way: In service to God, Jesus surrendered his life and died as "a ransom in place of many" whose lives were unconditionally forfeited to God because of their sin. These were released from indebtedness to God and therefore from guilt by Jesus' payment of their ransom. See further part 2, ch. 27.

20: AN ACTED PARABLE ABOUT A FIG TREE
(Mark 11:12–14, 20–25)

One likely date for the crucifixion of Jesus is Friday, April 6, AD 30. If we assume this chronology, we can tentatively reconstruct Jesus' movements for the first part of his final week, including his cursing of the fig tree and its subsequent withering.

- Sunday, April 1: Jesus enters Jerusalem on a colt and then returns to Bethany with the Twelve (Mark 11:1–11).

- Monday, April 2: While returning to Jerusalem, "Jesus was hungry. Seeing in the distance a fig tree in leaf, he went to see whether perhaps he would find fruit on it. When he reached it, he found nothing but leaves, because it was not the season for figs. Then he said to the tree in reply,

'May no one ever eat fruit from you again.' His disciples heard him say this" (Mark 11:12–14). Then followed the cleansing of the temple and a return to Bethany (Mark 11:15–19).

- Tuesday, April 3: As the disciples walked back to Jerusalem, they were amazed that the fig tree had completely withered so quickly (Matt 21:20; Mark 11:20–21). This prompted Jesus to teach them about the potency of faith in prayer (Mark 11:22–25).

In the life of a Palestinian fig tree, leaves appear in late March along with small knobs (called *taqsh*) that anticipate the real figs that arrive about six weeks later in early May. If there are leaves without these knobs ("nothing but leaves"), this is a sure sign the tree would be fruitless and was virtually dead. So the curse Jesus pronounced on the tree simply confirmed what was inevitable. It is certainly not the case that Jesus arbitrarily cursed a healthy tree in frustration at not finding fruit on it to satisfy his pressing hunger!

We should see Jesus' action as an acted parable, with the withered fig tree a symbol of the unresponsiveness of Jerusalem and Israel as a whole to the presence and message of God's Messiah. It was precisely because Jerusalem "did not recognize the time of God's coming" that Jesus wept over the city and predicted its violent downfall (Luke 19:41–44).

This acted parable matches Jesus' spoken parable about the fruitless fig tree recorded in Luke 13:6–9. A property owner visited his vineyard three years in succession hoping to find fruit on his fig tree, only to be frustrated on each occasion. So he directed his vinedresser to cut the tree down because it was wasting valuable space. The message of this parable, and the acted parable during Jesus' final week, is that judgment follows unproductivity.

21: "ELOI, ELOI, LEMA SABACHTHANI?"
(Mark 15:34)

This is the fourth of the seven sayings of Jesus on the cross. It was spoken "in a loud voice," probably slowly, given the great difficulty of uttering intelligible speech with a parched mouth and swollen tongue at the end of six hours of unspeakable agony. It was also spoken deliberately, for under intense emotion Jesus was quoting from the Scriptures (Ps 22:1) that he regarded as holy and authoritative.

It is uncertain whether Jesus spoke this in his native Aramaic (as Mark's Greek transliteration might suggest), in biblical Hebrew (as Matthew's Greek transliteration might suggest), or in a mixed Hebrew-Aramaic form. But the meaning of the Greek is clear: "My God, my God, why have you abandoned/forsaken me?" The doubly compounded Greek verb used in this "cry of dereliction" is *egkataleipō*, "forsake," "desert," "abandon." In derivation, it denotes the complete (*kata*) desertion (*leipō*) of someone who is in (*en*) a situation where aid is urgently needed.

The evidence that Jesus was abandoned by God was God's apparent "departure," his being "far off" as the psalmist expressed it (Ps 22:11, 19), and his apparent failure to intervene with support (contrast Ps 22:11) through the myriad of angels that Jesus himself had so recently spoken of (Matt 26:53). And it was not merely that Jesus *felt* deserted by God, as the psalmist had been (Ps 22:11, 19–21); in reality he *was* deserted by God. All active communion between Father and Son was suspended, although God was still Jesus' God ("my God"). God had actually hidden his face (cf. Ps 22:24) from his dearly loved Son, the constant joy of his heart. Given the fact that constant, undisturbed, blissful fellowship with the Father was the essence of Jesus' existence on earth, how can humans, even redeemed humans, begin to understand his agonizing spiritual trauma in being abandoned by his Father?

Thus far Jesus had been on the cross for about six hours (about 9 a.m. to 3 p.m.), with the darkness occurring from noon "until the ninth hour" (= 3 p.m.) as three Evangelists explicitly mention (Matt 27:45; Mark 15:33; Luke 23:44). Apparently, the period of abandonment coincided with the three-hour period of darkness.

But why would a holy God abandon his dearly loved and holy Son, even temporarily, especially since Jesus had earlier reassured his readers, "I am not alone, for my Father is with me" (John 16:32)? Two scriptural passages provide an adequate answer: 2 Corinthians 5:21 (see part 2, ch. 27) and Galatians 3:13. In both verses, God's abandonment of Christ is said to be "for us" (*hyper hēmōn*). When the Father totally identified his sinless Son with the sin of sinners (2 Cor 5:21) and so abandoned him, and when Christ endured the divine curse that rightly belonged to lawbreakers (Gal 3:13) and so was abandoned by God, the action was both "on our behalf" and "in our place." Substitution as well as representation was involved.

This is one of the most profound mysteries of the universe, yet the result of God's action is unambiguous. Christ was forsaken by God for a temporary but agonizingly long period on the cross so that believers may never be separated from God, either during life or after death (Rom 8:35–39; Heb 13: 5–6). As Elizabeth Barrett Browning wrote in her poem "Cowper's Grave,"

> Yea, once Immanuel's orphaned cry His universe hath shaken—
> It went up single, echoless, "My God, I am forsaken."
> It went up from the Holy's lips amid His lost creation,
> That, of the lost, no son should use those words of desolation.

LUKE

22: A DAUNTING JOURNEY
(Luke 2:1–6)

As Luke describes the circumstances of the birth of Jesus, he explicitly mentions only one reason for Joseph's decision to leave Nazareth in Galilee with Mary and set off for Bethlehem. He was obliged to comply with the edict of the Roman emperor, Caesar Augustus, that required people throughout the Roman Empire to be registered for taxation purposes. For such a census, it was usual to return to one's ancestral town. Joseph went to Bethlehem, the city of David (1 Sam 17:12, 58), because he belonged to the house and family line of David (Luke 2:1–4).

However, another reason why Joseph thought it necessary to return to Bethlehem at this time may have been his desire to spare Mary the emotional stress caused by hurtful gossip about her pregnancy that was probably circulating at Nazareth.

Mary was betrothed to Joseph (Luke 2:5); that is, she was "pledged to be married to him" (NIV) or "promised in marriage to him" (GNT). Betrothal was a formal marriage contract so that the betrothed couple were legally "husband" and "wife" (Deut 22:23–24). A betrothed woman was a "widow" if her fiancé died, and a betrothal could be dissolved only through death or a formal divorce. Betrothal became marriage in the full sense when the woman left her parents' home and commenced domestic and sexual relations with her husband (Matt 1:20, 24–25).

How far advanced Mary was in her pregnancy at this time, we do not know. We can infer she was beyond her first trimester, because after learning of her imminent conception (Luke 1:31, 35) Mary had stayed with her relative Elizabeth "for about three months" before returning home to Nazareth (Luke 1:56). On the other hand, it is extremely unlikely that Joseph would have risked taking a full-term woman on a prolonged journey. After all, the journey from Nazareth in the north of Palestine to Bethlehem in the south covers some ninety miles, and for fit adults it would take at least six days.

All Luke tells us is that Mary was pregnant ("being pregnant") and that she gave birth "while they were there" in Bethlehem (Luke 2:5–6). The participle in verse 5 (*ousē*, "being") may simply be adjectival: "(and she) was expecting a child." But it could be causal, indicating that Joseph went to Bethlehem "*because* she was pregnant." In this case, Joseph was concerned that Micah 5:2 be fulfilled by the birth of the Messiah in Bethlehem. A third option is that the participle may well be concessive in sense, indicating that Joseph went "*even though/in spite of the fact that* she was pregnant."

Whether Mary was in the second or the third trimester of her pregnancy, a six- or seven-day journey must have proved daunting. Imagine Mary sitting side-saddle or astride a donkey, swaying gently from side to side under Joseph's watchful gaze, until the terrain was so uneven that the pregnant Mary was given an uncomfortable jolt. Would she survive the rigors of this arduous pilgrimage? Both Joseph and Mary would have taken heart as they remembered the divine assurance each had received about the safe birth of their child (Matt 1:21; Luke 1:31, 35).

23: LOVING BECAUSE FORGIVEN
(Luke 7:47)

Consider these two sentences:

This woman is happy *because* she has won a competition.

This woman is happy *because* she is smiling.

Does the word "because" have the same meaning in both cases? No! In the first case, "because" introduces the ground or reason for the statement "This woman is happy" and bears the sense "for the reason that." In the second case, "because" introduces the proof or evidence for the statement "This woman is happy" and has the sense "as is shown by the fact that." One and the same Greek conjunction—*hoti*—can express both of these senses of "because."

This distinction is of special importance in Luke 7:47. Jesus had been invited to the home of Simon the Pharisee, who failed to extend the customary courtesies to Jesus on his arrival. A local prostitute, aware that Jesus was there, entered the house and wet his feet with her tears, wiped them with her hair, kissed them, and then poured perfume on them from an alabaster jar of perfume she had brought with her.

When Simon privately objected to Jesus' acceptance of the woman's effusive attention, Jesus addressed Simon with a story about the relation between forgiven debts and the intensity of gratitude and love: the greater the debt forgiven, the greater the loving gratitude. Applying the principle to the actions of the sinful woman, Jesus said, "Therefore, I tell you, her many sins have been forgiven because (*hoti*) she loved much."

Does this mean that great love by humans prompts great forgiveness by God? If this were the case, Jesus would have continued, "Whoever loves little has been forgiven little." But in fact he continued, "Whoever has been forgiven little loves little." And three verses later, he would have said, "Your love has saved you (= has brought about your forgiveness)," but in fact he said, "Your faith has saved you." So the proper sense of Jesus' statement is, "Therefore, I tell you, her many sins have been forgiven—as her great love has shown" (NIV), or, "Therefore, I tell you, her sins, which were many, have been forgiven; hence she has shown great love" (NRSV). Great forgiveness leads to great love.

Another example (of many) of this meaning of *hoti* is found in 1 John 3:14: "We know that we have passed from death to life because (= as is shown by the fact that, or because of which) we love our brothers and sisters/each other."

But a crucial question remains. How do we know we have been "forgiven much"? By recognizing the dreadful seriousness of our sin as an affront to an infinitely holy God, and by remembering the awful cost of our forgiveness that led Jesus to the suffering and shame of the cross.

24: WATCHING SATAN FALL FROM HEAVEN
(Luke 10:18)

In Luke 10:1–11, in anticipation of his imminent visit to various towns in Galilee, Jesus sent out seventy-two (some manuscripts have seventy) disciples to prepare the way by announcing the arrival and availability of the kingdom of God: "The kingdom of God has come near to you" (Luke 10:9, 11). On their return from their successful mission, filled with excitement, they said, "Lord, even the demons submit to us because of your name" (Luke 11:17). Jesus' response was dramatic: "I was watching Satan fall from heaven, like lightning. I have given you authority to trample on snakes and scorpions and over all the power of the enemy; nothing will harm you. However, do not rejoice at this, that the spirits submit to you, but rejoice that your names are written in heaven" (Luke 10:18–20).

Some identify this fall of Satan with the fall described in Isaiah 14:12, "How you have fallen from heaven, morning star (KJV: "Lucifer"), son of the dawn! You have been cast down to the earth—you who once laid low the nations!" But this is unlikely because this verse is part of the taunt-song against the king of Babylon (Isa 14:4–21).

Instead, Luke 10:18 should be understood in light of the immediately preceding verse: "Lord, even the demons submit to us because of your name" (v. 17). Jesus' word about Satan's fall was his response to his disciples' joyful claim. That is, the submission of Satan's agents to the disciples when they commanded the exorcism of demons in the name of Jesus was a certain sign of Satan's loss of power, his fall from temporary dominion. The driving out of demons was a sign, not only of the arrival of the kingdom of God (Matt 12:28) but also of the defeat of Satan. True, the final plundering of the "strong man's" house still lay in the future (Matt 12:29)—this would happen through the death of Jesus, as he makes clear in John 12:31—but a decisive victory in God's campaign to bring about the downfall of Satan and his demonic minions had taken place during the mission of the seventy-two. The unusual position of the participle "fall" (*pesonta*) at the end of the sentence, "I was watching Satan fall from heaven, like a flash of lightning," emphasizes this decisiveness.

Jesus couches his concluding word of advice to his rejoicing disciples in a typical Semitic contrast, where "not this, but that" has the sense "not primarily this, but principally that." "Do not rejoice at this, that the spirits submit to you, but rejoice that your names are written in heaven" (Luke 10:20; cf. Rev 20:12–15). He is telling his disciples that rejoicing in spiritual victory is legitimate.

Whether or not Jesus himself had received a vision during the disciples' missionary expedition, the imperfect tense (*etheōroun*), "I was watching" (NASB), reflects the vividness of his recollection of what he saw. One is reminded of the vision received by the apostle John on Patmos in which, when war broke out in heaven, "the great dragon was hurled down—that ancient serpent called the Devil, or Satan, who leads the whole world astray. He was hurled down to the earth, and his angels were hurled down with him" (Rev 12:9).

25: HATING ONE'S PARENTS?
(Luke 14:26)

In Luke 14:26, Jesus speaks the shocking words, "If anyone comes to me and does not hate father and mother, wife and children, brothers and sisters—yes, even their own life—such a person cannot be my disciple." Does this contradict the fifth commandment to honor one's father and mother (Exod 20:12)?

No, because here we confront another (see the previous chapter) vivid and distinctive Semitic idiom, in which "hate" means "love less." Jesus is insisting, in dramatic and unforgettable fashion, that his followers should regard family ties as secondary to the demands of the kingdom of God that he embodies.

There is an illuminating Old Testament instance of this use of "hate." Deuteronomy 21:15–17 deals with the inheritance of an Israelite man who had two wives, one of whom is "beloved," and the other "hated" (KJV). (Polygamy was tolerated but not endorsed in OT times.) The legislation defends the rights of a firstborn son against favoritism that could be shown toward a son born to the favorite wife. Even if the firstborn is the son of the wife whom the husband *loves less*, that son must still receive two-thirds of the father's inheritance. And the reason? "That son is the first sign of his father's strength" (Deut 21:17)—that is, he was proof of the father's ability to perpetuate the family line.

That this is the correct way to understand "hating" father and mother is clear from Matthew's version of the saying (perhaps spoken on a different occasion): "Whoever loves father or mother more than me is not worthy of me; and whoever loves son or daughter more than me is not worthy of me" (Matt 10:37).

Are there scriptural examples of this surrender to the primacy of God's claims even when this affects family relationships? One dramatic example occurred during the incident of the golden calf (Exod 32:17–29). After Moses challenged the sinning Israelites—"Whoever is for the LORD, come to me"—we are told, "all the Levites rallied to him" (Exod 32:26). They carried out God's instructions to execute all those guilty of rebellious idolatry, even when this involved their "own sons and brothers" (Exod 32:28–29). As a result, in the blessing Moses pronounced on the Israelites before his death, he blessed the Levites with the words, "He said of his father and mother, 'I have no regard for them.' He did not recognize his brothers or acknowledge his own children." So they became custodians of God's word and protectors of covenantal rites (Deut 33:8–10).

In the NT we have the case of the apostle Peter. From Mark 1:30, which speaks of his mother-in-law, we know that Peter was married when Jesus called him (Mark 1:16–18). And from the Gospel records we discover that he was always in Jesus' company. Some thirty years later, Paul notes that Peter was accustomed to take his wife along with him on his missionary travels (1 Cor 9:5). But apparently during Jesus' three-year public ministry, he was moving about with the other members of the Twelve, having left home and relatives for the sake of Jesus and the gospel (Mark 10:29–30).

Lest we be tempted to take this too far, alongside Luke 14:26 we also have the complementary NT injunction to give priority to the care of one's extended family over other obligations (1 Tim 5:8).

26: "THE KINGDOM OF GOD IS IN YOUR MIDST" (Luke 17:21)

Jesus' statement about the kingdom in this verse has the unenviable distinction of being the most disputed translation issue in the NT, to judge by the major English translations. Ten of these have a footnote giving an alternative rendering, four give two alternatives, and one (REB) lists three! The issue is how to translate *entos hymōn*. There are three defensible renderings.

First is "within you" (KJV, GNT, NIV 1984). "Within" is undoubtedly the essential meaning of *entos*. For example, *entos mou* means "within me" in Psalm 38:3 and 108:22 in the Greek OT (LXX). But even if we take "you" to be generic, the primary reference in the context is the Pharisees (Luke 17:20). It seems very unlikely, in light of Luke 11:37–54 (especially verses 52–54), that Jesus is affirming that within the experience of the Pharisees the kingdom was at work. And nowhere else does Luke speak of the kingdom as an internalized, subjective reality; people enter the kingdom rather than the reverse.

Second is "among you" (HCSB, NRSV). This rendering assumes that the preposition *entos* has the same sense as the preposition *en*, as in "God is among you" (*en soi*) in Isaiah 45:14 (LXX).

Finally, there is "in your midst" or "in the midst of you" (CSB, ESV, NASB, NIV). It is true that elsewhere Luke can use the longer explicit phrase *en mesō hymōn* to mean "in your midst" (as in Luke 22:7; Acts 2:22). But there certainly are parallels for *entos* meaning "in the midst":

- In Song of Songs 3:10 (LXX), "in the midst" of King Solomon's carriage was a mosaic pavement.

- In Polycarp's letter *To the Philippians* 3:3, "If anyone is in the midst of these (faith, hope, love) (= is engrossed in these virtues), he has fulfilled the commandment of righteousness."

This third option makes the best sense. In Luke 17:20a, some Pharisees asked Jesus when the kingdom of God would come, and his response (vv. 20b–21) related not to timing but to true and false ways of determining the kingdom's arrival. Recognition of the kingdom is not by studious observation of ambiguous signs (v. 20b) or by following other people's conflicting suggestions (v. 21a), but by recognizing its unambiguous presence: "The kingdom of God is in your midst" (v. 21b).

Jesus is directing a challenge to the Pharisees and soliciting a response: "I myself embody the kingdom you are inquiring about; it is right here before your very eyes." He is saying, in effect, "Look at what lies in front of you," to borrow a Pauline expression (2 Cor 10:7). They do not need to look elsewhere for the kingdom's presence.

Nor do we. As the church fathers used to say, "Jesus is *autobasileia*"—the kingdom itself.

27: FORGIVEN BECAUSE IGNORANT?
(Luke 23:34)

This first of the seven sayings of Jesus on the cross was uttered probably shortly after he had been crushed to the ground and his wrists and feet skewered to the cross by iron spikes: "Father, forgive them, for they do not know what they are doing" (Luke 23:34). Undoubtedly he used the word "Abba," "Dear Father," the way he normally addressed God (see part 2, ch. 32). This rich term contains ideas of simplicity, intimacy, security, and affection.

Some have suggested that the "them" who are forgiven were the Jewish authorities that pressed charges against Jesus before Pilate, or the Jewish nation as a whole, which failed to recognize and welcome their Messiah. On these views, Jesus was asking for the postponement of God's judgment on the nation or their representatives for their persistent unbelief, and God's response was to grant a generation of about forty years (AD 30–70), from the crucifixion to the fall of Jerusalem, during which time there was an opportunity for Jews to hear the gospel and embrace Jesus as Messiah. However, in early Christian preaching there was a call for Jews as well as Gentiles to repent "for the forgiveness of sins" (Luke 24:47); their forgiveness was not automatic. Jesus' request was not simply for a delay in divine retribution.

More probably, the persons for whom Jesus interceded were the four-man Roman execution squad and their supervising centurion. The present tenses, "they do not know" (*oidasin*) and "what they are doing" (*poiousin*), not "they did not know what they did," strongly support this view.

We gain important clues about the meaning of Jesus' request from the prayer of Stephen as he was stoned to death at the hands of the Sanhedrin. He directed a prayer to Jesus ("Lord") that is clearly modeled on Jesus' own prayer. "Lord, do not hold this sin against them" (Acts 7:60). He is not requesting that Jesus forgive all the sins of each member of the Sanhedrin but that he forgive their one corporate present sin of executing an innocent man.

In a similar way, the request Jesus addressed to God his Father was not for the blanket forgiveness of every sin committed by these Roman soldiers, but forgiveness for the one heinous sin of crucifying an innocent man. He was asking God to choose not to reckon this one sin against their account in the heavenly books.

But Jesus taught that forgiveness requires repentance (Luke 17:3; cf. Acts 2:48). So how could he appeal to the soldiers' ignorance ("forgive, *for* …"; HCSB, CSB: "forgive them, *because* …") as the reason God should forgive them? Perhaps the only explanation is that in the absence of any sufficient ground for forgiveness (such as acknowledgment of wrongdoing or repentance), Jesus finds it necessary to appeal to a mitigating circumstance: the soldiers' unawareness that they were in fact crucifying an innocent man who was God's Messenger. He transfers to his Father the responsibility for granting or withholding forgiveness, knowing there was, understandably, no contrition or repentance on the part of the soldiers. See also part 1, ch. 5.

28: WITH CHRIST AFTER DEATH
(Luke 23:43)

This is the second of seven statements made by Jesus while hanging on his cross. Although one of the criminals crucified with Jesus poured abuse on him and taunted him (Luke 23:39), the other reprimanded his fellow criminal and then directed a request to Jesus: "Remember me when you come into your kingdom" (Luke 23:42). "Remember me" is an earnest plea not simply for passing notice ("Spare a thought for me!") but for mercy in the royal court when Jesus assumes his kingly status and power.

Through his reply, Jesus was not only responding to the man's persistent request, indicated by the imperfect-tense *elegen* ("he said"). Jesus is also recognizing his confession of guilt (v. 41) and implied repentance, his assertion of Jesus' innocence (v. 41), and his belief in the afterlife along with Jesus' kingship and rule in that afterlife (v. 42). "I solemnly assure you, today you will be with me in paradise" (v. 43).

"Today" means "this very day," that is, "before the present day ends, when we are being crucified." The Greek word order shows that "today" belongs with the phrase "with me," not with "I solemnly assure you." "Paradise" here refers to the dwelling place of the righteous dead, which is either synonymous with the third (= the highest) heaven or located within the third heaven (see 2 Cor 12:4), the abode of God. Either way, it is a place of transcendent blessedness because of the presence of the resurrected Christ.

This verse is one of three NT texts that depict the status of believers between their death and their resurrection. In each passage, it is implied that there is no interval between the moment of death and the time of arrival in Christ's presence. To depart is to arrive.

We are confident, I repeat, and prefer to depart from this body and take up residence with (*pros*) the Lord. (2 Cor 5:8)

I am torn between these two alternatives. I am longing to break camp and so be with (*syn*) Christ, for this is a far, far better state. (Phil 1:23)

Today you will be with (*meta*) me in paradise. (Luke 23:43)

Although three different Greek prepositions are used in these verses (usually all translated by the English "with"), a single reality is represented—conscious fellowship with Christ after death. In themselves the prepositions need mean no more than "in the presence of" and contain no idea of reciprocity of action. But with this said, it seems inadequate to conclude that the believer's dwelling with the Lord implies no more than incorporation in Christ, or their spatial juxtaposition to Christ (as when a chair is said to be "with" a table), or their being in a state of suspended animation ("soul-sleep"). Prepositions that in themselves suggest simply a passive juxtaposition in space introduce, when applied to interpersonal relationship, the idea of dynamic mutual fellowship (see also part 2, ch. 60). What a prospect!

As to the locality of the Christian dead before their resurrection, there are two representations in the NT. From the viewpoint of the living who witnessed the burial of the dead and saw them disappear from view, they are resting in the grave (John 5:28–29; 1 Thess 4:16–17; cf. Acts 13:36) or residing in Hades (Acts 2:27, 31), the invisible realm in the heart of the earth (Matt 12:40) in which all the dead are temporary residents. From the viewpoint of faith, which sees the invisible, they are in proximity to God. This can be expressed as table fellowship with Abraham (Luke 16:23); as inhabiting resting places in the Father's house (John 14:2) or eternal abodes (Luke 16:9); as active fellowship with Christ in paradise (Luke 23:43) or heaven (John 12:26; 2 Cor 5:8; Phil 1:23); or, in the case of martyrs, as waiting under the heavenly altar (Rev 6:9).

But a question naturally arises. How is Jesus' implied ascent into paradise immediately after his death related to his "descent into Hades" (Matt 12:40; Acts 2:31; Rom 10:7) at his death? Perhaps the answer is that Jesus' sweeping cosmic movement from earth to exaltation in heaven was by way of a temporary visit to Hades where he announced to the "imprisoned spirits" his victory over death and Hades (cf. 1 Pet 3:19; Jude 6; Rev 1:18).

29: A JEWISH EVENING PRAYER
(Luke 23:46)

Many English versions suggest or affirm that Jesus uttered his last word on the cross "in a loud voice." For example, "Then Jesus, calling out with a loud voice, said, 'Father, into your hands I commit my spirit' " (ESV; similarly GNT, NASB, NIV, NLT, CSB). That is, the loud cry *was* the prayer.

The difficulty with such a rendering is that the participle rendered "crying out" (*phōnēsas*) is in the aorist tense, not the present, and an aorist participle that precedes a finite verb (here *eipen*, "said") normally indicates antecedent action. Thus the KJV and RV render this verse, "And when Jesus had cried out with a loud voice, he said …" (similarly JB). Here the loud cry is *not* the prayer. Instead, the loud cry was probably "It is finished" (John 19:30). It seems more probable that Jesus would have uttered his cry of victory "in a loud voice" than his final private prayer to his Father.

Among rabbis of a later time, this simple prayer from Psalm 31:5—"Into your hands I commit my spirit"—was part of a Jewish evening prayer that was to be repeated before sleep. This tradition probably reflects earlier practice, and Jesus himself may well have regularly used this prayer to end his own evening devotions. By addressing the prayer to his Father, Jesus was reverting to the address of his first saying on the cross ("Father, forgive them") after the ominous "My God, my God" of the fourth saying. His renewed use of "Father" is proof that full, conscious, and intimate fellowship with his Father has been restored after its agonizing suspension during the three hours of darkness.

Since the verb *paratithemai* means "entrust something/someone to the safe keeping of someone else," the word "hands" refers to protective care. But the expression "hand(s) of God" also regularly denotes God's unparalleled power (as in Ps 89:13; 95:4; Heb 1:10), so that voluntary surrender into God's hands expresses acquiescence in his gracious and omnipotent sovereignty. In particular, it indicates Jesus' confidence that God would deliver him from the dead by resurrection (cf. Luke 9:22; 18:33; 22:69; 23:43). "My spirit" refers to Jesus' inner person (cf. John 11:33; 13:21) or his incorporeal soul.

John notes that immediately before surrendering his spirit to God, Jesus bowed his head (John 19:30b). Apparently, the apostle John himself was close enough to the cross to observe this feature of Jesus' dying moments. This action of bowing his head indicates that Jesus faced death with calm restfulness and resoluteness. He was serene and content because he could say and had said, "It is finished."

As for the influence of this word of Jesus, recall that Stephen, the first Christian martyr, prayed, "Lord Jesus, receive my spirit" (Acts 7:59) while dying under a hail of stones. And some thirty or so years later, Peter concludes his discussion of Christian suffering with the injunction, "So then, those who suffer according to God's will should entrust themselves to their faithful Creator and devote themselves to doing good" (1 Pet 4:19).

30: "NOW YOU SEE HIM — NOW YOU DON'T!" (Luke 24:31)

Deep and awesome mystery surrounds three crucial events in the career of Jesus. His incarnation in the womb of Mary (see part 1, ch. 33) took place in the deep silence of God, and his actual resurrection was witnessed by neither angel nor man—it also took place in the deep silence of God. His appearances during the forty days between his resurrection and his final ascension into heaven are also awe-inspiring and beyond human experience and comprehension. Apparently one of the characteristics of the resurrected Jesus was his ability to appear and disappear at will.

Whenever Jesus appeared or disappeared, it was always at his initiative; he chose when he appeared and to whom he appeared. No one could ever say, "Today I am going to see Jesus!" Four Greek verbs point to his initiative in his appearances.

1. *Phaneroō*, "reveal" ("Jesus revealed himself," John 21:1 twice)

2. *Optanomai*, "appear" ("He appeared," Acts 1:3b)

3. *Paristēmi*, "present" ("He presented himself alive," Acts 1:3a)

4. *Horaō*, "see" ("He appeared," nine NT uses: Luke 24:34; Acts 9:17; 13:31; 26:16a; 1 Cor 15:5–8 four times; 1 Tim 3:16).

When this last verb is used in the aorist passive form (*ōphthē*) and is followed by the dative case, it bears an intransitive sense and means not "he was seen by X" but "he appeared to X." On this grammatical point all the authorities agree. The emphasis is on the action of the person appearing, not on the action of the one who sees. Interestingly, the same verbal form appears in Genesis 1:9, "the dry land appeared" (not "the dry land was seen").

The one understandable exception to the above rule regarding Jesus' initiative is found in Acts 10:40: "God raised him on the third day and allowed him to appear" (NRSV). Here "to appear" is literally "to become visible" (*emphanēs genesthai*). Its opposite, "to become invisible" (*aphantos genesthai*), is found in Luke 24:31: "Then their eyes were opened and they recognized him. And he became invisible to them." Or, "he disappeared from their sight" (GNT, NIV, HCSB). These two Greek expressions, "to become visible" and "to become invisible," are not found anywhere else in the Greek Bible. In a distinctive way they express the unique abilities of the resurrected Jesus, two remarkable characteristics of his resurrection body.

The question naturally arises: Where was Jesus during the long intervals between his appearances? We know he was in paradise on the day of his death (Luke 23:43; see part 1, ch. 28), and so we must assume his appearances were incursions from the heavenly realm where he had already been exalted to his Father's right hand. His ascension into heaven after forty days was a visible dramatization of this invisible enthronement, and it marked the end of his earthly resurrection appearances.

JOHN

31: "THE WORD HAD THE SAME NATURE AS GOD"
(John 1:1c)

The Greek article ("the" in English) is very versatile. Sometimes its presence with a noun is significant, sometimes its absence is important. John 1:1 is a fine example. Having affirmed that "in the beginning the Word was already in existence" (v. 1a), John declares that this Word was "with God" (*pros ton theon*, v. 1b), where the definite article *ton* is used with the noun *theon*. Throughout the Fourth Gospel the word *theos* with the article almost always refers to God the Father (see, for example, John 3:16). So verse 1b asserts that at the beginning of creation and time the Word was in the presence of the Father. For John, Jesus as the "Word" (*logos*) was the outward and personal expression of God.

But verse 1c differs in two ways. First, the Greek word order is changed from 1a and 1b, with the term *theos* preceding the subject ("Word"), indicating that *theos* is the predicate, not the subject, and is emphatic. Second, unlike *theos* in verse 1b, the noun *theos* in 1c is without the definite article.

What is the significance of this latter fact? When a Greek noun is used without the definite article, the omission often draws attention to the quality or character of the thing or person being spoken of. In our case, John is highlighting the distinctive nature of the Word, not identifying his person. Some translations capture this thought in a paraphrase: "What God was, the Word was" (NEB, REB); note, not "Who God was, the Word was." This rendering reproduces the Greek word order but has converted the predicate into the subject.

Other commendable paraphrases are "the nature of the Word was the same as the nature of God" (Barclay) and "the Word had the same nature as God" (P. B. Harner).

But most English versions opt for the simple rendering, "the Word was God." This has the advantage of being as simple and straightforward as the original, provided that we understand "was God" here as meaning "had the very nature of God" or "shared God's essential nature" or "possessed the divine essence." But that is the problem with this common translation. In normal English usage, "God" is a proper noun referring either to the person of the Father or to the three persons of the Godhead. But Jesus Christ as the personal Word is distinct from the person of the Father and the person of the Spirit.

How, then, should we render John 1:1c? The choice is between "the Word was God," which places a distinctive sense on a common English word, and "the Word had the same nature as God," which is a paraphrase that lacks the simplicity of the original.

32: BECOMING GOD'S CHILDREN
(John 1:12c–13)

Sometimes a straightforward, accurate translation of a Greek verse cries out for an illuminating paraphrase. John 1:13 is a prime example, referring to children of God "who were born not of bloods, nor of the will of the flesh, nor of the will of man, but of God."

The prologue of the Fourth Gospel (John 1:1–18) describes the mission of Jesus Christ, the preexistent Logos. He came into the world as the true Light in order to make God the Father known to humans, who, by believing in Christ, become the children of God. For the apostle John, believers in Jesus are called "the children of God" (*tekna theou*), not "the sons of God" (*huioi theou*, Paul's preferred term). As in John's first epistle, so in his Gospel Jesus alone is "the Son of God." Christ's sonship relates to his being or essence; the sonship of believers relates to their adoption. God has one Son by nature, many sons by adoption.

In John 1:13, the four uses of the Greek preposition *ek* (translated "of" above and in most English versions of this verse) may point to agency ("by" or "through") or source ("from") or cause ("as a result of") or any combination of these. The three negative phrases ("not … nor … nor …") are designed to highlight the climactic and positive phrase, "of God."

1. "Of bloods." This plural (*haimata*), unique in the NT, may be a generalizing or idiomatic use, simply meaning "blood." As a case of "concrete for abstract," the allusion will be to human descent or parentage. But if this is an actual plural, the reference is to "bloodlines" or even to the union of both male and female blood.

2. "Of the will of the flesh." As later in verse 14, the word "flesh" (*sarx*) has no negative overtones and refers to the purely natural or physical sphere. Also, here it is adjectival in sense, "human" or "natural." The whole phrase may refer to "human choice" or to "natural instincts" such as sexual desire.

3. "Of the will of man." Because *anēr* may mean "man" generically or "husband," this phrase could mean "a man's decision" or "a husband's will/initiative/design" in natural procreation.

Taken together, these three negated phrases affirm that believers in Jesus Christ did not become God's children by natural means. Rather, they owe their spiritual rebirth to the action of God himself and God alone. Divine procreation is totally unrelated to human parentage, human choice, or human design; spiritual generation has nothing to do with physical generation. It comes about solely "of God," that is, as a result of God's initiative and action.

33: WHEN DID THE WORD BECOME INCARNATE?
(John 1:14)

An ancient Christmas hymn written by St. Germanus (634–734) and translated by John M. Neale begins:

> A great and mighty wonder,
> A full and holy cure:
> The virgin bears the infant,
> with virgin-honor pure.

It continues in the second verse,

> The Word becomes incarnate
> And yet remains on high.
> And cherubim sing anthems
> To shepherds from the sky.

But did the incarnation take place at Bethlehem, as this carol and some others suggest? Consider these statements from prominent evangelicals (who shall remain nameless):

> It is important for us to see ... that what happened to Jesus happened to our humanity which he assumed at Bethlehem.

> Once again Christmas confronts us with birth. To God, the birth of Jesus was incarnation, an historic event of events when he became man to dwell among us.

If we believe that life begins at conception, it follows that Jesus' human life began at Nazareth after the announcement (the annunciation) to Mary that she would bear the Son of God. Luke 1:35 reads, "The angel (Gabriel) answered, 'The Holy Spirit will come on you, and the power of the Most High will overshadow you. So the holy one to be born will be called the Son of God." It is very significant—and appropriate—that on the western façade of the Church of the Annunciation in Nazareth there are two verses of Scripture—one is this verse, while the other is John 1:14. And if "the Word became flesh" (John 1:14) at Nazareth, not Bethlehem, what happened nine months before Jesus' birth is as important as December 25. It was in the deep silence of God that the incarnation of the Word took place. There was angelic singing at the birth of Jesus and seismic convulsions at his death, but silence surrounded his conception. In a sense not intended by the hymn writer, we can say, "How silently, how silently, the wondrous gift is given!"

The wonder of the incarnation is that God did not choose to deliver his final and perfect revelation to humankind through an awesome prophet with miraculous powers, or through a legion of angels who could superintend life on earth, or through the arch-angel Michael despatched directly from heaven with an infallible message. Nor was God's final word brought by a Son who suddenly appeared on the human scene as a mature man or as a full-term child miraculously implanted in a woman's womb. No, it was the divine plan that by a special action of the Holy Spirit a betrothed Jewish maiden would become pregnant, apart from any sexual relations with the man who was already deemed her husband in the eyes of Jewish law. "The Word became flesh" as a fertilized egg—a one-celled zygote, in biological terms—in the womb of Mary. It is only by being magnified half a million times that a fertilized egg can be seen by the human eye.

Even after two weeks the embryo of Jesus was only less than a tenth of an inch (2.5 mm) long. At eighteen days the heart of Jesus began to beat—the heart that would beat vigorously for over thirty years until he surrendered his spirit to his Father. At four weeks, Jesus' arm buds began to appear—the arms that would gently pick up and bless the children, the arms that would be outstretched on the cross. Also at four weeks, Jesus' eyes began to be formed—the eyes that would look on the crowds with compassion, the eyes that would gaze down from the cross at his mother. At five weeks, his nose began to take shape—the nose that would smell the delicate perfumes of "the flowers of the field," the nose that would smell the putrid odors of the crucifixion site. At six weeks, his leg buds appeared—the legs that would carry him through Judea, Samaria, and Galilee preaching and doing deeds of kindness, the feet that would be placed one upon another as an iron nail skewered him to the cross. At this stage, the embryo of Jesus was still less than ½-inch (12 mm) long, the size of the nail on your little finger. At seven weeks, he was ¾-inch (19 mm) long; he could move his hands, and his fingers were clearly defined. At eight weeks, his toe joints were apparent. At ten weeks, the fetus of Jesus was 2 inches (51 mm) long; at eleven weeks, 2-½ inches (64 mm); at twelve weeks, 3 inches (77 mm). At fourteen weeks, Jesus could turn his head, wrinkle his forehead, and suck his thumb.

Amazingly, the author of every human process himself underwent the same development as all humans experience in the womb. Here is a profound mystery that evokes astonishment, awe, and worship.

34: AFTER — YET BEFORE!
(John 1:15)

How can somebody come on the scene *after* someone else and yet also be *before* them with regard to time? This is the riddle and paradox of John 1:15.

If the prologue of John's Gospel (John 1:1–18) describes the mission of the Logos (1:1), its last section (1:14–18) depicts a crucial aspect of his mission—his unique role as the Logos-Son who reveals God the Father. Within this section, verse 15 records John the Baptist's testimony to the preeminence of his principal, Jesus the Messiah: "John testified about him and called out ..." This latter verb (*krazō*) reflects the prophetic style of proclaiming a message loudly and boldly so that all may hear.

The central affirmation of the verse falls into three parts, each defining a relationship between Jesus and John the Baptist.

1. "The One who comes after me." Although "the one who comes/is to come" is a title for the Messiah when it stands on its own (as in Luke 7:19–20; Heb 10:37), here it has a

verbal sense since it is followed by "after me." John the Baptist is portraying himself as the Messiah's forerunner.

2. "(The One who comes after me) has become before me" (literally). The word *emprosthen* was originally an adverb of place ("before," "in front of"), but here it is a preposition denoting not time ("before me," which would make the next phrase redundant) but rank or status ("ahead of me"). An example of this use of *emprosthen* is Genesis 48:20 in the LXX, "he set Ephraim ahead of Manasseh." The literal sense could be better rendered "he has taken precedence over me."

3. "Because he was earlier than me" (literally) = "because he was before me" or "because he existed before I did."

Three statements are here made about Jesus, the Logos-Son. He is *after* John with regard to time, *before* him in status, and (paradoxically) *before* him with regard to time. We would expect a forerunner to say he was inferior to his principal, but this is not the reason John gives for declaring the superiority of Jesus. For John the Baptist, the total supremacy of Jesus the Messiah was based on his preexistence: "He has taken precedence over me *because* (*hoti*) he existed before I did."

For John the Evangelist, the Messiah was not simply born before John the Baptist. He existed eternally in the presence of God the Father:

In the beginning the Word already existed, and the Word existed in the presence of God, and the Word was all that God was. (John 1:1)

"Very truly I tell you," Jesus answered, "before Abraham was born, I already existed." (John 8:58)

"And now, Father, glorify me in your own presence with
the glory I had in your presence before the world existed."
(John 17:5)

The One who came after John the Baptist (Matt 11:11) in time
surpassed him in rank and importance because he existed before
him in time.

35: UNINTERRUPTED GRACE
(John 1:16)

In the preceding verse (John 1:15), the apostle John has recorded the
testimony of John the Baptist regarding the superiority of Jesus: "The
One who comes after me has surpassed me because he was before me"
(see the previous chapter). Now in verse 16 the apostle confirms the
accuracy of that testimony by appealing to the uniform experience
of believers: "For from the fullness of his grace we have all received
a share—namely, grace in place of grace already received."

The crucial phrase is *charis anti charitos*, "grace in place of grace."
The term *charis* may be rendered "grace/favor/blessing/gift of love,"
and the preposition *anti* means "instead of" or "in place of" or the
equivalent. Because the whole expression is clearly condensed, a
wide variety of translations or paraphrases have been proposed, none
of which can be excluded as indefensible or inappropriate:

- "grace in place of grace"
- "grace upon grace"
- "grace after grace"
- "(new) grace instead of (old) grace"
- "one blessing after another"
- "blessing after blessing"
- "one favor in place of another"
- "gift after gift of love"

Some commentators relate each *charis* to a particular blessing. They find an allusion to the new covenant instead of the old, or the spiritual presence of the Holy Spirit instead of the physical presence of Jesus, or God's presence in Christ instead of his presence in the *Shekinah* (the visible glory of God), or the grace of freedom and sonship instead of the law of Moses.

However, more is implied than a single substitutionary exchange, X for Y, such as grace for law. The phrase refers to one blessing replacing another, to replenished grace, to a rapid and perpetual succession of blessings, as though there were no interval between the arrival of one blessing and the receipt of the next. A.T. Robertson sums this up in *A Grammar of the Greek New Testament*: "As the days come and go a new supply takes the place of the grace already bestowed as wave follows wave upon the shore" (574).

Precisely what is the nature of the constantly renewed grace remains undefined, but probably it is the multiplied spiritual benefits of the new covenant. "The law indeed was given through Moses; grace and truth came through Jesus Christ" (John 1:17). These benefits include direct and permanent and unparalleled access to God through our great high priest, Jesus Christ, the mediator of the new covenant, who is also able to empathize with our weaknesses (Heb 4:14–16; 9:15; 10:19–22); God's laws written on believers' hearts (Jer 31:33; Heb 8:10); and the hope of a second appearance of Christ to consummate salvation (Heb 9:28).

36: THE FATHER'S PERFECT EXPRESSION
(John 1:18)

As John concludes his prologue (1:1–18), he makes two complementary statements, one about invisibility, the other about visibility. The first is "No one has ever seen God" (1:18a), that is, God as he is in himself. God in his essence, God as God (*theos* without the definite article) has never been seen by either the physical or the spiritual eye of humans (cf. John 5:37; 6:46; Exod 33:20); he is invisible.

The second part of the verse (1:18b) speaks of his visibility, his becoming visible to humans through his self-disclosure in Christ the Revealer: "The only Son, who is God by nature and has his being in the Father's heart, has revealed him." Of the four main textual variants in 18b, the majority of textual critics and commentators rightly prefer the reading *monogenēs theos*, which brings together the two crucial terms found in verses 1 and 14 and may be rendered "the only Son, who is God by nature," or "the one and only Son, who is himself God" (NIV).

The term *monogenēs* refers to "the only member of a kin," so when it is used in a familial sense it means "of sole descent," "without siblings," referring to the only child in a family. Given the conjunction of "only" and "Son" in John 3:16, 18; 1 John 4:9 and the later reference to the Father, it is natural to understand "Son" with "only" in 1:18b. Jesus is without spiritual siblings and without equals. No one else can lay claim to the title Son of God in the sense in which it applies to Jesus Christ.

This "one and only Son" who shares God's divine nature (again *theos* without the definite article) "is in the bosom of the Father" (KJV, NASB) or "has his being in the Father's heart." The source of this imagery of the Father's bosom or heart may be festal (of reclining at a feast; cf. John 13:23), familial (of a child on a parent's lap or in a parent's or nurse's embrace), or conjugal (of the embrace of husband and wife). Whatever the source, it denotes the exclusive and privileged intimacy of a deeply affectionate interpersonal relationship where secrets can be shared.

The verb *exēgeomai* ("expound," "make known") was a common term in secular Greek for the communication of divine knowledge or the revelation of divine secrets. As a constative aorist here, it encompasses in a single glance the whole span of Christ's earthly life, including his death and resurrection. No object of this verb is expressed but "the Father" should be supplied from the context. It was Christ and no other (*ekeinos*) who fully "exegeted" or accurately revealed the Father. Jesus Christ made visible the invisible nature of God (cf. Col 1:15) and laid bare the heart of the Father.

In the whole of John's Gospel, 1:18 has a special function. It links the prologue and the remainder of the Gospel by highlighting the dual themes of the Father as fully and directly known to the Son, and the Son as the unique exegete of the Father—themes that are prominent throughout this Gospel. Having had eternal access to the innermost thoughts of the Father (John 1:1b; 6:46), Jesus is perfectly and uniquely qualified to give a full account of the Father's nature and purposes (John 3:32).

37: "BORN BY WATER AND THE SPIRIT" (John 3:5)

In his conversation with Nicodemus (John 3:1–15), Jesus tells him, "No one can enter the kingdom of God unless they are born by water and the Spirit" (John 3:5). This is the second of Jesus' two solemn affirmations of the necessity of the new birth for entry into God's kingdom (vv. 3, 5). In both of these verses he prefaces his statement with "I am telling you the solemn truth" or "Let me firmly assure you" (*amēn amēn legō soi*, literally, "Truly truly I say to you"). Whereas such solemn statements are always preceded by a single *amēn* in the Synoptic Gospels, in the Fourth Gospel the *amēn* is always repeated, twenty times followed by the plural "you" (*hymin*) and five times by the singular "you" (*soi*).

What does Jesus mean by this statement? Those who regard "water" and "the Spirit" as separate entities usually see "born of/by water" as a reference to physical birth, the "water" being amniotic fluid at birth or semen at conception, while "born of/by the Spirit" refers to the agent of spiritual birth. Alternatively, some link "water" with proselyte baptism or John the Baptist's baptism or Christian baptism as the means of rebirth, and regard "the Spirit" as the primary cause of regeneration.

But there is good reason to doubt whether two separate entities are being mentioned. First, *pneuma* ("Spirit") is without the definite article in verse 5 but has the definite article in verses 6 and 8, which suggests a distinctive emphasis in verse 5. Second, the preposition *ek* (*ex*) is omitted before *pneuma* in the phrase "by/of water and the Spirit," a fact that binds the two items closely together. That is, "water" and "the Spirit" form a single conceptual unit. No contrast is intended between an external element of "water" and a separate inward renewal achieved by the Spirit. Also, the focus is on the personal Spirit, not the impersonal water, for only the Spirit is referred to in verses 6 and 8. The Spirit produces rebirth by means of "water."

In Ezekiel 36:25–27 we find the same direct link between "water," as the agent of cleansing from impurity, and "the Spirit," as the agent who creates a new responsive heart and a new spirit of obedience to the divine decrees. Indeed, "by water and the Spirit" would be an apt summary of these three verses in Ezekiel that speak of spiritual renewal:

> I will sprinkle you with clean water, and you will be clean; I will cleanse you from all your impurities and from all your idols. I will give you a new heart and put a new spirit within you; I will take away from you your heart of stone and give you a responsive heart. And I will put my Spirit within you and cause you to follow my decrees and be careful to keep my laws.

On this understanding, "by water and the Spirit" refers to the cleansing and renewing role of the Spirit in producing the rebirth that is a prerequisite for entrance into the kingdom of God. The phrase expounds "being born again/from above" in John 3:3, 7, and "being born by God's work" in John 1:13.

38: UNIQUE GIVING BY UNIQUE LOVE
(John 3:16)

John 3:15 reads, "that everyone who believes may have eternal life through union with him (Jesus)." The next verse—the most famous sentence ever spoken or written—explains (hence it begins with "for," *gar*) why verse 15 is true: "For God so loved the world that he gave his one and only Son, that whoever believes in him shall not perish but have eternal life." Since the original Greek manuscripts did not indicate direct speech, there is some uncertainty whether these are Jesus' words or John's inspired reflection on Jesus' earlier words. Along with the majority of recent English versions, I believe Jesus' words end after verse 21.

"God so loved … that he gave." God the Father's love for the world, always present, was at one particular time expressed in a love-gift. The past tense (aorist) of "loved" matches the past tense (aorist) of "gave." God loved and gave. His gift expressed his love. The word "so" (*houtōs*) here means "to such an extent" or "so intensely," for the unusual position of "loved" in the Greek makes "so" particularly emphatic: this was no ordinary love!

There are only two places in the NT where the conjunction *hōste* ("that") is followed by the indicative mood in a dependent clause so that the emphasis falls on the result of the action. One is Galatians 2:13, where Paul notes Peter's unfortunate decision in Antioch to avoid contact with those Christians who happened to be non-Jews. He then comments, "Along with him (Peter) the rest of the (Christian) Jews there played the hypocrite, *with the result that* (remarkably) even Barnabas was led astray by their hypocrisy." The other example is found in John 3:16. Here the sense is, "If you can believe it, God did not spare his only Son but actually surrendered him for the benefit of his rebellious creatures!" That remarkable surrender, that momentous giving, involved sending him into the world (v. 17) as a fully human person (1:14) and also giving him over to a sacrificial death. As John says elsewhere, "God sent his Son to be the atoning sacrifice for our sins" (1 John 4:10). Both the incarnation and the crucifixion were involved in the giving.

In John's Gospel sometimes the Greek word *kosmos* refers to the whole universe (17:5) or planet earth (11:9) or the place where humans live (16:21) or even humanity as given over to evil (7:7). But in 3:16 "world" refers to all humans without distinction or exception (as in the third use of *kosmos* in 3:17).

God's giving was momentous because it was none other than his dearly loved, one and only Son that he gave, not some person that could easily be duplicated or replaced. As God's Son, Jesus had always been in his Father's presence, in intimate and loving dialogue with him, sharing all his secrets, embracing all his plans. That is why he was uniquely qualified to reveal his Father's character (John 1:18) and the giving was so extraordinarily generous.

"That whoever believes in him shall not perish but have eternal life." "That" (*hina*) expresses a purpose but implies a result; in God's economy a purpose is always realized. "Whoever believes" has the sense "Everyone who at any time believes"—the promise remains valid for all time. On "believing in," see the next chapter. The person in whom all people are invited to believe is the Son whom God gave. But believers in Jesus are not entrusting themselves merely to a crucified and buried Jewish prophet. He is a person who snapped the chains of death and now lives forever in his Father's presence, sharing God's throne (Rev 22:3).

Clearly, "perishing" and "having eternal life" are opposites, so "perish" will mean "suffer eternal death," that is, be permanently separated from God, the only source of true life. To be forever exiled from God is to "perish" or "be lost" as a result of being condemned in God's court and having his justified wrath resting on one's head. In the phrase "have eternal life," the word "have" has the sense "will obtain and enjoy the possession of," as in the sentence, "Everyone who pays the fee will *have* unlimited access to the gym." Getting eternal life lies in the future only in the sense that it is dependent on believing. But once there is belief, eternal life is a present reality.

"Life" (*zōē*) refers to *quality*: it is supernatural, spiritual life that comes from God and enables us to share his life. "Eternal" (*aiōnios*) refers to *quantity*: this "life" will continue forever. In this phrase "eternal life," the emphasis rests on "life" rather than on "eternal." And in the wider context of John 3, this obtaining of eternal life is the same as being "born again" or "born from above" (John 3:3, 7).

An expanded paraphrase of John 3:16 will incorporate many of the observations made above:

> (This rebirth from above is possible for everyone who believes,) because God the Father loved all humans to such an extraordinary extent that he actually sent his dearly loved one and only Son into the world and then gave him over to an atoning death, so that everyone, without distinction or exception, who believes in Jesus will not suffer God's wrath and thus be lost, but, on the contrary, will both now and in the hereafter enjoy intimate fellowship with God and actually share in God's own life.

39: "BELIEVING THAT" AND "BELIEVING IN" (John 3:36)

The verb "believe" (*pisteuō*) is very common in the Fourth Gospel (ninety-eight uses), so it is not surprising this Gospel has been called "the Gospel of Belief." Sometimes the verb refers to *facts* ("believe that," "be convinced that," as in John 9:18; 16:27) and sometimes *things* (4:50), but often it is a *person* who is believed (*pisteuō* with the dative case), where "believe" means "give intellectual credence to" (4:21) or "entrust oneself to" (5:24).

But John's characteristic idiom is "believe in" (*pisteuō* followed by the preposition *eis*). This construction is not found in Classical Greek or the Greek OT (LXX) or ancient Greek papyri. And only nine of the forty-five NT uses are found outside the Fourth Gospel and 1 John. It is used only of a divine object of faith (of God, only in John 12:44; 14:1, but usually of Christ), never of a human object of faith. It is in Christ that God meets the individual in salvation, so there are not two competing objects of human faith.

The preposition *eis* after *pisteuō* indicates the direction of the belief; it is faith focused on Jesus. But it is not simply believing certain facts about Jesus or that all his teaching is true. Belief involves not only recognition and acceptance of the truth, but also, and primarily, total and permanent adherence and allegiance to Jesus as the Truth (John 14:6), a commitment of one's whole self to the person of Christ as Messiah and Lord forever. This is anything but easy believism!

The differences between "believing that" and "believing in" may be set out as follows, but we should never forget that the former naturally and ideally leads to the latter.

Believing *that*	Believing *in*
Deals with facts	Deals with a person
Involves the mind	Involves the heart
Involves recognition of the truth	Involves allegiance to Jesus the truth
Can be momentary	Must be continuous
Alters nothing	Alters everything
Is a natural experience	Is a "rebirth from above"
Is a prerequisite	Is the proper outcome

To believe in Jesus is to come to him (John 6:35), to receive him (1:12), to drink the water he offers (4:13–14), to follow him (8:12), and to love him (14:21).

40: EATING FLESH AND DRINKING BLOOD
(John 6:53)

The last section (verses 30–58) of John 6 presents Jesus as the living bread from heaven. The dialogue took place in a synagogue gathering in Capernaum (John 6:59), where interruptions and discussion would be acceptable (see verses 28, 30, 34, 41–43, 52). Like the manna of old (Exod 16:1–3 5), Jesus the bread was supplied by God and came down from heaven (John 6:32–33). But unlike the manna,

- God's provision of bread is not simply in the past (*dedōken*, perfect tense) but also occurs in the present (*didōsin*, present tense) (John 6:32).

- Jesus is "the true bread from heaven" (John 6:32), "the real food" (John 6:55), the antitype of the wilderness manna.

- The bread supplied by God constantly provides (*didous*, present active participle) more than nourishment—it provides life (John 6:33, 58).

- This bread is intended for all people without distinction ("the world") (John 6:33, 51).

Verse 35 marks a transition from a somewhat abstract dialogue about "bread from heaven" (verses 30–33) to intensely personal claims ("I am … to me … in me"), and a transition from warm approval ("Sir, always give us this bread," v. 34) to vigorous complaint about Jesus' claims ("The Jews there began to grumble about him because he said, 'I am the bread that came down from heaven,'" v. 41). After all, he and his parents were known as simply Nazarenes (v. 42)!

Then Jesus issues the further claim that those drawn by the Father to believe in Jesus, and who by doing so eat the bread that descended from heaven, will never die (vv. 43–51). "Whoever eats this bread will live forever. This bread is my flesh, which I will give for the life of the world" (v. 51b). The relatively mild grumbling of these Galilean Jews (v. 41) now gives place to heated dispute (v. 52). They doubtless understood that Jesus was speaking figuratively (he was not advocating cannibalism!), but his language was still blatantly offensive; the spiritual appropriation of any person was mystifying if not incomprehensible.

But Jesus does not retreat from his amazing claim that immortality is guaranteed to anyone who eats his flesh (vv. 50–51); nor does he alter his metaphor to reduce misunderstanding. Rather, he adds to the scandal of eating his flesh the abhorrent idea of drinking his blood as the means of gaining eternal life and being included in the resurrection (vv. 53–56). The idea of drinking blood was anathema to Jews (Gen 9:4; Lev 17:10–14; Deut 12:16).

In the context of John 6, how are we to understand Jesus' cryptic words? We get help by noting three statements, each of which ends with "has/have eternal life":

- "Everyone who looks to the Son and believes in him shall have eternal life" (v. 40).

- "The person who believes has eternal life" (v. 47).

- "The person who eats my flesh and drinks my blood has eternal life" (v. 54).

This justifies the inference that "looking and believing" or "believing" is equivalent to "eating and drinking" as the prerequisite for possessing eternal life. To look to Jesus and surrender to him in faith is to eat his flesh and drink his blood, to participate in his life and enter into union with him (v. 56), and so come to share in the eternal life of God. Augustine summed it up succinctly: *Crede, et manducasti* ("Believe, and you have eaten," *Homilies on John* 26.1). In the expression "The person who feeds on me will live because of me" (v. 57b), we have the two ways of appropriating Christ (eating and drinking) merged into one ("feeds"), and the two items of sustenance (flesh and drink) merged into one ("me" = Christ). Jesus Christ fully satisfies the needs (food and drink) of a person's spiritual constitution.

Finally, commentators are divided over the presence or extent of language relating to the Lord's Supper in verses 50–58. On the one hand, there is no ground for believing, as some do, that verse 51c ("This bread is my flesh, which I will give for the life of the world") is John's version of Jesus' words at the institution of the Lord's Supper (Luke 22:19; 1 Cor 11:24), although it is true that the Fourth Gospel contains no record of that institution. What is significant is that "flesh," not "body," is used in verses 53–54. Perhaps we may safely say that words that were originally addressed to Jesus' Jewish audience and were potentially intelligible to them have been subsequently heard or read by Christians as alluding (rather than actually referring) to the Lord's Supper, at which believers in Christ feed on him in their hearts by faith.

41: LEGITIMATE ANGER
(John 11:33, 38)

There are five occasions recorded in the Gospels when Jesus reacts to a situation in anger or righteous indignation.

The first is Jesus' cleansing of the Jerusalem temple, which took place in the court of the Gentiles (John 2:13–17). Both at the beginning and at the end of his public ministry (Mark 11:15–18), Jesus cleansed the temple of hindrances to genuine Gentile worship in the form of noisy traders and clamorous moneychangers. His intense eagerness (*zēlos*, "zeal," John 2:17) for the sanctity of the temple and for the purity of worship so stirred up his anger that he vigorously expelled from the temple these commercial entrepreneurs: "Stop turning my Father's house into a market" (John 2:17).

Second is Jesus' healing of a man with leprosy in Mark 1:40–41. So far from crying out "Unclean! Unclean!" when Jesus approached, as was required, this leper himself came up to Jesus with his urgent request for healing if Jesus was willing. "Jesus was indignant" (v. 41 NIV) or "became angry," not at the man for asking (Jesus actually incurred defilement by touching him and then cleansed him) but at the ravages of disease as evidence of Satan's activity (see Luke 13:16).

Third is Jesus' healing of a man with a shriveled hand in a synagogue, probably in Capernaum (Mark 3:5). Jesus' anger was provoked by the perverse desire of his adversaries to spy on him and accuse him of violating the Sabbath if he healed the man on that day. But this anger gave place to grief at their stubborn hearts. His anger was short-lived: "He looked around (*periblepsamenos*, momentary aorist) at them in anger." His deep distress (*sullupoumenos*, continuous present) was prolonged.

The fourth is when Jesus' disciples rebuked people who were bringing little children to him for a blessing (Mark 10:13–16). This time Jesus' anger, or righteous indignation (v. 14), was aroused by his disciples' misguided protection of him from what they regarded as needless interruption, or by their desire to assert their authority by deciding who was worthy of their teacher's attention, or by their rejection of seemingly insignificant members of society—or for all three reasons.

Finally, there is Jesus' response to Lazarus' death in John 11:33, 38. It was precisely when Jesus saw Mary and other Jews weeping over the death of Lazarus that he "became angry in spirit" (v. 33). Some versions render this "was greatly disturbed in spirit" (NRSV) or "was moved with indignation" (REB). The verb involved is *embrimaomai*, which originally meant "snort with rage" and was used of animals and especially horses venting their fury. The same verb is used again in verse 38, describing Jesus' emotional state on arrival at Lazarus's tomb. In each case, his anger or deep distress apparently arose from his overpowering awareness of the ravages of sickness, suffering, death, and grief associated with Satan's reign in human affairs.

We can conclude from these that anger is not necessarily sinful. In Ephesians 4:26a, Paul wrote, "Be angry, but (in your anger) do not sin." When anger occurs—hopefully for a legitimate reason—sin must be avoided by not letting one's anger or indignation last until sunset (v. 26b). What caused the anger must be addressed promptly. Indeed, just as God is "slow to anger" (Jonah 4:2), so believers are to be "slow to become angry" (Jas 1:19) because love "is not easily angered" (1 Cor 13:5).

42: "JESUS BURST INTO TEARS"
(John 11:35)

In any language, some verbs express a particular state of being. For example, "I am thirsty" expresses the state of thirst. When you enter that state, you say, "I become thirsty." In Greek, entrance upon a state is expressed by what is called the "ingressive aorist." So when the verb *dakryō*, "I shed tears" or "I cry," is used in the aorist tense, the meaning can be "I began to cry" or "I burst into tears."

With this in mind, we can trace the relentless deepening of Jesus' emotions as the story of Lazarus's illness and death progresses (John 11:1–37).

First, Jesus was undoubtedly distressed that Lazarus was ill, for he loved him as a close friend (John 11:3, 5–6, 11). Even onlookers observed Jesus' intense love for Lazarus (John 11:36). Lazarus must have been seriously ill, because Jesus assured his worried disciples, "This sickness will not end in death" (John 11:4).

Then, Jesus became "deeply moved (some versions have "angry") in spirit and greatly shaken" at the sight of Mary's tears and the tears of the Jews who had come with her to meet Jesus (John 11:33). That is, he became profoundly agitated when he observed the grief caused by human suffering and death, evidences of Satan's reign.

Finally, when he actually stood in front of the tomb of Lazarus (John 11:34), those deep emotions spilled over—suddenly "Jesus burst into tears" (John 11:35). Jesus is one of us, fully human. John had noted in an earlier episode that Jesus, "exhausted from his journey," had sat down at Sychar's well, "just as he was" (John 4:6).

This whole Lazarus story shows us that in the face of death,

- *Grief is necessary.* The friends of Mary and Martha came to comfort them in their natural grief (John 11:19, 31).

- *Tears are appropriate.* They are a natural expression of human emotion (John 11:33, 35; compare Luke 19:41; Heb 5:7).

- *Questions are inevitable.* "If you had been here, my brother would not have died" (John 11:21, 32); "Could not he ... have kept this man from dying?" (John 11:37).

43: JESUS MY FRIEND?
(John 15:15)

A hymn written by Joseph Scriven (1819–1886) declares,

> What a friend we have in Jesus,
> All our sins and griefs to bear!

But is there scriptural justification for saying "Jesus is my friend"?

In the OT, Abraham is called God's friend (2 Chr 20:7; Isa 41:8). But this leads James to say, not that "God was called the friend of Abraham," but that "He (Abraham) was called the friend of God" (Jas 2:23). Moses, too, is called the friend of God by implication: "The LORD would speak to Moses face to face, as one speaks to a friend" (Exod 33:11 NIV).

But Jesus declares in John 15:14–15, "You are my friends if you do what I command you. No longer do I call you 'slaves,' because a slave does not understand what his master is doing. Rather, I have given you the name of 'friends,' because I have made known to you everything that I have heard from my Father." Doesn't this clearly authorize us to claim that Jesus is our friend?

We should observe, to begin with, that Jesus is not making a blanket affirmation that all his disciples are his friends. "You are my friends, *if* ..." Obedience to Jesus does not create his friendship, but it is a mark and proof of that friendship. Jesus' central point is that a slave obeys his master's orders without understanding his master's motives and plans; he has no intimate knowledge of his master's purposes. So then, because Jesus *did* disclose to his disciples a full knowledge of his Father's counsels (John 1:18; 8:38), they could not any longer be called "slaves." The only designation appropriate for them in this regard was "friends," for a friend has the privilege of intimate knowledge that is denied to a slave. No doubt Jesus' disciples would have called him their friend when introducing him to others, just as he spoke of "our friend Lazarus" (John 11:11).

But there is a radical difference between what was inevitable when Jesus was on earth—a mutual use of the term "friend"—and what is now appropriate with regard to the glorified Lord who shares God's throne as his plenipotentiary (Rev 22:3). His present titles stress his otherness and unparalleled majesty—he is, for example, the Alpha and Omega (Rev 22:13), just as the Lord God is (Rev 1:8; 21:6), and the bright Morning Star (Rev 22:16)—so that the notion of friendship or comradeship is demeaning when applied to him. It is not that the Father or Jesus is *un*friendly, but each remains a supreme Lord to be reverenced and obeyed.

A similar situation applies, I believe, with regard to whether we may call Jesus our brother. On the one hand, during his earthly life, Jesus did not hesitate to refer to his disciples as his brothers (Matt 28:10). And even now Jesus is graciously "not ashamed" to call believers his brothers and sisters (Heb 2:11–12) and be known as the firstborn of them (Rom 8:29). But on the other hand, that does not give us the right to call him our elder brother, which Scripture never does. Indeed, the apostle John describes Jesus as *monogenēs* (John 1:14, 18), the one and only Son, without siblings. He is the Son (*huios*) of God (3:18); believers are the children (*tekna*) of God (1:12).

44: "DEAR WOMAN, LOOK, YOUR SON!" (John 19:26)

Only three times in the Gospels do we read of Jesus directly addressing his mother.

In the first case (Luke 2:49), Joseph, Mary, and Jesus had traveled to Jerusalem to celebrate the Passover. As the Nazareth caravan of pilgrims returned home after the festival, Joseph and Mary wrongly assumed that Jesus was in the traveling party, while Jesus wrongly assumed his parents were still in Jerusalem. There was mutual misunderstanding, but Mary rebuked Jesus with a complaint, if not an accusation of betrayal or of filial insubordination: "Son, why have you treated us like this? Your father and I have been searching for you with great anxiety" (Luke 2:48). Jesus replied to both his parents, not simply Mary, with two probing questions that reflected his surprise at their reaction: "What made you search for me? Didn't you realize I had to be in my Father's house?" (Luke 2:49).

In the second case (John 2:4), Mary informs Jesus at the Cana wedding that the supply of wine has run out, clearly expecting and hoping that he would use his miraculous powers so that the hosts would be spared embarrassment. His response is (literally), "Woman, what (is there) to me and (at the same time) to you?" That is, "Your concern and mine are different," or "What has this concern of yours to do with me?" The right time for him to act in accord with his Father's will had not yet arrived.

In the third case (John 19:26), Jesus anticipates the loneliness of his widowed mother in the coming years without her firstborn and entrusts her to the tender and permanent care of her Son's closest disciple.

What is of special interest is that in none of these three cases does Jesus address Mary by the expected term of address, "Mother." In the two cases where Jesus uses a term of address in speaking to his mother, we find the form *gynai*, the address case of the word *gynē*, "woman." In modern English usage, the address "Woman ..." often has a negative sense, but in a Jewish setting this Greek form is simply a courteous formal address and is in no way disrespectful. Sometimes it has been appropriately rendered "Madam" or "Ma'am," or "Good woman," or "Dear woman." Moreover, this word Jesus chose to use was not preceded by an interjection as in Matthew 15:28 in reference to the Syro-Phoenician woman, "O woman (*ō gynai*), what great faith you have!" This absence of the expected "O" does not show an absence of emotion, but it does point to a certain matter-of-fact way of speaking.

If we examine the four episodes in the Gospels that involve Mary (Luke 2:41–52; John 2:1–10; Matt 12:46–50 and parallels; John 19:26–27), we can observe Jesus' readjustment of family and maternal ties at various junctures in his life and ministry. Mary was being gently led, like Mary Magdalene after Jesus' resurrection (John 20:11–18), from a temporary earthly relationship with Jesus toward a permanent spiritual relationship with him. This loosening of Jesus' links with his mother resulted from his establishment of a new family and of new relationships that supersede all others (Matt 12:46–50).

45: JESUS' REAL HUMANITY
(John 19:28)

The intense suffering of the previous three hours of darkness is over and Jesus has realized that "everything had now come to its appointed end" (Ernst Cassirer). This "everything" is all God gave Jesus to do, Jesus' complete carrying out of God's will that he had earlier described as his food (John 4:34) and his drink (John 18:11). Now, "so that Scripture would be fulfilled, Jesus said, 'I am thirsty.'"

The scriptural reference may be to Psalm 22:15 ("My mouth is dried up like a potsherd, and my tongue sticks to my gums; you lay me low in the dust of death"), but more probably the primary Scripture is Psalm 69:21, "They put poison in my food, and to alleviate my thirst they gave me sour wine to drink," because both the words "thirst" (*dipsaō*) and "vinegar/sour wine" (*oxos*) are found in the LXX of the psalm and are relevant to the whole passage John 19:28–30, where *dipsaō* occurs once and *oxos* three times. The psalmist is alluding to his dastardly betrayal by imagined friends or comforters.

John's record continues: "A jar full of sour wine was standing there. So they fixed a sponge full of the wine on a hyssop stem and held it up to his mouth. Then when Jesus had received the wine, he exclaimed, 'It is finished!'" (John 19:29–30a). "Sour wine" or "vinegary wine" (*oxos*) was more effective than water in quenching thirst and was a common drink among the poorer classes and especially soldiers.

Jesus would have had no fluids since the Last Supper, about eighteen hours previously. One of the physical causes of death by crucifixion was dehydration—expressed prophetically by the psalmist as having the mouth and throat as dry as a piece of dusty earthenware and the swollen tongue fused to the gums. Jesus' cry of physical pain, "I am thirsty," is testimony to his genuine humanity (cf. John 4:5–7), and also to his genuine humility, for it was a request to his executioners or others to provide temporary relief from the ravages of thirst. What a remarkable reversal of circumstances it is when the One who promised that all who drank his living water would never thirst again (John 4:10, 13–14) himself cries out, "I am thirsty"!

At an earlier time, when the execution squad arrived at Golgotha (Matt 27:33) but before Jesus was fastened to the cross (Mark 15:23–24), he was offered "wine (*oinos*) flavored with myrrh" (Mark 15:23), apparently a crude anesthetic ("drugged wine," Mark 15:23 REB). But once Jesus had tasted it, he *refused to drink* it (Matt 27:34b). He was determined to endure the agony of crucifixion without the dulling of his senses by a sedative. And it was for precisely the same reason that he later *accepted* the sour wine—to revive and sharpen all his senses and avoid the clouding of his physical and spiritual sensibilities, especially his mind, that so easily occurred with the passage of time under the torment of crucifixion. In this way he was ensuring that his final self-surrender to God in death (Luke 23:46) was a fully conscious act.

The ultimate outcome of Jesus' agonizing cry "I am thirsty" is portrayed in Revelation 7:16–17, where the numberless multitude whose robes have been made white in the blood of the Lamb stand before God's throne and before the Lamb. Of them it is said: "Never again will they hunger; never again will they thirst. ... For the Lamb seated in the center of the throne will be their shepherd; he will lead them to springs of living water."

46: MISSION ACCOMPLISHED!
(John 19:30)

In the previous chapter, we saw that anyone who is being crucified suffers from dehydration, with the mouth and throat unbearably dry and the tongue grossly swollen (see Ps 22:15). At first Jesus had refused the relief of the offered sour wine (Matt 27:34) so that all of his senses might be fully alert for his suffering. But hours later, the excruciating pain of crucifixion had begun to dull the senses and make speaking almost impossible, so Jesus accepted what he had earlier refused: "When Jesus had received the wine, he exclaimed, 'It is finished!'" (John 19:30).

This cry consists of a single word in Greek—*tetelestai*. It is in the perfect tense, which presupposes a past occurrence but focuses attention on the present results of that event, so the word may be translated "it stands complete" or "it is finished." It is a word an artist would use when she stands back after spending weeks perfecting what could become a masterpiece and gently whispers, with great relief and pleasure, *tetelestai*. Perhaps Jesus had used the word in his life as a carpenter when he had finished making a bedside table or plough for a client in Sepphoris. Running off to Joseph, he calls out "Abba, Abba, come quickly!" and proudly shows his foster father his completed carpentry. "*Tetelestai!*" "Splendid, *Yeshua*," says Joseph, placing an approving hand on Jesus' shoulder. "*Tetelestai.*"

The subject of the verb, the identity of the "it," is not stated, but it could refer to Jesus' life on earth, his work on earth, or both. Jesus realized that his death was imminent—perhaps only minutes away—when he would commit his spirit into his Father's care. When he exclaims, "*Tetelestai,*" he is speaking in anticipation, under the shadow of his atoning death. As he surveyed his earthly life, he knew he had completely and perfectly fulfilled God's will. He had earlier observed, "My food is to do the will of the One who sent me and to bring his work to completion" (John 4:34), and now he could affirm, "I have brought you glory on earth by finishing the work you gave me to do" (John 17:4). *Tetelestai!* This "work" involved his full and perfect exposure of God's heart (John 1:18) and his becoming God's paschal lamb (John 1:29), actions that brought salvation to humankind. From this perspective, "it" means the provision of salvation.

This cry was spoken in a loud voice. This is not said explicitly, but it is an appropriate inference from the Gospel accounts. According to both Matthew (27:48–50) and Mark (15:36–37), it was only *after* Jesus had been given the wine that he cried out again "in a loud voice" and *before* he yielded up his spirit. *Tetelestai* was a cry of triumph, not the lament or complaint of a defeated foe. The victim had become the victor. Significantly, this is the only cry of Jesus on the cross that was not spoken to somebody, but because it was spoken loudly, anyone within earshot could have heard this victorious shout.

47: IS DOUBT ALWAYS SINFUL?
(John 20:27)

Since doubt does not proceed from faith, is it not sinful? After all, did not Paul say, "Whatever does not proceed from faith is sin" (Rom 14:23)?

In Romans 14, Paul is insisting that all believers should be fully convinced in their own minds regarding dietary preferences and calendrical regulations (Rom 14:5), and then act in accordance with those convictions without judging others. His final observation (v. 23) is that any action that does not line up with a commitment to Christ as Lord (= "faith") is sinful. He is discouraging any actions about secondary matters such as food or observances that do not square with one's prior convictions, for by such hypocritical action a person stands self-condemned (as Peter was at Antioch; Gal 2:11–14).

In a psychological sense, doubt refers to natural uncertainty, being at a loss to understand some situation (John 13:22; Acts 2:12; 10:17; Gal 4:20). The doubter is unsure how to react or act without further information. Such hesitancy, being natural, is not sinful.

In a religious sense, doubt is a wavering between belief and unbelief, being in two minds, as when some of the eleven disciples worshipped Jesus, "but some doubted" (Matt 28:17). So doubt *may be* uncrystallized unbelief, but unbelief *actually is* crystallized doubt. In all faith, there seems to be an admixture of doubt; recall the exclamation of the father of the boy possessed by an impure spirit: "I do believe; help me overcome my unbelief!" (Mark 9:24).

The case of the apostle Thomas (John 20:24–29) dramatizes the journey to faith by way of doubt. His experience shows how secure faith can be hammered out on the anvil of vigorous skepticism.

Thomas was absent when Jesus appeared to the other ten disciples on the evening of his resurrection. He was not inclined to believe the testimony of Mary Magdalene (v. 18) or the assurance of his fellow disciples who "kept telling" (iterative imperfect) him, "We have seen the Lord" (v. 25). Instead, he remonstrated with them, "Unless I see the nail marks in his hands and put my finger in those nail marks, and put my hand into his side, I will certainly not believe (*ou mē* + future indicative)" (v. 25). To this vigorous denial Jesus gave a direct reproof: "Stop doubting (*mē* with the present imperative), but become a believer!" (v. 27). In response, "Thomas said to him, 'My Lord and my God!'" (v. 28).

How are we to account for Thomas's dramatic change of outlook from gloomy disbelief to ecstatic faith? First, for a week (see John 20:6) he was able to reflect on the claim of Mary Magdalene and his ten close friends that they had seen Jesus alive. Had they perhaps all experienced an identical vision? Were they all likely to be conspiring in telling a lie? Second, the appearance of the risen and transformed Jesus (John 20:26–27) would have seemed to Thomas to be a personal and gracious reply to his earlier semi-defiant assertion, "Unless I see ... I will never believe." Third, the personal invitation of Jesus to Thomas ("Put your finger here and examine my hands; put out your hand and place it into my side," v. 27) was couched in terms that implied Jesus' supernatural knowledge of the very language Thomas himself had earlier used (v. 25). Finally, the ultimate stimulus behind

Thomas's change of outlook and remarkable confession (v. 28) was the work of the Spirit (cf. Matt 16:15–17; 1 Cor 12:3).

Did Thomas take up Jesus' invitation and touch him? The text is silent on the matter, but it is highly unlikely. Sight and hearing provided evidence enough—he recognized Jesus, saw the wounds in his hands or wrists, and recognized his voice (as Mary Magdalene had earlier, John 20:16). Moreover, in verse 29 Jesus says simply, "Because you have *seen* me, you have believed."

In the confession of Thomas, "(You are) my Lord and my God!" (v. 28), the apostle John reaches the pinnacle of his Gospel and the zenith of his Christology. Just as the prologue ends as it begins (1:1, 18), so the Gospel ends as it begins (1:1, 20:28): with an assertion of the deity of Jesus Christ, who is both Logos and Son. On this, see further the next chapter.

48: A CLIMACTIC CONFESSION: "(YOU ARE) MY LORD AND MY GOD!" (John 20:28)

Scattered throughout the Fourth Gospel we find a number of titles for Jesus. For example, he is "Lamb of God" (John 1:29, 36), "Messiah" (1:41), "Son of God, King of Israel" (1:49), "teacher" (3:2), "prophet" (4:19; 7:40), "Holy One of God" (6:69), "Son of Man" (9:35), "the Messiah, Son of God" (11:27), and "King of the Jews" (19:19). But it is the confession of Thomas, "my Lord and my God!" that forms the climax of all these titles. John places this confession at the end of his Gospel as the point to which he wishes to bring his readers in their spiritual journey—a personal acknowledgment of the resurrected Lord.

When, after the resurrection, Mary Magdalene says, "They have taken my Lord away" (20:13), "my Lord" was a courteous and tender expression, referring to the deceased Jesus. For Thomas it was an exalted title of address, referring to the risen Jesus. Thomas recognized, or was beginning to recognize, that Jesus was supreme in the physical and spiritual realms as the One who shared his Father's authority, functions, and rights (see 5:17–18, 21–23, 26).

What does Thomas (and the author) imply when he addresses Jesus as "my God"? As used by a monotheistic Jew in reference to a person who was clearly human, the title "God" will point to Jesus' oneness with the Father, his sharing in the divine nature. John 20:28 is an advance on John 1:1, where Jesus as the Logos *was* "God" at the beginning of creation. But here in 20:28, the implication is that Jesus *is* "God." The essential deity of Christ is a present fact as well as a past reality.

It is of special interest that the evangelist records no rebuke by Jesus of Thomas for his worship. Jews considered the human acceptance of worship as blasphemous (see Acts 14:8–18; Rev 19:9–10). Far from rebuking Thomas, Jesus immediately commends Thomas's confession to others: "Blessed are those who have not seen me and yet have believed" (20:29).

Since chapter 20 ends with a statement of purpose ("These things are written so that you may believe that Jesus is the Messiah, the Son of God," 20:31), chapter 21 may be aptly treated as an epilogue. If so, 20:28 (with the following beatitude) marks the climax of the entire Gospel. We move from "God" (1:1) to "the only Son who is God" (1:18) to "my God" (20:28). That is, John regards Jesus as being appropriately called "God" in his preexistent, incarnate, and postresurrection states. See also the previous chapter.

49: A PAINFUL REINSTATEMENT
(John 21:15–17)

After his resurrection, Jesus encountered seven of his disciples on the shores of Lake Galilee. When their breakfast was finished, Jesus asked Peter a penetrating question: "Simon, son of John, do you love me more than these?" He does this two further times, each time beginning with "Simon, son of John" (vv. 15–17), not using his new name "Cephas" or "Peter" (John 1:42). The use of Peter's old name would have reminded him of an earlier word of Jesus (Luke 22:31): "Simon, Simon, listen! Satan has asked to have you (plural) (in his power; see Job 1:6–12) to sift you (all) like wheat (to discover who will fail under testing), but I have prayed for you (singular) that your faith may not fail. And when you (singular) have turned back (from your defection; see v. 34), strengthen your brothers."

"Do you love me more than these (*toutōn*)?" "More" here means "to a greater degree" and is followed by an abbreviated comparison. If the plural form *toutōn* is neuter, the sense is "(more than) these things," namely nets and fish, a career as a fisherman. If it is masculine, the meaning will be "(more than you love) these men" (= the other disciples), or "(more than) these men (love me)." This last alternative is the preferred understanding, since Peter had earlier boasted of a loyal love greater than his colleagues' love: "Even if all fall away on account of you, I never will" (Matt 26:33). Having made his point with "more than these," Jesus omits this phrase when he repeats his question "Do you love me?" twice more (vv. 16–17).

Jesus' threefold question corresponded to and was prompted by Peter's threefold denial that he was one of Jesus' disciples or knew Jesus at the time of Jesus' trial (John 18:17, 25, 27). In making his third denial, Peter had called down curses on himself and again had tried to guarantee his truthfulness by an oath (Matt 26:72, 74). Naturally, the repeated question evoked excruciatingly painful memories: "Peter was grieved or greatly pained (*elupēthē*)" (John 21:17).

To each of Jesus' questions Peter responded, "You know that I love you" (John 21:15–17). There is probably no significance to the fact that two verbs for "love" (*agapaō* and *phileō*) are used in these three verses, since (1) these verbs are interchangeable elsewhere in the Fourth Gospel, as (for example) when the Father is said to love the Son (3:35 and 5:20); and (2) in the present passage there are other stylistic variations (the words for shepherding, sheep, and knowing), a characteristic of John's style.

After each response that Peter gives, Jesus graciously recommissions him, this time as a shepherd: "Feed my lambs. ... Take care of my sheep. ... Feed my sheep." The two verbs used (*boskō*, "tend," "feed"; *poimainō*, "tend," "shepherd") remind us that a shepherd feeds, leads, and protects. Earlier, Peter had been commissioned to fish for people (Luke 5:10). To the evangelist's hook was now added the shepherd's crook, so that (as others have pointed out) he fulfilled his dual role "by hook and by crook"!

This gracious reinstatement also does not imply Peter's elevation to pastoral primacy, for Jesus remains "the chief shepherd" (1 Pet 5:4) and Peter, the "fellow elder," is one of many undershepherds (1 Pet 5:1–4).

Finally, this whole episode throws light on the question, "Can Christian leaders who are guilty of wrongdoing that is widely known, whether to Christians or others, ever be reinstated to public Christian service?" The answer is "Yes!"—provided the wrongdoing is confronted and its repercussions for the Christian cause are recognized, and there is genuine repentance. This repentance should be shown by (1) full reparation or compensation to all the parties involved, as far as this is possible; and (2) submission to an extended period of supervised spiritual rehabilitation that will indicate humility and a desire for ultimate restoration to some form of specialized service to be determined by Christian colleagues.

50: FIRST THINGS FIRST!
(John 21:15–22)

It is perilously easy for Christian workers to become preoccupied with either the amount of service rendered to the Master or gaining an adequate knowledge of the faith. But our preoccupations and priorities are readjusted when we listen to two questions and two commands in John 21.

The immediate background to the first question is this. Late one night, some time after the resurrection, Peter and six other disciples were strolling along the shores of the Sea of Galilee, perhaps discussing the implications of the commission Jesus had so recently given them: "As the Father has sent me, even so I send you" (John 20:21). Gazing out into the mist that had enveloped the lake, Peter is overcome by happy memories of the past. True to his impetuous nature, he declares, "I'm off fishing! Who's coming?" "We're with you," comes the reply. But toil as they might, to their embarrassment they caught nothing (John 21:1–3).

After fishing, they joined Jesus for breakfast on the shore. When they all had enjoyed the breakfast he had prepared, Jesus addressed *a legitimate and necessary question* to Peter: "Do you love me more than these (your fellow disciples)?" To Peter's grief, Jesus repeated his question three times (John 21:9–17), reminding Peter of his threefold denial of Jesus (John 18:17, 25, 27; see the previous chapter). When Peter answers Jesus, "You know that I love you," the Lord says to him, "Feed my sheep!" (John 21:17). Before we obey Jesus' command to serve, we must hear his question about love for him. Love is the inspiration of acceptable service. Service is the expression of genuine love.

The immediate context of our second question and command is this. Having charged Peter with the task of shepherding, Jesus prophesies Peter's death by martyrdom, and probably even his death by crucifixion (John 21:18–19). And as Peter now follows Jesus in literal obedience, he turns and sees John following (John needed no recommissioning!) and seeks to satisfy his curiosity about his close friend by asking Jesus *a natural but illegitimate question:* "Lord, what about him?" To this Jesus replies, "If it is my will that he should remain alive until I return, what is that to you? As for you, follow me!" (John 21:20–22).

Certainly, Jesus is not discouraging the spirit of legitimate inquiry; curiosity is the mother of knowledge. But it was not Peter's place to enter into the divine counsels—to pose a question that related to the faithfulness and destiny of another, particularly when that other person had never ceased "following." What Peter needed at that moment was not to have his attention diverted to speculation about what the future had in store for the beloved disciple, but to face resolutely the demanding task that Jesus had just entrusted to him—the responsibility of feeding and guarding the flock.

First things first! Love comes before service: "Do you love me?" "Care for my sheep!" Personal love for Christ should always have precedence over Christian service.

And obedience comes before knowledge: "Lord, what about this man?" "As for you, follow me!" Personal obedience to Christ should always have precedence over the gaining of knowledge.

ACTS

51: "UNDER NEW MANAGEMENT"
(Acts 8:16)

A shop that has recently changed owners will sometimes display a notice in the window that reads "Under New Management." This is a perfect picture of the nature of Christian conversion that is reflected in Christian baptism "into the name of Jesus Christ" (Acts 8:16).

Twice in the book of Acts we read of baptism "in the name of Jesus Christ" (Acts 2:38; 10:48), where "in" (*en* or *epi* in Greek) points to a ceremony in which the name of Jesus Christ was invoked or confessed by the person being baptized or the one baptizing or both. But of special interest are the five NT passages where baptism is said to be "into (*eis*) the name" of someone (Matt 28:19; Acts 8:16; 19:5; 1 Cor 1:13, 15). In commercial usage, this Greek phrase, *eis to onoma*, meaning "into the possession of," denoted the establishment of a relationship of belonging, and so a transference of ownership. It was used when money was paid into the account of an individual whose name stands over the account, or money was credited to the name of someone in banking transactions or commercial sales.

Against this background, the person being baptized passes into the possession of the Triune God (Matt 28:19) or the Lord Jesus (Acts 8:16; 19:5), and comes under new control and special protection. Support for this understanding comes from 1 Corinthians 1, where Paul equates being baptized in his name (*eis to onoma*) with belonging to him: "One of you says, 'I belong to Paul.' ... Were you baptized into the name of Paul? I am thankful that I did not baptize any of

87

you except Crispus and Gaius, so that no one can say that you were baptized into my name" (1 Cor 1:12–15).

Just as in commercial usage payment "into" someone's name indicated a transfer of money into someone's account, so in baptism there is signified a transference of believers into the permanent possession and safekeeping of the omnipotent Trinity. The baptized person is "under new management." In baptism God says to the believer, "You belong to me. You are my adopted son, my adopted daughter, forever." And in response, the believer says to God, "I belong to you. I will be your willing slave forever." Believers are Christ's indentured slaves in the sense that, through baptism, they have become eternally bound to him by mutual agreement. Like the Hebrew slave whose earlobe was pierced with an awl to signify that he loved his master and wished to be his slave for life (Exod 21:5–6; Deut 15:16–17), the disciples of Jesus submit to baptism as an indication that they love their new Master and pledge to serve him wholeheartedly as long as they live.

It is a remarkable fact that the NT records no case of baptism in the triune name ("in the name of the Father and of the Son and of the Holy Spirit," Matt 28:19), only of baptism "into the name of the Lord Jesus" (Acts 8:16; 19:5) or "in the name of Jesus Christ" (Acts 2:38; 10:48). Perhaps we can explain this apparent anomaly by observing that Luke's formulas may be abbreviated forms of Matthew's formula, not indicating the precise words used in Christian baptism—actually the trinitarian form—but highlighting the point that in the baptismal "transference of ownership" a person becomes the property of Christ and his slave (cf. Rom 1:1; 1 Cor 6:19b–20; 7:22–23) and calls on Christ's name when being baptized. See also part 2, ch. 26.

52: A SHARP DISPUTE — AND BEYOND
(Acts 15:37–39)

Paul and his close friend Barnabas returned from a very profitable missionary journey in South Galatia and reported back to their home church of Antioch and also to the mother church of Jerusalem

(Acts 14:26–27; 15:12). Paul then proposed that they should make a return visit to check on the converts they had made in the towns they had recently evangelized. Barnabas agreed with the idea and suggested that his cousin John Mark (Col 4:10) should accompany them as he had earlier.

Now, John Mark had left Paul and Barnabas in the lurch at Pamphylia on the first journey, deserting them when they were about to penetrate inland through robber-infested mountains known for their dangerous rivers. He had then returned to the safety of Jerusalem (Acts 13:13). Because of this, Paul was of the opinion that they should not risk having with them all the time (*sumparalambanein*, present infinitive) someone who earlier had let them down and could do so again. Barnabas apparently wanted to give his cousin a second chance and simply take him along (*sumparalabein*, aorist infinitive). It must have been a fascinating and vigorous exchange of views.

But Luke tells us that the ensuing discussion degenerated into a *paroxysmos*, a sharp and acrimonious dispute between the two friends. This colorful Greek word, which gives us our English word "paroxysm," a fit of disease or rage or laughter, regularly has connotations of irritation and even exasperation. In the only other New Testament use (Heb 10:24) it means a "stirring up" or "provoking." But here it refers to a contention or disagreement that became sharp and harsh. We can hardly excuse either of these stalwarts of the early church from any blame for this dishonoring altercation.

The result? The friends parted company. Barnabas took John Mark and sailed for Cyprus, while Paul chose Silas and traveled through Syria and Cilicia, strengthening the churches (Acts 15:39–40). In God's providence, two missionary expeditions replaced the planned one!

There will always be disagreement among Christians, even among mature believers and those in leadership, regarding matters that involve the kingdom of God and the church. These disagreements should not descend into a sharp or bitter dispute. Even if this happens, however, God reigns supreme and can create good out of human weakness, perversity, or sin.

53: MUTUAL DEVOTION IN MARRIAGE
(Acts 18:2–3)

Luke introduces Aquila as a refugee Jewish tentmaker who had recently arrived in Corinth with his wife Priscilla as a result of an edict of the emperor Claudius that expelled all the Jews from Rome (Acts 18:2–3). In his three references to Aquila's wife (Acts 18:2, 18, 26), Luke uses the name Priscilla, the diminutive form of Prisca, whereas Paul always uses her formal name, Prisca (Rom 16:3; 1 Cor 16:19; 2 Tim 4:19). She may have been related in some way to the renowned Roman family the *gens Prisca.* Given the name, we can assume she was probably freeborn, and given the word arrangement in Acts 18:2, we can assume she was not Jewish. Here was a racially mixed marriage, but both were believers (Acts 18:26; Rom 16:3–5).

Priscilla and Aquila formed an ideal Christian marriage. Over their lives could be inscribed the words "Total Mutual Devotion." There are three indications of their wholehearted commitment to one another.

First, when Claudius's edict (of AD 49) expelled the Jews from Rome, Prisca the Roman, under no compulsion by reason of race to leave the capital, accompanied her Jewish husband in his departure.

Second, when Luke says that "because he (Paul) was of the same trade he stayed with them, for by trade they were leatherworkers" (Acts 18:3), the plurals "they" and "them" both refer to Aquila and Priscilla. Whether or not Priscilla was a woman of high birth, the fact that she toiled at the same trade as her husband indicates the compatibility and cooperation between the pair, especially if she learned her craft from her husband after their marriage, although this cannot be demonstrated.

Third, Aquila and Priscilla are mentioned six times in the New Testament—three times by Luke in the book of Acts (18:2, 18, 26) and three times by Paul in his letters (Rom 16:3; 1 Cor 16:19; 2 Tim 4:19). They are always mentioned together, never separately. This reflects the inviolate unity of their lives. As we trace their movements, Rome—Corinth—Ephesus—Rome—Ephesus, they are always found side by side, toiling at their craft, adjusting to new situations, and creating new circles of friends, always in unison. For them, mutual love and respect as well as marital fidelity were corollaries of being Christ's slaves.

On four occasions, Priscilla is named before her husband: twice by Luke (Acts 18:18, 26) and twice by Paul (Rom 16:3; 2 Tim 4:19). It was customary in first-century society for the wife to be mentioned after her husband. Why, then, this unusual reversal of order? Priscilla may have been better known or more prominent in the church, having greater visibility because her giftedness lay in the more public arena. But even if she was more conspicuously gifted than her husband, their constant association in joint Christian ministry would suggest that relations between them were harmonious rather than strained.

54: DEVOTED TO CHRISTIAN DOCTRINE
(Acts 18:24–26)

When Paul left Corinth and traveled to Ephesus, Priscilla and Aquila accompanied him (Acts 18:18–19), perhaps to establish a new branch of their tentmaking business there and to afford Paul support for his pioneering evangelism in the city, where they hosted part of the infant church (1 Cor 16:19). It was there in Ephesus that they met Apollos.

Acts 18:24 gives a fourfold description of Apollos. He was Jewish, an Alexandrian by birth, and a learned man, with a thorough knowledge of the Scriptures. His knowledge of Jesus and the Jesus movement, incomplete as it was (Acts 18:25), may have been gained from his home city, Alexandria, or possibly from John the Baptist's disciples. "With burning zeal" he used to speak and teach (habitual imperfects) accurately about Jesus. At a later time he resoundingly refuted the Corinthian Jews in public debate as he proved the messiahship of Jesus from the Scriptures (Acts 18:28).

When Priscilla and Aquila heard this learned professor skillfully debate with the Jews in the synagogue in Ephesus (Acts 18:26), they were evidently deeply impressed by his ability as an exponent and defender of the gospel. However, he knew of no baptism except John's. Instead of criticizing him for his defective understanding of Christian doctrine or comparing him unfavorably with their close friend Paul, they apparently discussed the matter together and decided to invite him to their home so that the three of them could talk at length about "the way of God" (v. 26). Luke's use of the compound verb *proslambanō* ("take aside") highlights the sensitivity and graciousness of this Christian pair. It was not in public, where Apollos might be embarrassed, that they supplemented his accurate knowledge of Jesus, but "aside" or "privately." Moreover, it is a tribute to the humility of this distinguished Jewish Christian scholar that he was willing to learn from a woman and her husband.

This Christian couple were engaged in the process of the transmission of orthodoxy, the guarding and handing on of the apostolic deposit (cf. 2 Tim 1:14; 2:2). They themselves were so well versed in the (Old Testament) Scriptures and Christian tradition that they were able first to identify the deficiencies in Apollos's knowledge and then to rectify those deficiencies by convincing him of the truth of their teaching, especially about Christian baptism and what it signified. Just as Luke's next episode (Acts 19:1–7) shows Paul's concern to bring certain Ephesian disciples (perhaps the nucleus of the church at Ephesus) into line with normative Christianity as represented by the Jerusalem church, so Acts 18:24–26 illustrates Priscilla and Aquila's concern to ensure the orthodoxy of a man whom they recognized to be an outstanding apologist for the faith.

From this episode, we can see that Priscilla and Aquila were knowledgeable believers, gracious team-teachers, and champions of orthodoxy. What was said of the early Christians in Jerusalem was also true of this couple in Ephesus: "They devoted themselves to the apostles' teaching" (Acts 2:42). See also the previous chapter.

55: A TRINITARIAN PROJECT
(Acts 20:28)

Acts 20:3–21:6 narrates Paul's journey to Judea in the company of the delegates of the Gentile churches (Acts 20:4; cf. 1 Cor 16:3) for the purpose of delivering the collection for "the poor among the saints at Jerusalem" (Rom 15:26). While his ship was harbored at Miletus for several days, some thirty miles from Ephesus, he summoned the Ephesian elders (Acts 20:17) and delivered to them his "farewell speech" that Luke records in abbreviated form in Acts 20:18–35, the only Pauline speech in Acts that is directed to a Christian audience.

In verses 25–31 Paul issues his challenge to the Ephesian elders to be alert to their responsibilities as guardians of their flock. He reinforces his challenge by reminding them of their divine appointment to shepherd a church that had been acquired by divine blood (v. 28). This latter verse well illustrates the complexity of two issues that are relevant to NT study.

First is the textual issue. After Paul's directive, "Be shepherds of the church," there are more than nine variant readings, but only two have weighty manuscript support: "of the Lord" and "of God." Having considered what are called "transcriptional probabilities" and "intrinsic probabilities," the majority of textual critics prefer the reading "(the church) of God" as being the original text. Another textual issue relates to the word "his own" (*idios*). Is it here an adjective, "(the church of God which he obtained with) his own blood," or a titular noun, "(with the blood) of his Own (Son)"? The manuscript evidence strongly supports the latter reading.

Second is the translational issue. Even though most textual critics, commentators, and English versions prefer the reading "of God," there remains the problem of the translation of the last part of the sentence. Here are the four possibilities:

1. "To shepherd the church of God (the Father) which he acquired with his own blood." The concepts of "the blood of God" and "the sufferings of God" became common fare in the second and third centuries AD, but nothing resembling these expressions has been found in the first century. Nowhere in the NT, for example, do we read of "the cross of God" or that at Golgotha "they crucified God" or that "God died and rose again." Nor is it appropriate to say that Christ's shed blood was in effect his Father's blood or was the heart blood of the Father.

2. "To shepherd the church of God (= Jesus) which he acquired with his own blood." This is a defensible and common understanding, for Paul can on occasion use the title "God" of Jesus (Rom 9:5; Titus 2:13), and he depicts Jesus as acquiring the church through his death (Titus 2:14).

3. "To shepherd the church of God (the Father) which he (Christ) acquired with his own blood." Some have suggested that there is a "sliding" in thought here. The action of the Father is so closely associated with the action of the Son that the reader can pass from one to the other without any mark of transition. But the fact remains that there is no explicit change of subject, and the Father may be said to have "acquired" the church (see Eph 1:4–6 or 1 Pet 2:9–10).

4. "To shepherd the church of God (the Father) which he acquired with the blood of his own Son." On this view, "God" refers to the Father, as regularly throughout the NT, and *ho idios* may be a title of Christ ("his own" or "his own one"), or, better, it may be an abbreviation of

"his own Son" (as NJB, NRSV; cf. Rom 8:32). Just as God had originally acquired a people to be his treasured possession through a covenant ratified by blood (Exod 19:5–6; 24:3–8), so now he had secured for himself the church to be his distinctive people by means of the shed blood of his own dearly loved Son.

This last option is the best. Thus, addressing the Ephesian elders, Paul emphasizes the high privilege and onerous responsibility of the pastoral office: "Keep watch over yourselves and over all the flock, of which the Holy Spirit has made you overseers, to shepherd the church of God that he obtained with the blood of his own Son" (NRSV). God, Christ, and the Holy Spirit are all acting in unison. Eldership involves participation in a magnificent Trinitarian enterprise.

56: TO GO OR NOT TO GO?
(Acts 21:4)

In Acts 19 and 20, we find that the Spirit has directed Paul to go to Jerusalem (19:21) but warns him of coming afflictions (20:22–23). Thus far all is clear. But then we discover Acts 21:4: "Through the Spirit they (the Tyrian disciples) urged Paul not to go on to Jerusalem."

"Through the Spirit"! How are we to explain this apparent contradiction?

Some have suggested that Paul simply disobeyed the Spirit's further direction and proceeded with his own plans to travel to Jerusalem. But this is out of keeping with what we know of Paul, who said, "Do not ever stifle the Spirit" (1 Thess 5:19).

Others propose that Paul doubted whether these Tyrian believers were really directed by the Spirit. This doubt made him all the more determined to follow the Spirit's previous clear leading (cf. Acts 21:12–14).

Or, with A.T. Robertson, we could distinguish between duty and warning: "In spite of this warning (Ac 21:4b) Paul felt it his duty as before (Ac 20:22) to go on. Evidently Paul interpreted the action of the Holy Spirit as information and warning although the disciples at Tyre gave it the form of a prohibition. Duty called louder than warning to Paul even if both were the calls of God" (*Word Pictures* 3:360).

Finally, in the phrase *dia tou pneumatos*, usually rendered "through the Spirit," the preposition *dia* may indicate attendant circumstances: "while under the inspiration of the Spirit." The believers at Tyre evidently had been given a prophecy about Paul's suffering in Jerusalem—else why their exhortation?—that was given at the direction of the Spirit, as also later to Agabus at Caesarea (Acts 21:11). This prediction of the Spirit immediately prompted the Tyrians' urgent plea to Paul ("they kept telling Paul," iterative imperfect) not to persist in going to Jerusalem.

Thus, in his condensed statement, Luke has not mentioned the prophecy, only the exhortation that was based on it. Not long after, at Caesarea, a similar prophecy and a similar exhortation are both described (Acts 21:11–12). Paul's response to the exhortation at Caesarea not to go up to Jerusalem (Acts 21:12), presumably also expressed at Tyre, was "What are you doing, weeping and breaking my heart? For I am ready not only to be bound but even to die in Jerusalem for the name of the Lord Jesus" (Acts 21:13).

57: "GET YOUR SINS WASHED AWAY"
(Acts 22:16)

There are three accounts in the book of Acts of the conversion of Saul of Tarsus: 9:1–19 (Luke's account), 22:1–21, and 26:1–23 (Paul's own accounts). In Acts 22, with the permission of Claudius Lysias, the garrison commander of the Antonia Fortress in Jerusalem (see Acts 23:26), Paul addresses the rioting Jerusalem crowd. In 22:12–16 he recounts the intervention of Ananias, a highly respected local Jew, to restore his sight and announce his divine commission. Then Ananias continues, "And now, what are you waiting for? Get up, get yourself baptized and your sins washed away, as you call on his (the Lord's) name" (Acts 22:16). Was Ananias telling Paul to baptize himself or wash away his sins through his own merits?

In ancient Greek, there are three "voices" (ways the subject relates to the action)—active (*x* sees *y*), passive (*x* is seen by *y*), and middle (*x* sees to this for himself). The middle voice indicates that the action described affects the subject of the action in some particular way, whether directly or indirectly. Apart from its use in so-called deponent verbs, the middle voice is not common in NT Greek, so when it occurs there is usually some special reason.

In our verse, there are two significant middles—*baptisai*, which many translations render "be baptized," and *apolousai*, often rendered "wash away." But the middle voice is perhaps best brought out by the translation "get/have yourself baptized," and "have/get (your sins) washed away."

It is not the case that Ananias was directing Paul to do these things on his own. Rather, it was a direction to arrange to be baptized (presumably through the help of Christian leaders in Damascus; see Acts 9:18), and to do what was necessary to be forgiven (namely, confess and repent of sin). Both of these actions—being baptized and securing forgiveness—involved calling on the name of the Lord Jesus. So the participle *epikalesamenos* ("calling on/invoking") probably refers to attendant circumstances, "as you call on the Lord's name." We also see this on the Day of Pentecost, when Peter challenged his hearers, "Repent and be baptized, every one of you, in the name of Jesus Christ, upon the forgiveness of your sins" (Acts 2:38). Note also Romans 10:13 (citing Joel 2:32), "Everyone who calls on the name of the Lord will be saved" (see also Acts 9:14, 21).

PART 2
EPISTLES AND REVELATION

ROMANS

1: THE HIGHEST PRIVILEGE OF ALL — TO BE A SLAVE OF THE SUPREME MASTER (Rom 1:1)

Word order can often be significant, especially when it is surprising. For example, Paul's letter to the Christian believers in Rome is the flagship of the Pauline fleet. The apostle greatly treasured his special calling to be an apostle that came through the direct appearance of the resurrected Christ to him outside the city of Damascus. So we might have expected Paul to introduce himself right at the beginning of Romans as someone "called to be an apostle of Christ Jesus." But no! His chosen self-description is this: "Paul, a slave (*doulos*) of Christ Jesus, called to be an apostle" (Rom 1:1). Similarly, Peter begins his second letter, "Simon Peter, a slave (*doulos*) and apostle of Jesus Christ" (2 Pet 1:1), and not "an apostle and slave of Jesus Christ."

Doulos is the distinctive Greek word for "slave." It is unfortunately true that many modern English versions avoid translating *doulos* with "slave" and opt for the less-specific term "servant." There are, in fact, some six NT Greek words that can be rendered "servant," but there is only one special word for "slave." From their preference for it, then, is it not fair to infer that these two towering figures in the early church both believed that it was a higher calling to be Christ's slave than even to be his apostle?

A similar inference may be drawn from the initial self-description of two of Jesus' half-brothers (see Mark 6:3), who each understandably might have been tempted to call himself "the brother of Jesus." But Jude describes himself as "a slave (*doulos*) of Jesus Christ and a brother of James" (Jude 1), while James begins his letter, "James, a

slave (*doulos*) of God and of the Lord Jesus Christ" (Jas 1:1). Did Jude
and James not believe that it was a more exalted privilege to be the
slave of Christ than even to be his brother?

But what is a slave (*doulos*)? A slave is someone whose person
and service belong wholly to another. In the case of Paul, Peter, Jude,
and James—and all Christians—the Another is the Lord Christ who
paid the supreme price to redeem us, with the result that we are not
our own masters (1 Cor 6:19–20). As Christ's purchased possession,
the believer is the exclusive property of the Master. "Whether we
live or die, we belong to the Lord" (Rom 14:8). And since this Master
is himself the Lord of the universe (Acts 10:36), slavery to him is a
consummate privilege and joy, not debilitating drudgery (see further part 2, ch. 34).

As the apostle John describes the final state of believers in the city
of God, the site of the throne of God and of the Lamb, he observes
that the slaves (*douloi*) of the Lord God will perpetually serve him
in worship and see his face (Rev 22:3–4).

2: "BY FAITH TO FAITH"
(Rom 1:17)

Paul is the master of the abbreviated phrase that the reader could
understand in different ways. A notable and important example is
ek pisteōs eis pistin in Romans 1:17, which may be literally translated
"by faith to faith."

We find the theme of Romans clearly expressed in Romans 1:16–
17—the divinely powerful gospel that reveals the righteousness God
provides for everyone who has faith in Christ, both Jew and Gentile.
Although "the righteousness *of God*" could refer to the holy character
and righteous actions that belong to God (the genitive denoting possession), here the genitive case "of God" expresses the source of the
righteousness, "a righteousness from God," as in Philippians 3:9 ("the
righteousness that comes from [*ek*] God"). It is a right standing before
God that he himself provides. In the message of the gospel, this
"righteousness" is revealed and made available to everyone (v. 17a),

a righteousness that is "by faith to faith." In support of these affirmations, Paul appeals to Habakkuk 2:4b.

Habakkuk 2:4–20 contains God's indictment concerning the ruthless Babylonians, a "revelation" given to the prophet (vv. 2–3). Verse 4b is parenthetical, contrasting the perverse desires of the proud Babylonians (v. 4a) with the uprightness of the person whose life will prosper by his trust in God and adherence to his ways. "The righteous person will live by *his* faithfulness." The Greek OT (LXX) rendering of the phrase is "by *my* (= God's) faithfulness" or "by faith *in me* (= God)." Significantly, in his citation of Habakkuk 2:4b Paul has omitted any personal pronoun—either the Hebrew's "his" or the LXX's "my" or "in me." This suggests that Paul wants the Greek reader to take "by faith" with "the person who is righteous" and also with "will live," in an intentional double sense.

In English translation, we cannot incorporate both ways of understanding "by faith" at the same time. So we have the NAB rendering, "the one who is righteous by faith will live," alongside the NRSV, "the one who is righteous will live by faith" (similarly NIV). The former translation certainly coheres with Paul's insistence that a right standing before God comes by human faith, as in Romans 3:22; Galatians 2:16; and Philippians 3:9. In each of these cases, *dia pisteōs* bears the same sense as *ek pisteōs,* "by faith." The latter rendering fits well with Paul's belief that the believer's journey is "through the realm of faith" (2 Cor 5:7) and his confession that "the life I now live in the body, I live by faith in the Son of God" (Gal 2:20b).

Perhaps the clearest indication that Paul understood the Habakkuk passage in a double sense is his phrase "by faith to faith." If Paul is repeating the word "faith" (*pistis*) for rhetorical emphasis or to express exclusiveness, we could render *ek pisteōs eis pistin* by a paraphrase: "(a righteousness that is) by faith from first to last" (NIV), or "through faith from beginning to end" (GNB), or "from start to finish by faith" (NLT), or simply "entirely through faith." But is preferable to retain the two uses of "faith" and render the expression "on the basis of faith and leading to faith."

That is, faith in Christ characterizes the Christian's life in every circumstance such as initial belief, prayer, witness, and hope.

3: THE MOST IMPORTANT VERSE
AND WORD IN THE BIBLE? (Rom 3:25)

If you were asked (quite unfairly!) to decide whether the OT or the NT was the more important part of the Bible, you may well decide in favor of the NT. And if the questions continued:

"Who is the most important author in the NT?" Paul.

"And Paul's most important letter?" Romans.

"And the most important section of Romans?" Romans 1–8.

"And the most important chapter within Romans 1–8?" Chapter 3.

"And the most important section within chapter 3?" Verses 21–26.

"And the most important verse within 3:21–26?" Verse 25.

"And the most important word within verse 25?" *Hilastērion*.

In a nutshell, the theme of Romans 3:21–26 is "the redemption that came by Christ Jesus" (v. 24b) or "a righteousness before God that comes from God apart from the law" (v. 21a). The challenge of verse 25a is how best to translate three expressions.

The first is *proetheto*. A literal rendering such as "(God) set before himself" or "proposed" makes the action too personal, as if God were simply engaged in an individual drama. The verb depicts a public exhibition, open for all to see, so that the NASB rendering "displayed publicly" is apt. Both here and in Galatians 3:1 ("Before your very eyes Jesus Christ was publicly exhibited as crucified"), the emphasis rests on the clear and vivid verbal portrayal of Christ's crucifixion or sacrifice of atonement as being at the heart of the gospel.

The second is *hilastērion*. In Greek and Roman usage, the term refers to a propitiatory gift or votive offering given to a deity as a way of regaining the deity's goodwill. The distinctive element in the NT is the fact that God himself takes the initiative in removing the obstacle to reconciliation—human sin.

In the first use of *hilastērion* in the Greek Bible (Exod 25:17), it describes as "atoning" the lid of pure gold on the ark of the covenant in the most holy place. This cover was the "place of atonement," where the high priest sprinkled blood to atone for the sins of the people on the day of atonement (*Yom Kippur*) once a year (Lev 16:13–16). This accounts for translating *hilastērion* as "mercy seat" in the KJV (following Tyndale, and Luther's translation *Gnadenstuhl*) of Romans 3:25 and Hebrews 9:5 (the only two uses of the word in the NT).

From a grammatical point of view, in Romans 3:25 *hilastērion* could be an adjective ("atoning") with *thyma* ("sacrifice") understood; thus "a sacrifice of atonement" (NIV and NRSV). If, as in Hebrews 9:5, it is a neuter noun, the sense will be "means of expiation" or "place of propitiation" (the renderings in the principal NT Greek lexicon, with the former preferred in Rom 3:25), or "propitiatory sacrifice" (in the principal two-volume commentary on the Greek text of Romans).

In English, "propitiate" means "make gentle in manner," and "expiate" means "make amends for." Behind propitiation is the NT concept of the wrath of God. Expiation involves the removal of sin through sacrifice. God is propitiated and sin is expiated; propitiation is through expiation. In other words, God's wrath against sin was averted when he provided Jesus Christ as a propitiatory sacrifice to remove sin. Is not *hilastērion* the most important word in the Bible—if we must choose?

The third expression is *en tō autou haimati*, "in/by his own blood." This phrase immediately follows "through faith" in the Greek word order. Some translations reverse the order and make both phrases dependent on *hilastērion*: "a propitiation in His blood through faith" (NASB), "a sacrifice of atonement by his blood, effective through faith" (NRSV). It is preferable to retain the Greek word order, "through faith in his blood," as in the KJV and NIV. It is true that in Paul's writings the word "faith" (*pistis*) is normally followed by a person and the genitive case, as in verses 22 and 26, not by a preposition (here "in"). But the difficulty is eased if we recognize Paul's shorthand in both these phrases: "a propitiatory sacrifice accomplished by the shedding of his (Christ's) blood and effective through (the believer's) faith (in Jesus Christ, vv. 22, 26)."

In the second part of verse 25, Paul goes on to observe that the purpose of God's provision of Christ as a propitiatory sacrifice was to demonstrate his justice or righteous character that needed vindication, because in his patience (not his indifference) God had refrained from exacting the full and proper penalty for acts of sin committed in the time before the cross.

4: "ABRAHAM BELIEVED GOD"
(Rom 4:3)

In three NT passages (Rom 4:3; Gal 3:6; Jas 2:23) Genesis 15:6 is quoted in the Greek OT form: "And Abram believed God, and it (Abram's faith) was credited to his account (by God) as righteousness." Abraham believed God in four areas:

- in his departure from Ur (Gen 13:1; Heb 11:8);

- that Sarah would bear a son (although he was childless when the promise was given and was beyond the age of fatherhood, just as Sarah was beyond the age of motherhood—Rom 4:18–19);

- that he would have innumerable descendants (Gen 15:5); and

- in the surrender of Isaac (Gen 22:1–18; Heb 11:17–19).

In the crucial phrase *eis dikaiosynēn* (literally "to/for/as righteousness"), the preposition *eis* may legitimately be expanded in various ways: "as equivalent to righteousness"; "as a substitute for (law-based) righteousness"; "as giving a status of righteousness"; or "as bringing righteousness" (= a right standing before God).

Paul cites Genesis 15:6 in Romans 4:3 as providing in the case of Abraham an OT precedent for the principle of "justification on the basis of faith apart from works of the law" (Rom 3:28; see also

4:6). Abraham was justified, Paul argues, (1) apart from works (Rom 4:4–8); (2) apart from circumcision (vv. 9–12); and (3) apart from the law (vv. 13–17). The apostle can say both that "faith was reckoned to Abraham as righteousness" (4:9; cf. 4:3, 5, 22) and that righteousness was reckoned to the account of Abraham on the basis of faith (4:6, 11, 13, 23; cf. 9:20; Phil 3:9) because he regarded faith and righteousness as correlatives. Verses 18–19 describe the outworking of Abraham's faith, which is a model for all his spiritual children to follow (vv. 23–25).

In Galatians 3:6, Paul appeals to this OT verse (1) to validate the implied answer to the question he posed in verses 2 and 5—in effect, "Did God give you the Spirit because of your law-observance or because of your faith in the gospel?"; and (2) to preface his demonstration in verses 6–14 that those who believe are children of Abraham (v. 7) and that "the righteous will live by faith" (v. 11) and receive the promised Spirit (v. 14).

In James 2:14–26, the author is seeking to establish the inseparability of faith and actions. Abraham's example (Jas 2:23) shows that the two are complementary (v. 22), since Abraham "offered his son Isaac on the altar" (v. 21; cf. Gen 22:1–18) in what Paul calls an "obedience inspired by faith" (Rom 16:26). He had already acted on the basis of faith in departing from Ur and traveling to Canaan in obedience to God's call (Gen 12:1–3; 13:1). See also part 2, ch. 56.

5: TWO CONTRASTING WAYS OF LIVING
(Rom 8:4–5)

In Paul's writings, sometimes the term "flesh" (*sarx*) can have a neutral sense and refer to human life on earth, as when he says "we live in the flesh (= we live in the world/as human beings/in the body)" (2 Cor 10:3a). In a similar way, the word "spirit" (*pneuma*) sometimes has a neutral sense (as opposed to an "evil spirit") and refers to the human spirit, the immaterial part of humans, as when he speaks of "everything that contaminates body and spirit" (2 Cor 7:1).

But when these two words are used in close proximity and contrasted with each other, they denote stark opposites, with "flesh" referring to the sinful human nature and "spirit" referring to the Holy Spirit of God. Such is the case in Romans 8:4b–5, which may be rendered literally as follows.

> ... in us, who do not walk according to the flesh (*kata sarka*) but according to the Spirit (*kata pneuma*). For those who are according to the flesh (*kata sarka*) set their minds on the things of the flesh (*ta tēs sarkos*), but those who are according to the Spirit (*kata pneuma*) set their minds on the things of the Spirit (*ta tou pneumatos*).

In Paul's letters, the verb "walk" (*peripateō*) regularly is a metaphor for "conduct one's life" or "habitually behave and think." "Set the mind on" (*phroneō*) means "give careful consideration to," "be intent on," or "totally espouse," while "the things" twice referred to here are the desires or aims or dictates of the flesh, or those of the Spirit.

So then, what is being contrasted here are two diametrically opposed patterns of conduct and thinking. On the one hand, there is a life lived under the control of the unregenerate human nature that pursues everything that this human nature wants and is preoccupied with satisfying those desires. On the other hand, there is a life lived under the domination of God's Spirit that pursues everything the Spirit wants and is preoccupied with satisfying those desires. No two patterns of life could be more different! Hence Paul's exhortation, "Let the Spirit guide your lives, and you will not gratify the cravings of your sinful nature" (Gal 5:16).

This same contrast is expressed differently in Galatians 6:8, where the idea of sowing replaces the concept of walking or living: "The person who sows to please his sinful nature (*eis tēn sarka*)" is contrasted with "the person who sows to please the Spirit (*eis to pneuma*)." Or again, the contrast may be expressed in reference to outcomes: "actions prompted by the sinful nature (*ta erga tēs sarkos*)" (Gal 5:19); "fruit produced by the Spirit (*ho karpos tou pneumatos*)" (Gal 5:22).

Thus a paraphrase of our passage would read as follows:

… in us, whose lives are not ruled by the human nature (cf. v.13a) but by the Spirit. For those whose outlook and conduct are dictated by the sinful nature focus their attention on what that nature desires, but those whose outlook and conduct are dictated by the Spirit focus their attention on what the Spirit desires.

6: CHRIST AS "GOD BLESSED FOREVER"
(Rom 9:5)

There is certainly no other NT verse, and probably no other sentence in all of literature, that has come under more intense scrutiny than Romans 9:5 with regard to punctuation. This verse should give pause (!) to those who doubt the importance of periods and commas. The issue is this: Does the verse apply the title "God" (*theos*) to Jesus Christ, or is the word "God" part of a doxology? That is, should we place a period in the Greek after *kata sarka* ("with regard to human ancestry"), or a comma?

In the history of a prominent English translation we discover the punctuation issue at stake—and a significant change. The RSV, both the 1946 and 1971 editions, has "from them [the Israelites], according to the flesh, comes the Messiah. God who is over all be blessed forever." By contrast, the NRSV (1989) has "from them, according to the flesh, comes the Messiah, who is over all, God blessed forever."

What are the reasons why the verse might end, not with a doxology to God the Father (as in the RSV), but with an affirmation of the deity of Christ (as in the NRSV)? First, the participial phrase ("the one who is," *ho ōn*), which is in the nominative (subject) case, most naturally refers back to the immediately preceding nominative (subject) case, "the Messiah/Christ" (*ho christos*). A sudden change of subject is improbable. Second, the word order "God blessed" (*theos eulogetos*) makes it very unlikely that a doxology ends the sentence, because the usual word order in a doxology that is not explicitly linked with what precedes is "Blessed be God." Third, if there is a doxology, the participle *ōn* is superfluous; in Greek, "God who is over all" is simply *ho epi pantōn theos*, without the participle. And finally, the phrase "according to the flesh" or "with regard to human ancestry" (*to kata sarka*) expresses a limitation and anticipates the complementary and contrasting word "God," both in reference to Christ.

It is of interest to note that of the fifty-six principal commentators on Romans in the major European languages (including Latin) that I consulted (up to 1995), thirteen favored a reference to God the Father, thirty-six a reference to Christ, and seven were undecided. This dominant view, found in commentators of widely divergent theological persuasions, can now also claim the support of the textual editors of the *Novum Testamentum Graece* of Nestle-Aland (26th and 27th editions) and the *Greek New Testament* published by the United Bible Society (3rd and 4th editions), along with the translators of the NRSV (see above). All of these are significant reversals of previous positions.

Given the high Christology of the Pauline letters—according to which Jesus shares the divine name ("Lord," Rom 10:13) and nature (Phil 2:6), exercises divine functions (e.g., Col 1:16; 3:13), and is the object of human faith (Rom 10:8–13) and adoration (Phil 2:9–11) and the addressee in petitionary prayer (1 Cor 1:2; 16:22)—it should bring no surprise if on occasion, as here in Romans 9:5 and in Titus 2:13, Paul should refer to Jesus by the generic title "God." For Paul, Jesus shares intrinsically in the divine nature: "to them [the Israelites] belong the patriarchs, and from them, as far as human descent is concerned, came the Messiah, who is over all, God blessed forever. Amen."

7: CHRIST, THE END OF THE LAW?
(Rom 10:4)

"For Christ is the end of the law for righteousness to everyone who believes" (ESV, CSB). A simple literal translation of this verse calls out for expansion to produce clarity.

After all, did not Jesus say, "Truly I tell you, until heaven and earth disappear, not an iota, not a dot, will by any means disappear from the law until everything is accomplished" (Matt 5:18)? An *iota* (ι) is the Greek equivalent of the smallest letter, *yod* (ʾ), in the Hebrew/Aramaic alphabet. A "dot" (literally "horn") is a very small mark attached to a letter to distinguish it from another similar letter, such as O and Q in our alphabet.

And did not Paul also affirm that "the law is holy, and the commandment is holy, righteous and good" (Rom 7:12)? Even if we recall that for Paul the word *nomos* can refer to a specific Mosaic law (Rom 7:2) as well as the Mosaic law in general or even the whole OT, the ambiguity of "the law for righteousness" is not removed. The focus of attention naturally moves to the Greek word *telos*, which can mean "end" in the sense of "termination," or "goal" in the sense of "end in view" or "culmination."

It is certainly defensible to say that Christ is the goal of the law, if the law's purpose was to produce righteousness (Gal 3:22), for Christ himself fulfilled the law (Matt 5:17) and so has become believers' righteousness (1 Cor 1:30). What the law was intended to do—but in the event was unable to do, given human frailty and sinfulness—Christ was successful in accomplishing for others. In that sense, he achieved the law's goal. The NLT rendering reflects this understanding. "For Christ has already accomplished the purpose for which the law was given. As a result (Greek *eis*, denoting an outcome) all who believe in him are made right with God."

But perhaps the immediate context lends support to the sense that Christ's provision of righteousness in salvation marks the end/termination of the law in its imagined potency to produce righteousness. In Romans 9:30–32, we find a stark contrast between the Gentiles, who did not pursue righteousness but have obtained it, and the people of Israel, who pursued the law as the way of righteousness but did not attain their goal because they pursued it as if it were by works. Then in 10:3 Paul states that the Israelites did not know or submit to God's righteousness but sought to establish their own righteousness—by keeping the law (9:32; 10:5).

Thus, 10:4 would be rendered as "Christ has brought the law to an end in its connection with righteousness in the case of everyone who believes," where *eis* is referential, meaning "in its relation to" or "in its connection with." That is, the work of Christ marks the end of law-keeping regarded as a way of gaining righteousness.

On this view, it is possible that "until everything is accomplished" in Matthew 5:18 looks forward to Christ's own accomplishment—his provision of a right standing before God (= righteousness) for everyone who believes.

8: "JESUS IS LORD"
(Rom 10:9)

At first sight, Romans 10:9 appears to state two simple, straightforward requirements to gain salvation—one a verbal declaration, the other an inward belief, both requirements being individual and private: "That if you declare with your mouth, 'Jesus is Lord,' and believe in your heart that God raised him from the dead, you will be saved."

But if we view the verse against its context in Paul's letter and the NT as a whole—as we must—requirements that might seem to be simple and undemanding become profound and challenging. The somewhat strange reference to "mouth" and "heart" stems from a quotation Paul has just made from Deuteronomy 30:11-14, which he cites to illustrate the point that gaining salvation does not require some Herculean effort but is readily available owing to God's gift received by faith: "'The word is near you; it is in your mouth and in your heart,' that is, the message concerning faith that we are proclaiming: That if you declare ..." (Rom 10:8-9). Then, lest his readers imagine that the declaration is more important than the belief, Paul reverses the "mouth—heart" order and explains, "For it is with your heart that you believe and so are justified, and it is with your mouth that you declare your faith and so are saved" (Rom 10:10). Saving faith is as near as one's heart and mouth.

These two requirements are so closely related that we may speak of them as two sides of the same coin, namely, recognition of the resurrection of Jesus. Philippians 2:9–11 makes it clear that when God the Father raised and exalted Jesus he bestowed on him the unparalleled name of "Lord." That is, recognition of the supreme lordship of Jesus dates from his resurrection, so that in declaring Jesus' supremacy as a result of his resurrection, the believer is simply concurring with God's prior action. Jesus does not become Lord when the believer follows Thomas in declaring "(You are) my Lord and my God!" (John 20:28). The lordship of Jesus is a universal fact apart from and prior to any individual's recognition of the fact. This declaration of Jesus' lordship made by the believer is not some private act but a public confession, probably made at the time of one's baptism in the presence of witnesses (this tradition is represented in a secondary manuscript reading in Acts 8:37—see KJV).

The two earliest Christological confessions were "Jesus is the Christ/Messiah" (Acts 18:5, 28; cf. 2:36; 9:22; 17:3), and "Jesus is Lord" (Rom 10:9; 1 Cor 12:3; cf. Phil 2:11). They are combined in Colossians 2:6, "You have received Christ Jesus as Lord."

When believers declare "Jesus is Lord" at the time of our conversion or baptism as the result of the Holy Spirit's enlightenment (1 Cor 12:3), we are:

- acknowledging the deity of Christ (John 20:28; Phil 2:6, 9–11);

- declaring that the risen Jesus is absolutely supreme in the universe (Col 1:15–16) and in the church (Eph 1;22), over both Jews and Gentiles (Acts 10:36; Rom 10:12) and over individual believers (Rom 14:8);

- asserting everyone's accountability to the Lord (1 Cor 4:5; 2 Tim 4:1, 8); and

- pledging our willing servitude as the Master's slaves (1 Cor 7:22; 2 Cor 4:5; Jas 1:1). See part 2, ch. 1.

9: REPAYING SPIRITUAL INDEBTEDNESS
(Rom 15:26–27)

How can one repay a spiritual debt to a fellow believer—be it the person God used to bring you to faith, a stimulating Bible class leader, a spiritual mentor, or a pastor or priest?

From AD 52–57 a considerable proportion of Pauls' time and energy was devoted to organizing a financial collection among his Gentile churches for special needs in Jerusalem. In Romans 15:26 he describes the intended recipients of this gift as "the poor among the saints in Jerusalem." It is just possible that the Jerusalem believers referred to themselves as "the poor" (in spirit, Matt 5:3; cf. Gal 2:10) and that verse 26 means "the poor, namely the saints in Jerusalem," *tōn hagiōn* ("the saints") being a defining genitive. But more probably this genitive is partitive, denoting the whole of which a part is specified, "the poor among the saints in Jerusalem" (thus most EVV). "The poor" is simply a sociological term, referring to those who were financially poor or economically depressed.

Several factors account for their continuing poverty. First, after their conversion to Christianity many Jews in Jerusalem would have been ostracized socially and economically. Second, persistent food shortages in Palestine because of overpopulation culminated in the famine of AD 46 in the time of the emperor Claudius (Acts 11:27–30). Third, as the mother church of Christendom, the Jerusalem church was obliged to support a proportionately large number of teachers and probably to provide hospitality for frequent Christian visitors to the holy city. And finally, Jews in Palestine were subject to a crippling twofold taxation—religious (Jewish) and civil (Roman)—that may have been between thirty and forty percent of total income. But it is probable that the collection was designed not only for poor Jerusalemites within the church but also other indigent believers in Judea (note "all the others" in 2 Cor 9:13).

Who were the contributors to Paul's collection? We find from Acts 20:4 that Paul was accompanied by delegates from several Gentile churches on his final visit to Jerusalem when he was delivering the collection—representatives of the Roman provinces of Macedonia, Galatia, and Asia (and also Achaia, Rom 15:26).

Paul was prompted to spend so much travel time and energy in organizing this collection because, first, he saw the offering as an act of brotherly love (Rom 12:13; 13:8; Gal 6:10) and a tangible expression of the interdependence of the members of the body of Christ (1 Cor 12:25–26) that would honor Christ (2 Cor 8:19) and help effect equality of provision of the necessities of life (2 Cor 8:13–15). Second, the collection effectively symbolized the unity of Jew and Gentile in Christ (Eph 2:11–22) and may have been designed to win over those Jewish Christians who were still suspicious of Paul's Gentile mission (see Acts 11:2–3). Third, it dramatized in material terms the spiritual indebtedness of Gentile believers to the church in Jerusalem (Rom 15:19, 27; cf. 1 Cor 9:11). Fourth, it was a visible sign of Paul's fulfillment of his promise to James, Cephas, and John, the "pillars" of the Jerusalem church, to continue to remember the poor (Gal 2:9–10), and perhaps was a way of partially compensating for his earlier obsession to persecute the Jerusalem saints (Acts 8:3; 9:1; 26:10–11; 1 Cor 15:9; Gal 1:13; 1 Tim 1:13). Finally, it was a fitting climax of his ministry in the eastern Mediterranean as he planned to turn westward after visiting Rome (Rom 15:24, 28).

Was the collection a success? Paul had some misgivings about the outcome of the enterprise, for he asked the Christians in Rome to "pray that I may be kept safe from the unbelievers in Judea and that the contribution I take to Jerusalem may be favorably received by the Lord's people there" (Rom 15:31). Paul's fear was that if his own life was threatened by Jewish unbelievers during his forthcoming visit, Jerusalem Christians might feel compelled to refuse the collection lest, by accepting it, they provoke a fresh wave of persecution or compromise their efforts to win fellow Jews to Christ. However, Acts 21:17 suggests the collection delegation was warmly welcomed and the collection itself gratefully received: "When we arrived at Jerusalem, the brothers received us warmly." Indeed, after hearing Paul's detailed report of what God had done among the Gentiles through his ministry, which would have included reference to the "service" of the collection (Rom 15:31), James and all the elders "praised God" (Acts 21:18–20a).

Paul's "collection for the poor" suggests an answer to our original question: How can one repay a spiritual debt to a fellow believer? Determine a special ongoing practical need of the potential recipient, and then make plans to meet that need with creativity, enthusiasm, and persistence, possibly enlisting the help of others.

1 CORINTHIANS

10: BOASTING IN THE LORD
(1 Cor 1:31; 2 Cor 10:17)

In both of these passages Paul is quoting a phrase based on the LXX version of Jeremiah 9:23 (EVV 9:24), which reads "But rather, let the person who boasts, boast about this: understanding and knowing that I am the LORD who exercises mercy, judgment, and righteousness on the earth, for my pleasure resides in these, says the LORD."

In adapting the LXX text, Paul has omitted the initial "But rather" that looks back to verse 22: "This is what the LORD says, 'Let not the wise boast of their wisdom or the strong boast of their strength or the rich boast of their riches." Also, instead of "about this," he has substituted "in the Lord," which aptly sums up what follows in verse 23 about the character of the Lord ("I am the Lord ... my pleasure") and his actions ("who exercises mercy, judgment, and righteousness").

So behind Paul's "Let the one who boasts, boast in the Lord" (1 Cor 1:31; 2 Cor 10:17) is a contrast between improper and proper boasting. To boast of human qualities or achievements or advantages as though these derived from oneself is to usurp God's glory and reject dependence on him. But to boast of who God is, and what he does or has done, is wholly appropriate. "Glorying in God" is at the heart of both OT and NT religion. If, then, we understand Paul's "in the Lord" against its OT background, the expression may be regarded as shorthand for the character and deeds of the Lord. And grammatically, the preposition "in" (Greek *en*) will specify the object of the boasting: "Let the one who boasts, make the Lord the object of his boast."

In 1 Corinthians 1:31, "Let the one who boasts, boast in the Lord" serves to counteract prideful boasting in human wisdom, power, pedigree, and strength (1 Cor 1:26–29). But in 2 Corinthians 10:17, its function is to counteract improper boasting about someone else's successful ministry carried out in someone else's God-assigned sphere of activity (2 Cor 10:12–18).

But who is the "Lord" in Paul's modified citation? Is it God or is it Christ? There are compelling reasons for believing "Lord" refers to Christ.

1. The concept of "boasting in Christ" is found elsewhere in Paul: "We are the true circumcision ... who boast/glory in Christ Jesus" (Phil 3:3); "I glory in Christ Jesus in my service to God ... what Christ has accomplished through me" (Rom 15:17–18); "May I never boast except in the cross of our Lord Jesus Christ" (Gal 6;14); "so that I may share abundantly in your boasting in Christ Jesus through my coming to you again" (Phil 1:6).

2. In 1 Corinthians 1:31, "boasting in the Lord" is taking pride in the salvific work of "righteousness, sanctification, and redemption" that Christ accomplished as believers' true wisdom (1 Cor 1:30).

3. The prepositional phrase "in the Lord" (*en kyriō*) regularly refers to Christ in Paul's letters (some twenty-eight times).

4. Paul sometimes applies to Christ OT passages that refer to Yahweh (e.g., Isa 28:16 in Rom 9:33; 10:11; Isa 45:23 in Phil 2:10–11; Joel 2:32 in Rom 10:12–13; Ps 68:18 in Eph 4:8).

In Paul's view, then, for boasting to be legitimate, it must be about who the Lord is or what he has accomplished. Self-promotion or self-glorification, the opposite of "boasting about the Lord," disqualifies a person from receiving divine approval: "For it is not those who commend themselves who are approved, but those whom the Lord commends" (2 Cor 10:18). To gain Christ's approval during life and after death at Christ's tribunal was Paul's goal (2 Cor 5:9). See part 2, ch. 25.

11: SANCTIFICATION BY IMITATION
(1 Cor 4:16)

In 1897, Charles Sheldon published his bestselling book *In His Steps*, the story of a church that was revolutionized when members followed their pastor's exhortation to ask the question "What would Jesus do?" before making any major decision. But in seeking to discern God's guidance in a particular circumstance, is it appropriate to ask the question "What would Jesus do?" given the great differences between his circumstances and ours—and his resources and ours?

As Paul expresses it, the final destiny of those on whom God has set his love is to be conformed to the image of his Son (Rom 8:29). In John's words, we shall be "like" Christ, "for we shall see him as he is" (1 John 3:2); the vision of Christ will produce likeness to Christ. We may describe this conformity to the image of Christ, this becoming like Christ, as "Christification." Currently believers are being transformed into Christ's image "with ever-increasing glory" (2 Cor 3:18), so that this Christification is both an ongoing process and a final climax. If so, we could view believers' future bodily resurrection as the acceleration and completion of Christification, and sanctification as progressive Christification.

"The imitation of Christ" is one of the ways in which "becoming like Christ" takes place. Sometimes this imitation is *direct*, with the call to follow the example of Christ in his patient endurance of unjust suffering, his refusal to retaliate, and his entrusting of himself and his cause to God (1 Pet 2:21–23).

In Paul's letters, the imitation is usually *indirect*: "Be imitators of me, as I am of Christ" (1 Cor 11:1), or "Follow my example, as I follow the example of Christ." Apart from three passages (Heb 6:12; 13:7; 3 John 11), all the NT uses of the phrase "to be or become an imitator" (*mimētēs ginesthai*) or the verb "to imitate" (*mimeisthai*) are Pauline. He never uses the noun "disciple" (*mathētēs*) or the verb "to follow" (*akolouthein*), both so common in the Gospels as descriptions of the process of "becoming like Christ."

Paul realized that his own imitation of Christ, although imperfect, was more accessible to his converts than was the historic life of Jesus. (They did not have the four Gospels as we do!) So their imitation was mediated, and it was qualified. "Be imitators of me, just as I imitate Christ" implies "to the extent that I imitate Christ." This indirectness in the imitation of Christ is found when Paul holds himself up as a model to follow (1 Cor 11:1; Phil 3:17; 4:9; 1 Thess 1:6) because he himself models his life on Christ: "Even if you had ten thousand guardians in Christ, you do not have many fathers, for in Christ Jesus I became your father through the gospel. Therefore I appeal to you, be imitators of me" (1 Cor 4:15–16).

In addition to the call to imitate Christ, or Paul as a follower of Christ, we sometimes find a directive to imitate some particular Christian virtue, especially as it is enshrined in another believer. So the addressees in the book of Hebrews are encouraged "to imitate those who through faith and patience inherit what has been promised" (Heh 6:12), and are advised, "Remember your leaders who spoke the word of God to you; consider the outcome of their way of life and imitate their faith" (Heb 13:7). And in more general terms, Gaius, the addressee in 3 John, is instructed, "Do not imitate what is evil, but imitate what is good" (3 John 11), and Paul can admonish the Philippians, "Put into practice whatever you have learned or received or learned from me, or seen in me" (Phil 4:9; cf. 2 Tim 3:10–11). He can also appeal to his own diligent toil night and day to avoid financial dependence as a model for the Thessalonians to imitate (2 Thess 3:7–9).

Only when Paul was unacquainted with his addressees did he exhort them directly to imitate God: "Be imitators of God, as dearly loved children, and live a life of love, just as Christ loved us and gave himself up for us as a fragrant offering and sacrifice to God" (Eph 5:1). Ephesians was probably an encyclical letter, copies being sent from the church in Ephesus to various churches in the hinterland that Paul had never visited.

The NT evidence leads us to conclude that imitating Christ, whether directly or indirectly through some Christian leader, is one important ingredient in living the Christian life, along with other aspects such as living lives controlled by the Spirit (Rom 8:4; Gal 5:16), clothing oneself with the Lord Jesus Christ (Rom 13:14), or letting the message of Christ find a home in one's heart (Col 3:16).

12: SEXUAL SIN IS UNIQUE
(1 Cor 6:18)

We are sometimes told that sexual sin is no different from any other sin and therefore is no more serious than, say, stealing or lying. All sin is against God and is serious, so we should not distinguish (it is claimed) between one particular sin and another.

The apostle Paul does not agree.

In 1 Corinthians 6:12–20, Paul is opposing some libertines at Corinth who apparently believed that visiting prostitutes was quite permissible. After all, one's physical body was designed to bring sexual pleasure, and "I have the right to do anything I wish with my body" (see v. 12). Paul's primary response to them is "make it your habit to flee from sexual immorality" (v. 18a) and "honor God with your bodies" (v. 20).

The apostle gives several reasons why any form of sexual immorality must be vigorously rejected.

- The bodies of Christians are members (= limbs and organs) of Christ (v. 15).

- Becoming one with a prostitute does not fit with being one with the Lord (vv. 16–17).

- Sexual immorality is a sin against one's own body (v. 18).

- The Christian's body is a sanctuary in which the Holy Spirit resides (v. 19a, b).

- Christians were purchased at a great price and so are not their own masters (vv. 19c–20a).

- Consequently, they are obligated to honor their new owner, God, in the way they use their bodies (v. 20b).

But what is it about sexual sin that sets it apart from all other sin? It is "outside the body" (1 Cor 6:18b). All other sins do not involve the whole person, body and spirit, as the sexual act uniquely does. Sins such as drunkenness, gluttony, or drug abuse certainly affect the physical body both inwardly and outwardly. But the stain left on the whole personality by sexual sin is both deep and permanent, since it is a repudiation of God's intent for sexual relations. That is, sexual sin adversely affects the character more directly and severely than all other transgressions, and it is irreversibly damaging in its effects. Paul saw the sexual act (and marriage) as more than an outward physical encounter involving only physical organs. It is an outward and inward bonding and unification involving both body and spirit, a reciprocal communication between two individuals on both a physical and a spiritual plane. To be joined with a prostitute was to become not only "one body" or "one flesh" with her (v. 16) but in some real sense "one spirit" with her (see v. 17).

Any sexual liaison with someone other than one's spouse (see Eph 5:22–33) is "against the body" (v. 18c). This is true not only because of its self-destructive effects mentioned above but also in the sense that it violates the believer's prior union with the Lord in spirit (v. 17). It amounts to taking away from Christ what forms part of his body (v. 15) or belongs to him (v. 19c) and giving it to an illegitimate and immoral competitor (v. 15). "Perish the thought!" says Paul.

13: DIVORCE AND REMARRIAGE
(1 Cor 7:15)

A proper starting point for any discussion of this unpleasant topic is the Christian view of marriage as a divine institution involving an exclusive, lifelong, mutual commitment between a man and a woman that is sealed in physical intercourse.

There are three main NT passages relevant to the topic.

First is Matthew 5:32, where the main point is not that divorce for "sexual immorality" (*porneia*, here "adultery") is permissible but that divorce for any other reason is impermissible. "I tell you that anyone who divorces his wife, except for sexual immorality, forces her into an adulterous situation" (if she remarries, for she would have been divorced on impermissible grounds). The issue of the remarriage of the husband is not raised.

Second is Matthew 19:9, where Christ authorizes divorce for "sexual immorality" (*porneia*, "adultery") but does not make it mandatory. Divorce is a concession to "hardness of heart" (v. 8); the way of forgiveness and reinstatement is to be preferred, provided there is evidence of genuine repentance (see part 1, ch. 13): "I tell you that anyone who divorces his wife, except for sexual immorality, and marries another woman commits adultery." Most agree that we may make a legitimate inference from this statement—namely, that the man who divorces his wife for adultery does not commit adultery himself if he remarries.

The reason this "exceptive clause," found only in Matthew, is absent from Mark (10:2–12) and Luke (16:18) is that: (1) Mark and Luke are focusing attention on the essence of Jesus' teaching (namely, the sanctity of marriage and his discouragement of divorce); and (2) adultery was assumed to be a legitimate ground for divorce in the Roman, Greek, and Jewish worlds.

That brings us to 1 Corinthians 7:15. In 1 Corinthians 7:12–16, Paul is addressing the marital situation of "the rest" (v. 12)—believers who find themselves in a "mixed marriage" as the result of one partner coming to faith after marrying. Since Paul knows of no definitive pronouncement of Christ on this particular situation (cf. vv. 10a, 12a), he gives his own judgment as someone guided by the Spirit of God (v. 40). If the unbelieving partner is willing to live with the believing spouse, the believer should not initiate a divorce (vv. 12–14). On the other hand, if the non-Christian partner initiates a separation (probably on the ground of religious incompatibility), the Christian partner "*is not bound (ou dedoulōtai)* in such cases, for God has called us to live in peace. How can you be sure, wife, whether you will save your husband? Or, how can you be sure, husband, whether you will save your wife?" (vv. 15–16).

Some commentators have supplied after "is not bound" the phrase "by Christ's prohibition of divorce" or "to refrain from remarriage," and speak of "the Pauline permission," his provision of an additional ground for divorce and so remarriage—the desertion of the unbelieving spouse. But the immediate context rather suggests an added phrase like "to persist in seeking reconciliation," for the previous sentence has encouraged acquiescence in the unbeliever's choice ("if the unbelieving partner leaves, let it be so") and the following sentence gives the reason why a believer in these circumstances should not feel bound to keep on trying to be reconciled: "for God has called us to live in peace," not wrangling.

In fact, the only places that the issue of remarriage explicitly arises in 1 Corinthians 7 are in verse 11, where it is forbidden ("if a wife does separate, she must remain unmarried or else be reconciled to her husband"), and in verse 39, where it is permitted ("if a woman's husband dies, she is free to marry anyone she wishes, provided that he too belongs to the Lord").

14: A CHRISTIANIZED SHEMA
(1 Cor 8:6)

Chapters 7–16 of 1 Corinthians contain Paul's replies to questions the Corinthians posed in a letter delivered probably by three of the church's representatives: Stephanas, Fortunatus, and Achaicus

(1 Cor 16:17). Each question begins with, "Now concerning" (*peri de*, 7:1, 25; 8:1; 12:1; 16:1, 12).

Addressing the Corinthians' question about the legitimacy of eating "food offered to idols" (8:1), Paul contrasts in 8:4–6 the un- reality of idols and the plurality of so-called gods and lords with the reality and oneness of God and Jesus Christ, with a view to show- ing that although food sacrificed to idols is not defiled (cf. 1 Cor 10:25–26), it should be avoided if consuming it wounds the weak conscience of a Christian brother or sister (8:7–13). The first part of the *Shema*, the basic Jewish confession of faith, reads, "Hear, O Israel; the LORD our God, the LORD is one" (LXX, *kyrios ho theos hēmōn kyrios heis estin*; Deut 6:4). Paul concurs with the Corinthians in this basic affirmation, citing a phrase from their letter: "We know that ... 'There is no God but one.'"

But he proceeds in 1 Corinthians 8:6 to restate the Shema by dis- tinguishing "the Lord" and "God" in a binitarian formulation: "one God, who is the Father ... and one Lord, who is Jesus Christ":

> one God, who is the Father,
>
> from whom all things proceed
>
> and for whom we exist, and
>
> one Lord, who is Jesus Christ,
>
> through whom all things were created
>
> and through whom we exist.

This indicates that in Paul's view, "the Father" + "Jesus Christ" = "one God." That is, Paul did not regard "one Lord" as an addition to the Shema but as a constituent part of a Christianized Shema. It seems, then, that the solution the apostle is proposing to the theological problem posed by the "Christ event" is to use the expression "one God" only of the Father (cf. Eph 4:6, "one God and Father of all"), never of Jesus, although "God" (*theos*) could occasionally be used of Jesus (Rom 9:5; Titus 2:13), while the expression "one Lord" was applied exclusively to Jesus (Eph 4:5), never to the Father, although "Lord" was often applied to the Father (e.g., Rom 11:34):

1. Singularity of person	one God	one Lord
2. Description (in apposition)	the Father	Jesus Christ
3. Relationship to "all things"	"from whom"	"through whom"
4. Relationship to "us"	"for whom"	"through whom"

With regard to categories three and four, God and Christ both operate in the spheres of creation and redemption, nature and grace, cosmology and soteriology, but their function in these realms is distinguished. The Father is the origin or source or fount ("from whom," *ex hou*) of creation, and the purpose and goal ("for whom," *eis auton*; lit. "for him") of Christians' existence, so that they live/exist to serve him. The Son, on the other hand, was and is God's intermediary ("through whom," *di' hou*) in creation, and is God's agent ("through whom," *di' autou*; lit. "through him") in maintaining the existence of Christians. Each use of the preposition *dia* ("through") in reference to Christ indicates that he acts as an intermediate agent on God's behalf. Further, his agency with respect to "all things" implies his personal existence prior to creation and therefore to time (cf. Rom 8:3; 2 Cor 8:9; Gal 4:4; Phil 2:6).

15: RAISED — NEVER TO DIE AGAIN
(1 Cor 15:4)

The verbal form *egēgertai* is fascinating because seven of its nine NT occurrences are found in a single chapter (1 Cor 15). In form, it is the perfect passive of the verb *egeirō*, "raise," so it means "he [Jesus] has been raised." Being in the perfect tense, it implies a past act ("he rose" or "he was raised") but focuses our attention on the present and ongoing results of that past fact, namely that "he is risen."

In one of the two NT uses of *egēgertai* not found in 1 Corinthians, Jesus solemnly affirms that "among those born of women there has not risen (*ouk egēgertai*) anyone greater than John the Baptist" (Matt 11:11). In the other instance, Mark 6:14 reports that to explain Jesus' miraculous powers "some were saying, 'John the Baptist has been raised (*egēgertai*) from the dead.'"

But it is in Paul's "resurrection chapter" (1 Cor 15) that we find most NT uses of *egēgertai*. He was totally convinced of the past fact of Christ's rising from the dead—after all, the risen Jesus had appeared to Paul in person (1 Cor 15:8)—and by the use of this perfect tense he wants to emphasize that this historical event has permanent consequences. Jesus died, but he is no longer dead. He was buried, but he is no longer in the grave. He is alive, and will always remain alive. As the apostle expresses it elsewhere, "We know that Christ, once raised from the dead, will never die again; death no longer has any power over him" (Rom 6:9). It could be said that Lazarus rose from the dead, but not that he has been raised, never to die again. Indeed, John 12:10 indicates that shortly after Jesus had reanimated Lazarus "the chief priests made plans to put Lazarus to death."

An interesting problem of translation arises the first time Paul uses *egēgertai* in 1 Corinthians 15, where he adds "on the third day" (v. 4). We cannot say in English, "he has been raised on the third day" or "he is risen on the third day," only "he was raised on the third day" (so most EVV). If we are to be successful in bringing out the sense of the perfect tense here, we have no option but to use a paraphrase such as "he was raised on the third day—and remains alive." After all, it was the resurrected Jesus himself who said, "I am the Living One. I was dead, but see, I am alive for ever and ever! And I have, secure in my possession, the keys that unlock Death and Hades" (Rev 1:18).

What already is true of Jesus will also become true of his people. Believers are destined to be "raised immortal" (1 Cor 15:52). That is, when they are raised from the dead, they will be forever free of the ravages of decay and death because they will be sharing God's eternal life. See part 2, ch. 20.

16: CHRIST AS "FIRSTFRUITS" (1 Cor 15:20, 23)

In the OT the firstfruits were the initial part of the annual production of grain, wine, oil, and sheared wool that was offered to God to acknowledge that he owned all the produce of the field and flocks and to thank him for his generous provision.

Thus, when something or someone is said to be the firstfruits, twin ideas are suggested by this agricultural analogy: unity and distinction, similarity and difference. The firstfruits were part of the harvest (unity), yet not the whole harvest (distinction).

1. Unity. As the first part of the harvest, the firstfruits were representative of the whole harvest. That is, the total harvest was representatively and potentially present in the firstfruits. To affirm Christ's resurrection is to affirm the resurrection of "those who belong to Christ" (1 Cor 15:12, 20, 23). To deny their resurrection is to deny his (1 Cor 15:13, 15–16). Paul cannot conceive of the firstfruits without the full harvest any more than he can think of the full harvest without the firstfruits. "As is the heavenly man, so also are those who are of heaven. ... We shall bear the image of the heavenly man" (1 Cor 15:48–49).

There are also basic similarities between the resurrection of Christ and that of believers. Both have a single cause—the creative power of God (1 Cor 6:14 regarding Christ; 2 Cor 4:14 regarding believers). For both, resurrection involved reanimation (Mark 16:6; John 5:28–29), transformation (Acts 1:3; 1 Cor 15:42–43), and exaltation (Acts 2:32–33; 2 Tim 2:12). In each case, resurrection led to the possession of a glorified body (Phil 3:21) and residence in heaven (Eph 1:20; 2 Cor 5:8).

2. Distinction. The very term "*first*fruits" implies priority in time. Firstfruits were gathered before the remainder of the harvest was ripe or mature or had been gathered. Using a military metaphor, Paul names two "orders" or "ranks" that are related by succession: "each in his own rank—Christ the firstfruits, then, at his coming, those who belong to Christ" (1 Cor 15:23). Christ was raised "on the third day" (1 Cor 15:4), but his people experience their resurrection on the last day. As Paul expressed it in his speech before Herod Agrippa II, Christ was "the first to rise from the dead" (Acts 26:23), never to die again (Rom 6:9).

Although believers first acquire immortality through their resurrection (1 Cor 15:53–54), when Christ rose from the grave he regained the immortality that he had surrendered when he became "obedient to death" (Phil 2:8). Moreover, when Jesus is described as "the firstborn of the dead" (Rev 1:5) and as "the firstborn from the dead" (Col 1:18), the thought is that he enjoys a supreme status, a superior rank, as the first and most important part of a series. Only of Christ is it true that resurrection meant his appointment as universal Lord and Judge (Acts 17:31; Rom 14:9; Eph 1:20–21). So then, these two resurrections differ with regard to their time, their nature, and their significance.

17: HOW SHOULD CHRISTIANS VIEW DEATH?
(1 Cor 15:26, 54–55; 2 Cor 5:8)

For some people, death is a terrifying prospect—entrance into the Great Unknown. For others, it will be a monumental relief, bringing an end to relentless pain.

There are no fewer than four ways in which the NT speaks of "death."

1. *Physical death* generally denotes the irreversible cessation of bodily functions (Heb 9:27) but occasionally the gradual weakening of physical powers (2 Cor 4;12, 16).

2. *Spiritual death* describes our natural alienation from God, our lack of responsiveness to God, or our hostility to God, all because of sin (Rom 6:23; Eph 2:1).

3. *"Second death"* refers to the permanent separation from God that is the destiny of the unrighteous (Rev 20:6, 14).

4. *Death to sin* involves the suspension of all relations with sin that results from being alive to God through dying and rising with Christ (Rom 6:4, 6, 11).

The first of these, physical death, is our focus here. There are three reasons why Christians should not be distressed by it. First, physical death should not be feared by the Christian, since by Christ's first advent death was robbed of its power (Rev 1:18) so that the believer is emancipated from the law that issues in sin and death (Rom 8:2). Believers have been set free from the bondage caused by fear of death (Heb 2:15).

Second, physical death should not be dreaded because at Christ's second advent death will be finally destroyed, being the last enemy to be subdued by the reigning Christ (1 Cor 15:23–26). Death's sting will be drawn when death is swallowed up in victory (1 Cor 15:54–55).

Third, fear of death is misplaced because it immediately ushers in deepened fellowship with Christ (2 Cor 5:8; Phil 1:23). As well as remaining "in Christ," deceased believers will then be "with Christ." Death marks the termination of the believer's temporary exile from the Lord and the end of the pilgrimage of faith (2 Cor 5:6–8).

On the other hand, death should not be embraced as a friend, since physical death as a biological necessity is one evidence of God's curse on humankind for their sin (Rom 5:12; 6:23). Also, we should not welcome death because it is destructive. It deprives humans of their God-given embodiment and their sense of belonging to the human race. By death they are totally removed from the securities of life on earth.

So Christians' attitude to death should be ambivalent. We should neither fear nor welcome physical death. But we should eagerly welcome what death brings—enriched communion with the glorified Christ in his immediate presence. See further part 1, ch. 28; and part 2, ch. 60.

18: BAPTISM FOR THE DEAD
(1 Cor 15:29)

Verses 1–34 of 1 Corinthians 15 treat the *that* of the resurrection (*hoti*, vv. 4, 12), and verses 35–58 the *how* of the resurrection (*pōs*, v. 35). Paul first enunciates the premise he shares with his opponents, namely, the resurrection of Christ (vv. 1–11), and then proceeds to draw a conclusion from this premise, that the dead in Christ will rise (vv. 12–32). At the end of this latter section he gives two ad hominem ("relating to the particular person") arguments supporting this conclusion—baptism for the dead (v. 29) and apostolic peril and danger (vv. 30–32). Then he adds a warning to avoid bad company and conduct (vv. 33–34).

He writes in verse 29, "Otherwise (i.e., if there is no resurrection of the Christian dead), what will those people do who are baptized for the dead? If the dead are not raised at all, why are people baptized for them?" What does this mean?

To be satisfactory, any proposed interpretation of the crucial phrases "for the dead" and "for them" must meet two requirements: (a) the preposition *hyper* ("for") should not be given a sense unparalleled in the Greek Bible (since the customary meaning of this preposition affords a suitable, even if strange, sense in this context); (b) the resulting meaning of the verse should contribute to Paul's argument in the chapter. It is highly improbable, for example, that *hyper* means "in memory of" or "out of respect for" or has a local sense, "over (the graves of the dead)"; or that "people who are baptized" refers to new converts who were being baptized "in the place of (the dead)," thus filling up the ranks left depleted by Christian martyrs. Nor should we find a final or purpose sense here: converts to Christianity were getting themselves baptized "in order to (be united with)" their departed relatives and friends at the resurrection.

If we give *hyper* its most common sense, "on behalf of," we arrive at this strange scenario. Some baptized Corinthians who had a semi-magical view of baptism were having themselves rebaptized on behalf of, and for the benefit of, certain deceased Christians who were thought to be at a disadvantage because they had not been baptized before being overtaken by death. Note that Paul says, "What will *they/those people* do ..." not "we" or even "you." Such a practice is otherwise unknown to us in first-century Christianity. On this interpretation, Paul is using an ad hominem argument in support of a conclusion already established (that the dead in Christ will rise), without giving it his approval. That Paul could occasionally argue in this way, on the basis of concession, is evident from 1 Corinthians 8:10 (cf. 10:20–21).

Another option is to take this preposition here as bearing an uncommon causal sense, "because of," as in Romans 15:9, where "for (*huper*) his mercy" means "because of his mercy." In this case, Paul is referring to those who became believers and so were baptized "because of the dead," that is, because of the earlier verbal or life witness of Christians no longer alive. If this is the preferable way to understand this much-debated verse, it is a salutary reminder of the power of Christian witness, sometimes even after the witnesses have died.

19: WHAT IS A "SPIRITUAL BODY"?
(1 Cor 15:42–44)

There have always been some who believe that the highest good is to be released from any form of embodiment. This is summed up in the quaint Greek aphorism *sōma sēma*, "the body is a tomb." Now, while it is true that conscious existence in a bodiless state is possible—God himself exists as a pure spirit—the Christian's goal is not to be free from the body but to gain a new, improved form of embodiment, a "spiritual body" (1 Cor 15:44)

Paul's distinctive expression, "spiritual body" (*sōma pneumatikon*), might sound like a contradiction in terms. Are not "spirit" and "body" opposites? Not for Paul. Since Greek adjectives ending in *–ikos* (here the neuter *–ikon*) denote an ethical or dynamic relation, not a material one, *sōma pneumatikon* means not "a body composed of spirit," but "a body animated by the spirit" or "a body controlled by the spirit." This "spirit" refers either to the Holy Spirit or to the human spirit as transformed by the Holy Spirit. If the latter, we may say that in the resurrection state the believer will have a body enlivened by and responsive to their redeemed spirit, which in turn will be completely and permanently amenable to the power and guidance of God's Spirit.

This being so, the "spiritual body" will be free from sinful inclinations. Gone forever will be the conflict between the flesh and the Spirit (see Gal 5:17). Apparently, too, it will be without physical instincts, not needing food or sleep, for "flesh and blood cannot inherit the kingdom of God" (1 Cor 15:50).

So then, Paul rejects both a materialistic view of resurrection—it is a *spiritual* body—and a spiritualistic view of immortality—it is a spiritual *body*. But the resurrection body whose architect and builder is God (1 Cor 15:38; 2 Cor 5:1–2) has other characteristics. It is:

- imperishable (1 Cor 15:42, 53–54), free from any form of decay or sickness;

- glorious (1 Cor 15:43a), free of physical indignity ("dishonor") and beautiful in form and appearance;

- powerful (1 Cor 15:43b), with limitless energy and perfect health; and

- angel-like (Luke 20:35–36), not because the resurrection body is sexless (sexual identity, an essential element in personality, is retained in the resurrection) but because it is deathless (Luke 20:35–36) and without sexual passions and procreative powers (Matt 22:30; Mark 12:25).

This assured destiny is of incomparable encouragement to all Christians, but especially to elderly believers whose physical powers are diminishing, and to disabled believers who face the daily challenge of coping with restricted resources.

20: ARE HUMANS IMMORTAL?
(1 Cor 15:52)

There is one area of thought where most Christians follow Plato rather than Paul. When asked whether humans are naturally immortal, most would answer "Yes!" In giving this reply they are, perhaps unwittingly, following Plato, who taught that in its rational form or function the soul is both eternally preexistent and immortal. Even when people prove themselves incurably guilty and so are condemned to eternal punishment in Tartarus without hope of rebirth, still the soul is not annihilated, for it never loses its natural property of immortality.

Paul, on the other hand, taught that "God ... alone is immortal" (1 Tim 6:15–16), and that believers will be "raised immortal" (1 Cor 15:52), that is, they will be "raised and so become immortal," not "raised as they already are, immortal."

Clearly, the issue depends how you define the terms "immortal" and "immortality." If we take "human beings are immortal" to mean "humans will live forever," both Plato and Paul would agree with this statement. But if "immortal" refers to being free from decay and death as a result of sharing God's life, immortality is a future acquisition, a privilege reserved for believers in Christ.

How does Paul use these terms? *Aphtharsia* (seven uses) is by derivation "non-decaying-ness," and so a good translation would be "incorruptibility" or "imperishability." *Athanasia* (three uses) is by derivation "non-dying-ness," and so "deathlessness" would be a good translation. The adjective *aphthartos*, "incorruptible" or "imperishable," occurs four times in Paul and three times in 1 Peter. Seven of Paul's uses of these terms are found in 1 Corinthians 15, where the future nature of immortality becomes apparent; the reference is always to a state that commences after death.

> The dead will be raised imperishable. ... For this perishable body must put on imperishability, and this mortal body must put on immortality. When this perishable body puts

on imperishability, and this mortal body puts on immortality, then the saying that is written will come true: "Death has been swallowed up in victory." (1 Cor 15:52–54)

Whether the term "immortality" is applied to God (1 Tim 6:16) or humans, it denotes the immunity from decay and death that results from having (in the case of God) or sharing (in the case of humans) the eternal divine life. See part 2, ch. 59.

According to Paul, then, it is death or a propensity to death, not immortality, that humans inherit from Adam (Rom 5:12; 1 Cor 15:22). And it is "those who belong to Christ," not all who are in Adam, who at Christ's coming will be made alive by a resurrection transformation that issues in immortality (1 Cor 15:22–23, 42, 52–54). Immortality is not a gift bequeathed to all by the first Adam but an inheritance won for the righteous by the second Adam. Possession of immortality is dependent on our relation to the second Adam, not the first Adam.

21: REGULAR PROPORTIONATE GIVING
(1 Cor 16:2)

In preparation for his forthcoming visit (1 Cor 4:18–19; 15:5–6), Paul gives directions to the Corinthians concerning his collection "for the poor among the saints in Jerusalem" (Rom 15:26; see part 2, ch. 9). He had already given these directions to his Galatian churches (cf. Acts 18:23), so that no special collections would need to be made in Corinth after his arrival (1 Cor 16:1, 2b): "On the first day of every week, each of you should set aside at home and store up some money in proportion to how they are prospering."

From these directions, we may deduce Paul's concept of giving, at least for one of the churches he founded. Christian giving should have the following characteristics.

It should be *regular*. "On the first day of every week" = "every Sunday/Sunday by Sunday." "The first day of the week" (John 20:1, 19; Acts 20:7), "the Lord's day" (Rev 1:10), had become or was becoming the holy day for Christians, being the day of Christ's resurrection. The verb *tithetō* ("set aside") is a present imperative with the implication, "let this be your habit."

It should be *individual*. Although any collecting of the offerings before Paul arrived might be done in public, the "setting aside" was an individual act.

It should be *voluntary*. As a third-person imperative, this verb *tithetō* is an exhortation ("each of you should ..."), not a formal command; giving cannot be mandated. This is in keeping with Paul's later directions regarding the same collection: "I am not commanding you" (2 Cor 8:8) and "I am simply giving you my advice" (2 Cor 8:10).

It should be *financial*. Both the term *logeia* ("collection," 1 Cor 16:1) and the verb *tithetō* ("set aside") relate to money.

It should be *private*. A regular setting aside of unspecified sums of money "at home" (*par' heautō*) would avoid any competitiveness and ensure privacy.

Finally, it should be *proportional*. Literally, the relevant phrase may be rendered "with regard to whatever way he is prospering." The verb "he is/they are prospering" refers not to profit ("in proportion to his gains," NEB) or to income ("in proportion to what you have earned," GNT)—both of which would be anachronistic given the presence of slaves in the Corinthian church—nor to what one can afford ("whatever he can afford," REB; "as much as each can spare," NJB), but to general financial prospering week by week. The "proportion" is not some percentage, but conformity to whatever degree of prosperity one has enjoyed. Paul expresses a similar sentiment in 2 Corinthians 8: giving is to be "as resources permit" (2 Cor 8:11) or "according to/in proportion to whatever on has" (2 Cor 8:12).

2 CORINTHIANS

22: EQUIPPED TO DISPENSE COMFORT
(2 Cor 1:4)

We are sometimes told that unless we have experienced the same trial as someone else, we are unable to give that person genuine sympathy and encouragement. For example, only a parent who has lost a very young child can really sympathize with parents who lose a child who is born prematurely.

Paul's words in 2 Corinthians 1:4, however, show that sentiment to be false.

The small Greek adjective *pas* is common in the New Testament. When it is used with the Greek definite article (English "the") in the singular, it means "all" or "the whole of." But when it stands alone with a singular noun, it means "every" in the sense "any you might think of" or "any you care to specify." The first use points to totality, the second to comprehensiveness.

These two uses of *pas* are found side by side in 2 Corinthians 1:4 in reference to "distress." Paul first describes the Father of the Lord Jesus Christ as "the compassionate Father and the God who always gives comfort." Throughout 2 Corinthians the verb "comfort" (*parakaleō*) does not denote some weak sympathy but rather refers to strengthening, consolation, encouragement, and even intervention to deliver (see Isa 51:9, 12). Paul then proceeds to affirm that God comforts and encourages in "all our distress (regarded as a whole)" (*epi pasē tē thlipsei hēmōn*). But there was a special divine purpose when God dispensed his comfort—it was so that Paul might always be able to bring comfort and encouragement to those in "any kind

137

of distress" (*en pasē thlipsei*). Paul's own affliction was specific to him but his experience of divine comfort equipped and obligated him to mediate God's comfort to those in any and every imaginable kind of distressing circumstance.

The crucial issue, then, is whether we are open to experiencing the divine comfort that qualifies and obligates us to bring God's comfort to others. Sometimes we gain God's comfort through prolonged meditation on the Scriptures, other times through reflective prayer. Perhaps on occasion it comes through direct divine intervention, as when Paul was taken up into the third heaven and paradise (2 Cor 12:2, 4; see part 2, ch. 30) in order to strengthen and encourage him for his constant apostolic suffering (see 2 Cor 6:4–10; 11:23–27).

Significantly, God's comfort very often comes to us by way of the words and actions of fellow believers. In 2 Corinthians 7:6, Paul recalls with gratitude that "God, the comforter of the depressed, comforted us by the coming of Titus," who brought good news about the spiritual state of the church at Corinth. Paul himself had been depressed (this is clearly implied) about the Corinthians' spiritual welfare, but Titus's safe arrival with reassuring news about Paul's converts had the effect of replacing the apostle's dejection with unbridled joy (2 Cor 7:7). See further part 2, ch. 28.

23: THWARTING SATAN'S STRATAGEMS
(2 Cor 2:11)

One of the Christian's defenses against the devil's stratagems is prior awareness of his purposes and methods. In 2 Corinthians 2:5–11, we discover several of those devilish schemes for outwitting and defrauding believers, culminating in Paul's statement in verse 11: "And we do all this so that Satan might not outwit us; for we are not unaware of his designs" (2 Cor 2:11).

The background to this episode in Paul's relationship with his converts in Corinth was this. Evidently, after Paul's most recent visit to Corinth, a serious insult of some description had been directed against him or one of his representatives (vv. 5, 10) by a member of the church at Corinth who may have headed up the opposition to the apostle there. Some unidentified disciplinary measures (possibly the temporary suspension of church privileges) had been inflicted on "the individual in question" (v. 6) by "the majority," but now Paul counsels the church to terminate the discipline and so rescue the repentant man from inordinate grief, and to complete his reformation by forgiving and encouraging him and by a public reaffirmation of their love for him (vv. 6–8). The implied minority of church members were probably a pro-Pauline clique, "ultra-Paulinists," who regarded the penalty as insufficient.

In these circumstances, what can we infer about Satan's designs or stratagems? First, Satan was bent on creating discord and wreaking havoc within the church at Corinth, either between the church at large and a dissident minority or between the repentant wrongdoer and his fellow Christians. Against this, as Paul elsewhere exhorts believers, "Make every effort to maintain the unity engendered by the Spirit by binding peace on yourselves" (Eph 4:3).

Second, the devil fostered an unforgiving spirit, at least among the minority at Corinth, in spite of the culprit's repentance. Against this, Jesus' direction was this: "If your brother or sister sins against you, rebuke them; and if they repent, forgive them" (Luke 17:3).

Third, the evil one wanted the man's punishment to continue in retribution, so that he was "overwhelmed by excessive sorrow" (cf. v. 7). Against this, Christian discipline, administered in love, is not simply punitive or retributive; it is also remedial or reformative (1 Cor 5:5; 11:32; 2 Cor 7:9–10; 13:10). It aims at reinstatement after repentance, through forgiveness and reconciliation.

Fourth, Satan always wants to turn good (the man's repentance) into evil (the man's downfall through excessive grief over his wrongdoing). Against this, God specializes in converting evil into good (Gen 50:20).

Prior awareness of Satan's techniques is part of the armor of God that enables believers to stand firm against the tactics of the devil (cf. Eph 6:11).

24: PARTICIPATING IN GOD'S TRIUMPHAL PROCESSION (2 Cor 2:14)

In the second chapter of 2 Corinthians, Paul begins what has rightly been called "the great digression" (2 Cor 2:14–7:4), for there are travel references to Macedonia in 2:13 and 7:5. What prompted this unparalleled digression was Paul's memory of Macedonia as the place where he gained relief from his unnerving restlessness (2:13) through the safe arrival of his messenger Titus, who brought a welcome report of the further triumph of the gospel in the lives of the Corinthians (7:5–7).

He begins this digression saying, "But thanks be to God, who always leads us as captives in his triumphal procession through our union with Christ, and through us diffuses everywhere the sweet odor of the knowledge of Christ." By using the colorful verb *thriambeuō* ("lead in triumphal procession"), Paul likens the irresistible advance of the gospel, in spite of temporary frustration, to a Roman *triumphus* ("triumph"), a victory procession celebrated by Roman generals on their return to Rome after a successful foreign campaign. About 350 triumphs are recorded in Greco-Roman literature. The procession began with trumpeters, who were then followed by prisoners of war from the conquered territory driven in chains in front of the ornate chariot of the general and thus exposed to public ridicule. The victorious soldiers followed, shouting "*Io triumphe*" ("Hail, triumphant one!").

When this verb is followed by the accusative case (denoting the direct object), it means "lead (someone) as a captive in a triumphal procession." Paul therefore sees himself not as a partner but as a prisoner of the *triumphator* (the one honored by the triumph), not as an exultant soldier but as a willing and privileged captive, a trophy of the general's victory, a onetime enemy who has been conquered. His implied prior "defeat" was his Damascus encounter when he surrendered to Christ (compare Phil 3:12, "Christ Jesus has made me his own").

The only other NT use of this picturesque verb is in Colossians 2:15: "After disarming the powers and authorities, he boldly displayed them in public by leading them in triumphal procession through Christ." These powers and authorities—hostile forces, whether cosmic, angelic, or demonic—were driven, as it were, before the victor's chariot as defeated enemies and as silent testimony to the superior might of their conqueror. While *thriambeuō* has the same meaning in both verses (2 Cor 2:14; Col 2:15), the two objects differ (Paul, his fellow apostles, and by implication all believers, on the one hand; and hostile powers and authorities on the other). In one case they are (paradoxically) willing, joyful captives and vocal witnesses to the general's victory (cf. 2 Cor 2:14b), while in the other case they are involuntary, sullen captives and silent witnesses to the commander's conquest.

The transition from "us" in verse 14a to "through us" in verse 14b is interesting. Paul the passive captive is also the active evangelist. God's agent is none other than God's prisoner. These two motifs are united in Paul's self-description, "I am an ambassador in chains" (Eph 6:20). The Greek word order, "To God be thanks" (v. 14a), not the usual "Thanks be to God" (as in 2 Cor 8:16; 9:15), throws special emphasis on God whose action, "always" and "everywhere," has prompted the thanksgiving. His activity is ongoing and universal, without temporal or national boundaries.

25: PLEASING THE MASTER
(2 Cor 5:9)

Here Paul states unambiguously his principal aim in life. "That is why we make it our aim to be pleasing to him (Christ), whether we are at home or away." In Classical Greek, when the verb *philotimeomai* ("be ambitious") was used positively, it carried the sense "show patriotic zeal for"; if used negatively, it meant "contend in rivalry." But in the later Hellenistic period it came to mean "strive eagerly" or "have as one's ambition." Thus Paul says elsewhere that "it has always been my ambition to proclaim the gospel where Christ was not known" (Rom 15:20). Paul's aim to win Christ's approval was continuous: "We constantly make it our ambition (present tense) to please him"—and this in the midst of all the trials of his apostolic ministry, "troubles, hardships and distresses ... beatings, imprisonments, and riots" (2 Cor 6:4–5).

We have seen that Paul's classic self-description was "a slave of Christ Jesus" (see part 2, ch. 1). There were two essential ingredients in a slave's service to his master. First, there is obedience. Obedience to commands was not simply required of slaves; it was assumed to be their principal role. In fact, the degree of a slave's faithfulness was determined by the extent of his obedience; a perfectly obedient slave was a completely faithful slave. The verdict on their lives that all Christians hope to hear from their heavenly Master is just this: "Well done, good and faithful slave (*doulos*)" (Matt 25:21, 23). His warm congratulations will be offered to slaves who have been industrious ("good") and obedient ("faithful"). This link between slavery and obedience is perhaps clearest in Romans 6:16 and Ephesians 6:5–6.

The second ingredient in a slave's service is pleasing the master. Where there are no particular commands to follow, it is the slave's prerogative to use his initiative in seeking to please his master (see Matt 25:14–23). Paul instructs Titus, "Urge slaves to be submissive to their masters (= obedience) and to please them in every way" (Titus 2:9). Whereas most slaves served under some degree of compulsion and expected punishment for disobedience, Christ's slaves serve voluntarily so that what motivates their service is not fear of punishment, or even principally the prospect of reward, but their desire to please their Master, the desire "to please him in everything" (Col 1:10). An explicit link between slavery to Christ and divine pleasure is found in Romans 14:18: "The person who acts as Christ's slave (*ho ... douleuōn tō Christō*) in this way (by exhibiting righteousness, peace, and joy in the Holy Spirit, Rom 14:17) pleases God and wins people's approval." To please God is to please Christ, and prompting divine pleasure can be a constant experience. One may recall Eric Liddell's memorable statement in *Chariots of Fire*: "God made me fast. When I run, I feel his pleasure." When we use our God-given gifts for his honor, we bring God pleasure.

In both these respects—obeying and pleasing a master—Christ himself is the model to imitate. "He emptied himself by assuming the form of a *slave* (*doulos*) ... and became *obedient* to the point of death, even death on a cross" (Phil 2:7–8). "I always do what is pleasing to him (God)" (John 8:29).

The apostle Paul, then, had an exclusive preoccupation with pleasing Christ. This was his magnificent obsession, an obsession that had the effect of expelling inferior—albeit legitimate—pursuits. Believers give satisfaction to their Master not only by obeying him promptly and implicitly, but also by devising innovative ways of pleasing him.

May I be permitted to mention an innovative way by which I sought to please the Master? On my retirement from regular teaching, I gifted my specialist biblical studies library of 7,000 books and 700 journals, accumulated over forty years, to the Nairobi Evangelical Graduate School of Theology (now part of Africa International University), keeping only some basic reference works necessary for my ongoing writing.

In our verse, something must be supplied after "at home" to clarify what is ambiguous. Clearly, "home" does not have a literal sense here, for the same pair of opposites ("be at home," "be away from home") has just been used metaphorically in verses 6 and 8. If "with the Lord" is supplied from verse 8, we have the anomaly of a future state being mentioned before a present condition. It is better to supply "in the body"; thus, "whether resident in the body or absent from it." This preserves the natural order of "present condition—future state," as in verse 6 (cf. Rom 14:8; Phil 1:20) and anticipates "through the body" in verse 10. The phrase "absent from it" (= the body) does not imply that it is possible to perform actions in a bodiless intermediate state that are pleasing to Christ, but rather points forward to verse 10 with its reference to the tribunal of Christ before which all believers will stand. Accordingly, "whether we are at home or away" may bear the sense "whether today during life on earth or tomorrow at Christ's judgment."

Finally, our verse illustrates how crucial the context is for a proper understanding of an isolated verse. Verse 9 looks back to verse 8 ("We prefer to depart from this body and take up residence with the Lord"): "*That is why* (*dio kai*) we make it our aim to be pleasing to him." But verse 9 also looks forward to verse 10: "We always aim to please him ... *for* (*gar*) we must all appear before Christ's tribunal." What prompted Paul's eager striving to have Christ's approval? His future destiny of dwelling with the Lord in person-to-person communion (v. 8), and his coming accountability to Christ for actions performed through the body (v. 10). Eschatology and ethics are interwoven.

26: A DRAMATIC CHANGE OF OUTLOOK
(2 Cor 5:16–17)

Both of these verses begin with the conjunction *hōste*, "for this reason," "so," "so then," that introduces two consequences of the death and resurrection of Christ and Paul's having a new life lived for Christ's benefit, not his own (vv. 14–15). One outcome was a radically altered outlook on fellow human beings and on Christ: "So then, from now on we regard no one from a human perspective. Even though we once viewed Christ from a human perspective, yet now we no longer do so" (v. 16). Paul had ceased making superficial judgments about people "from a human perspective" (*kata sarka*, literally "according to the flesh"), just as he now repudiated his superficial preconversion estimate of Jesus as a misguided messianic pretender, a crucified heretic, whose followers must be rooted out (Acts 9:1–2; 26:9–11). He had come to recognize Jesus as the divinely appointed Messiah and fellow humans as those for whom Christ had died (vv. 14–15). People were viewed not primarily in terms of nationality, but in terms of spiritual status. The time-honored division of people into Jew and Gentile, while remaining, was less important for Paul than the believer/unbeliever distinction (Rom 10:12–13; Eph 2:11–22; Col 3:11). *Adelphos* ("brother") now signified not only "fellow Israelite" (Acts 28:17) but also "fellow believer" (Jew or Gentile) in Jesus of Nazareth (Rom 10:1). It was Paul's encounter with the risen Lord on the Damascus road (Acts 9:1–19) that effected this dramatic twofold change in attitude "from now on": he now acclaimed Jesus as Messiah and Lord (Acts 17:3; Rom 10:9), and he now viewed Gentile believers as Abraham's offspring (Gal 3:26–29) and Jewish unbelievers as needing salvation in Christ (Rom 10:1–4). Both people and events were now seen (he implies) *kata pneuma*, "from a spiritual perspective," or *kata stauron*, "in the light of the cross."

If verse 16 states a negative consequence of Christ's death and resurrection and Paul's new motivation in life (vv. 14–15), verse 17 describes the positive outcome: "So if anyone is in Christ, there is a new creation: the old order has passed away; see, a new order has begun." Whenever any person, Jew or Gentile, comes to be part of the body of Christ by faith, there is a new act of creation on God's part. (On the "in Christ" expression in Paul, see part 2, ch. 48.) It is true that *ktisis* can mean "creature," so that the sense may be "he or she is a new creature" or "he or she is a newly created being." But since Paul has already in this letter depicted conversion as a creatorial act of God, comparable to the initial creation of light (2 Cor 4:6), perhaps *ktisis* here means "act of creation." Either way, with the adjective *kainē* ("new," in the sense of "freshly made") Paul is emphasizing the completely altered nature of the converted person or the total newness of God's creative action. The rendering "there is a new creation" (REB) reproduces the ambiguity of the Greek.

In this new creation, "the old order," the whole set of conditions and relationships belonging to former times, "has passed out of existence" (*parēlthen*, aorist expressing total removal, "has come and gone"). "A new order," a brand-new set of attitudes and relationships, qualitatively superior to the old set, has arrived and will stay (*gegonen*, a perfect tense, "has come to stay"). When a person becomes a Christian, they experience a total restructuring of life that alters its whole fabric—thinking, feeling, willing, and acting. Anyone who is "in Christ," the safest place in the universe, is "Under New Management" (see part 1, ch. 51) and has "Altered Priorities Ahead," to use the wording sometimes found (in Britain) in shop windows and on roads.

27: THE SINLESS ONE FOR THE SINFUL
(2 Cor 5:21)

In 2 Corinthians 5:18–20, Paul has broadly outlined the drama of reconciliation. Now in verse 21 he explains, as far as human language
and imagery permit, the "how" of reconciliation: "He made him who
knew no sin to be sin for us, so that by being in him we might become
the righteousness of God." The evangelistic watch-cry, "Get reconciled to God" (v. 20), leads the apostle to specify the basis (v. 21a) and
the result (v. 21b) of reconciliation. The fifteen Greek words, carefully
balanced, almost chiastic, defy final exegetical examination, dealing
as they do with the heart of the atonement.

"Him who knew no sin." Behind the Greek verb *ginōskō* ("know")
lies the Hebrew verb *yāda'*, "have personal acquaintance or experience with." This "knowing" denotes knowledge gained by personal
participation. Although Christ was aware of the reality of sin and
observed sin in others, he himself "never knew sin" (TCNT); he was
"the sinless one" (JB), with the negative particle *mē* signifying "not
(ever)" = "never." Neither outwardly in act nor inwardly in attitude
did Christ ever sin, so that at no time was his conscience stained by
sin (cf. Heb 4:15; 7:26; 1 Pet 2:22; 3:18; 1 John 3:5).

"He made him … to be sin." As we reverently consider the meaning of what is without doubt the most profound and incomprehensible statement in all of Scripture, we can question the view that
Paul is saying that God regarded and treated the sinless Christ as
a sinner; the crucial word used in this verse is "sin" (*hamartia*), not
"sinner" (*hamartōlos*). Nor should we argue that, since two Hebrew
sacrificial terms, *hattā't* and *'āshām*, can mean both "sin" and "sin
offering," the first use of the word *hamartia* in our verse means "sin"
while the second means "sin offering." The regular Greek for "sin
offering" is *peri hamartiōn thysia* (Heb 10:26, "a sacrifice for sins"),
or simply *peri hamartias* (Rom 8:3; Isa 53:10 [LXX], "[an offering] for
sin"). Also, nowhere else in Paul or the NT does the word *hamartia*
have the meaning "sin offering." Or again, it is unlikely that Paul is
speaking simply of the incarnation when Christ assumed human

nature "in the likeness of sinful flesh" (Rom 8:3) and was subject to the consequences of sin, namely, suffering and death.

Paul is thinking of the crucifixion, not the incarnation, and the sense is not exactly "God made the sinless one into sin" (JB), but "God *caused* the sinless one *to be* sin" (not the ambiguous English "made him sin"), pointing to divine appointment. God treated Christ on the cross as if he were sin, or, in a pregnant mysterious sense, God actually caused Christ to be sin, that is, to be the very personification of sin and so to be estranged from him and the object of his wrath (see part 1, ch. 21). Verse 21a stands in stark contrast to verse 19b. Because of God's transference of sinners' sin onto the sinless one—because sin was reckoned to Christ's account (v. 21a)—sin is not now reckoned to the believer's account (v. 19b). This total identification of the sinless one with sinners at the cross, in assuming the full penalty and guilt of their sin, leaves no doubt that substitution as well as representation was involved. God's action was "for us," that is, both "on our behalf" and "in our place."

It is perhaps not surprising that while Paul can boldly say "God was in Christ" (v. 19), apparently his awareness of this awe-inspiring mystery makes him draw back from the dreadful statement "God made Christ to be sin," instead opting to leave the subject and object unstated—"he made him to be sin"—although the referents are clear.

The second part of our verse states the purpose, and by implication the result, of God's total alignment of Christ with human sin. It is not that believers themselves come to share God's inherent righteousness. Rather, "becoming the righteousness of God" refers to gaining a right standing before God that God himself bestows ("of God" is a subjective genitive; cf. Rom 5:17; Phil 3:9). The term "righteousness" is here an "abstract for concrete," meaning "righteous" in a forensic rather than an ethical sense. By being united to the risen Christ through faith ("in him"), believers are "constituted righteous" (Rom 5:19) by God in the heavenly court.

28: PAUL'S THREE LOW POINTS
(2 Cor 7:5–7)

Because the apostle Paul made such a massive contribution to early Christianity as a pastoral writer and missionary statesman, Christians tend to elevate him to an almost unreal status as a "super-extra" Christian without fluctuation of feelings and desires. But in reality, like all believers, he had his emotional and spiritual highs and lows.

From Paul's letters we can identify three occasions when he felt alone and discouraged. Significantly, all these occurred in his maturity (assuming he was born early in the Christian era).

1. In Macedonia in about AD 56 (2 Cor 7:5–7). Paul had sent his deputy, Titus, to Corinth with a no-longer-extant "severe letter" (cf. 2 Cor 2:4; 7:8) that called for the Corinthian believers to repent of their support of those who were opposing Paul. When Titus did not arrive in Troas with news of Corinth, Paul "had no peace of mind" and went on to Macedonia (2 Cor 2:12–13). There, his restlessness continued and he was "harassed in every way—outwardly there were conflicts, and inwardly fears" (2 Cor 7:5).

What were Paul's fears? A haunting uncertainty about Titus's reception at Corinth (cf. vv. 13, 15); a persistent apprehension about the Corinthian reaction to the "severe letter" delivered by Titus, especially given Titus's failure to meet Paul in Troas (2:13) and initially in Macedonia (7:5); anxiety that he had caused the Corinthians unnecessary pain by his "severe letter" (cf. 7:8) with its call for disciplinary action against the wrongdoer; concern that his boasting to Titus about the Corinthians might prove unfounded and therefore acutely embarrassing (cf. 7:14); anxiety about the safety of Titus in travel; apprehension that on his forthcoming visit to Corinth he might find some members indulging in un-Christian conduct (12:20–21).

Relief came to Paul in his downcast, anxious state only by the safe arrival of Titus with favorable news of the Corinthians' positive response to the "severe letter" (2 Cor 7:6–13). "God, the Comforter of the depressed, comforted us (= me, who was depressed, by implication)" (v. 6). When the adjective *tapeinos* is used of an emotional state, it means "downcast," "dejected," "disheartened," or "depressed." With Titus' arrival and his news about Corinth, Paul's dejection gave way to consummate relief and deep joy (vv. 8–13).

2. In Jerusalem in about AD 59 (Acts 23:1–11). Shortly after Paul's arrival in Jerusalem, some Jews prompted a popular uprising against Paul that led the Roman military commander to arrest Paul and finally have him address the summoned Jewish Sanhedrin. Paul unwisely began his defense with a vigorous assertion of his innocence before God (v. 1). When the high priest Ananias illegally ordered Paul to be struck, the apostle (who had not been charged, let alone found guilty) lashed out verbally, "God will strike you, you whitewashed wall!" But then, just as abruptly, he apologized for his ill-considered outburst (vv. 3–5). Then he engineered a stratagem that effectively divided the Sanhedrin but prompted a violent dispute that endangered his own life (vv. 6–10).

After all this, Paul was undoubtedly despondent as he sat alone in his cell in the Antonia Fortress. When he recalled the calm demeanor of Jesus and Stephen before this same Sanhedrin (Matt 26:59–63; Acts 6:15; 7:54–56, 59–60), Paul must have felt saddened by his own dismal performance in the same arena. He had put his own life in danger by his divisive maneuver (v. 10), and he may have doubted whether his longstanding desire, as a Roman citizen (Acts 22:27) and Christian, to visit Rome would be fulfilled.

These precise concerns were graciously addressed by the risen Jesus: "The following night the Lord stood near Paul and said, 'Take courage! As you have testified about me in Jerusalem (see Acts 22:1–21; 23:6), so you must also testify in Rome'" (v. 11).

3. In Rome in about AD 64 (2 Tim 4:9–18). For the second time in his career, Paul was in Rome under guard (for the earlier occasion, see Acts 28:16, 30–31). But this time there were differences: he was awaiting a final trial but anticipated legal delays that would permit visits from his colleagues (2 Tim 4:9, 11, 13, 16, 21); he was not making plans for travel after his release (compare Phlm 22) but expected conviction after his trial and death as a martyr (2 Tim 4:6–8).

What hints are there in the text that he was grappling with loneliness, frustration, and despondency? First, his immediate circle of colleagues had broken up—Demas had gone to Thessalonica, Crescens to Galatia, Titus to Dalmatia, and he had sent Tychicus to Ephesus (vv. 10, 12). Second, Demas, his onetime coworker (Col 4:14; Phlm 24), had deserted Paul because of his "love of the present world"— perhaps departure from the faith, perhaps unwillingness to face martyrdom with Paul. Third is his request that Timothy should join him "quickly," because of Demas's desertion (vv. 9–10; cf. vv. 11, 21). Fourth, at his first defense, probably a preliminary investigation of his case prior to his formal trial, there was no support of any kind from the local Roman believers, a serious sin of omission ("May it not be counted against them!" v. 16). And finally, twice Paul uses a colorful verb to depict his sense of being let down (vv. 10, 16). In derivation, *egkataleipō* denotes the complete (*kata*) desertion (*leipō*) of someone who is in the midst of (*en*) a situation where aid is urgently needed (see part 1, ch. 21). Paul had felt abandoned, "left in the lurch." Like Jesus, who was abandoned by his disciples in his hour of need (Mark 14:50), Paul felt forsaken by those who ought to have stood with him (cf. 1:15).

But once again, the Lord Jesus stood by his side and gave him strength (v. 17; cf. Acts 18:9–10; 22:17–21; 23:11). In the second and third instances mentioned above, God the Father or the Lord Jesus intervened directly to bring the needed comfort, while in the first case the divine comfort was mediated through Titus.

When we find ourselves in emotional turmoil and traumatic circumstances, sometimes God will come to our rescue directly, often through the Scriptures. At other times, his intervention will be mediated through fellow believers.

29: PAUL'S FAVORITE WORD
(2 Cor 8:9)

It is probably not fair to ask a writer or speaker to sum up his message in a single word. But if we were to ask Jesus this unfair question, my guess is that his answer would have been "Abba" (see part 2, ch. 32). As for Paul, my guess is he would say "grace" (*charis*).

It is one of the most remarkable features of Paul's letters that the word *charis* occurs at or near the beginning and the end of each letter, forming the opening chord and dying refrain of every Pauline symphony. No one definition of *charis* does justice to the word's wealth of meaning, although the common proposal that it refers to "God's unsought and unbought favor" captures important aspects of its meaning.

Second Corinthians 8–9 is Paul's clarion call to the Corinthians to bring to completion their contribution to his collection for "the poor among the Lord's people in Jerusalem" (Rom 15:26; see part 2, ch. 9). *Charis* is a key term in these two chapters, occurring no fewer than ten times in six different senses:

1. "Grace," referring to Jesus' unconditional kindness lavishly displayed (8:9), or to God's enablement, especially his enablement to participate worthily in the collection (8:1; 9:8, 14)

2. "Privilege" or "favor," used of the honor or opportunity of participating in the offering (8:4)

3. "Act of grace," denoting the collection itself as a charitable and generous act (8:6)

4. "Grace of giving," referring to the virtuous act of sharing or of affording help (8:7)

5. "Offering" or "charitable work," describing the collection as an expression and proof of goodwill (8:19)

6. "Thanks," the verbal expression of gratitude for an act of benevolence (8:16; 9:15)

There are two uses of *charis* found in Classical Greek but not the NT. It can denote something's inherent beauty (such as a spectacular sunset) and someone's being charmed or fascinated by that beauty. The four main NT uses of *charis* may be classified this way:

1. Unconditional kindness: "By *grace* you have been saved" (Eph 2:8); "The *grace* of God has appeared …" (Titus 2:11)

2. Act of unconditional kindness: "You know the *grace* of our Lord Jesus Christ, that though he was rich, yet for your sake he became poor" (2 Cor 8:9)

3. Gratitude for an act of unconditional kindness: "singing to God with *gratitude* in your hearts" (Col 3:16)

4. Verbal expression of gratitude for an act of unconditional kindness: "*Thanks* be to God for his indescribable gift" (2 Cor 9:15)

30: AN INTENTIONAL PROLONGED SILENCE
(2 Cor 12:2)

Paul begins 2 Corinthians 12 by reasserting that he had no choice but to go on boasting (v. 1a; cf. 2 Cor 11:1, 16, 30; 12:6). By insisting that their teachers display their "credentials" (cf. 2 Cor 11:21–29), the Corinthians were forcing him to break a fourteen-year silence and describe a vision and revelation the Lord Jesus gave him (v. 1b): "I know a man in Christ who fourteen years ago was caught up to the third heaven." In the third heaven or paradise, he was given an inexpressible revelation that no mortal was permitted to repeat (v. 4), what he later calls "the stupendous grandeur of the revelations" (v. 7). None of Paul's visions recorded in Acts can be identified with this visionary revelation, since it occurred fourteen years before the time of writing (fall AD 56)—that is, about AD 43 by inclusive reckoning, during the ten so-called silent years (AD 35–45) that Paul spent in Syria and Cilicia (Gal 1:21) and that Acts says nothing about.

Is Paul recounting his own experience when he writes enigmatically, "I know a man in Christ (= a Christian man)"? Undoubtedly so, for several reasons. He knew the exact time the revelation took place (v. 2) and that its content was beyond words (v. 4). The revelation was directly related to the receipt of a "thorn" that was given, says Paul, "to me" (v. 7). The reference to a lack of awareness whether he was in the body or not at the time of the revelation (vv. 2–3) also points to a personal experience. Or again, he would be unlikely to feel embarrassment (v. 1) about boasting on another person's behalf (v. 5a).

But why does the apostle objectify his experience and speak in the third person in verses 2–4, even distinguishing between himself and "the man involved" in verse 5? Probably he saw this as a convenient way of distancing himself from this necessary but futile boasting that in itself did not contribute to the common good (cf. 12:19; 1 Cor 12:7). He also may have wanted to dispel any idea that his privileged experience added anything to his status or importance.

Paul's silence about his revelatory vision was *prolonged*, not only because the silence lasted for fourteen years, but also because from a Corinthian viewpoint there had been at least four occasions when Paul could have informed them of his extraordinary experience but chose to remain silent:

- his initial eighteen-month visit on his second missionary journey from fall AD 50 to spring AD 52 (Acts 18:1–18);

- his writing of 1 Corinthians (spring AD 55);

- his "painful" visit in summer or fall AD 55 (2 Cor 2:1; 13:2); or

- his "severe letter" in spring AD 56 (2 Cor 2:3–4; 7:8, 12).

Clearly, then, the previous silence was *intentional.* His silence was broken only because in the present contest with his rivals, brought on by the Corinthian disloyalty to him, he was forced to match his rivals' foolish boasting (11:18, 21–23), and because an account of his heavenly rapture was a necessary prelude to the description of his immediate receipt of the "thorn in the flesh" that God gave him to curb any inordinate pride in the revelation he received in paradise (v. 7). Paul could date his extraordinary heavenly experience so precisely because he could not forget how long he had been grappling with his painful and frustrating "thorn" that the Lord Jesus had declined to remove, assuring him, "My grace is sufficient for you" (12:8–9; see part 2, ch. 31).

The apostle's skillful handling of his privileged ascent to heaven illustrates the truth of the aphorism, "There is a time for everything ... a time to be silent and a time to speak" (Eccl 3:1, 7). But it is also a potent example of his pastoral sensitivity. His prolonged and intentional silence about his remarkable privilege demonstrates his conviction that ecstatic experiences, as private encounters with God, were not to be publicized unnecessarily, and, as God-given privileges, added nothing to a person's standing or role in the church (cf. 2 Cor 12:6).

31: "A THORN IN THE FLESH"
(2 Cor 12:7)

Both in 2 Corinthians 11:30 and 12:5 Paul indicated his (reluctant) willingness to boast about his weaknesses. His first dramatic example was his humiliating exit from Damascus (11:32–33); the second was his permanent receipt of a debilitating "thorn." Being both past and present, "weakness" was integral to Paul's experience.

The exit was a single episode that nevertheless was emblazoned on his memory because of its ignominy. The "thorn," on the other hand, was a recurrent trial that could incapacitate and humiliate him at any time: "And because of the extraordinary nature of the revelations, therefore, to keep me from being too elated, there was given me a thorn in the flesh, a messenger of Satan sent to pummel me, to keep me from being too elated." From 2 Corinthians 12:7–10 we may deduce that this "thorn" had certain characteristics.

1. It was given to Paul as a direct consequence of the revelations he received in paradise (v. 7).

2. It caused him acute pain, either physically or psychologically, which prompted him to seek its removal (vv. 7–8). In Classical Greek, the word *skolops* commonly meant "stake," but in the LXX, as also in the papyri, it means "splinter" or "thorn." "In the flesh" (*en sarki*) has the sense "embedded in/driven into my body."

3. He regarded it, paradoxically, as simultaneously given by God ("was given" is a "theological passive") and yet a "messenger" or instrument of Satan (see part 1, ch. 2).

4. It was a permanent condition, as implied by the two present tenses, "to keep me from being too elated" and "to pummel." Yet its exacerbations were intermittent, as implied by the "three times (I implored the Lord)" in verse 9.

5. It was humbling, for it was designed to curb or prevent spiritual arrogance (note the repeated "to keep me from being too elated") over the "extraordinary nature" (or "stupendous grandeur," Weymouth) of the revelations received.

6. It was humiliating, comparable to receiving vicious blows about the face. The colorful verb *kolaphizō* means "strike with the fist," or, more generally, "maltreat violently," "batter," "knock about."

7. It caused Paul to feel weak (vv. 9–10), yet the weakness it caused became an object of boasting (v. 9; cf. v. 5) and a source of pleasure (v. 10).

The proposed identifications of the "thorn," legion in number, can be classified under three main headings: spiritual or psychological anxiety; opposition to Paul in general or at Corinth in particular;

or a physical malady, often unspecified but sometimes identified as malaria or defective vision.

Some kind of physical ailment most easily accommodates the seven characteristics of the "thorn" outlined above. In 1 Corinthians 5:5 (cf. 1 Cor 11:30; 1 Tim 1:20), Satan appears as God's agent for the infliction of disciplinary illness (cf. Job 2:1–10). Certainly a recurrent and tormenting illness could be considered "a messenger of Satan," for it might bring Paul within the shadow of death (cf. 2 Cor 1:8–9) or hinder the advance of the gospel either by arousing the contempt of the hearers (cf. Gal 4:13–14) or by frustrating his travel plans (cf. 1 Thess 2:18). Be that as it may, behind any and every machination of Satan, Paul could discern the overarching providence of a God who perpetually creates good out of evil.

If Paul had identified his "thorn," Christians of subsequent generations who lacked his particular affliction would have been tempted to regard his experience, as summarized in 2 Corinthians 12:8–10, as largely irrelevant to their situation. As it is, multitudes of believers with a variety of "thorns" have been challenged and consoled as they have made Paul's experience their own.

GALATIANS

32: SHOULD ABBA BE TRANSLATED AS "DADDY"? (Gal 4:6)

On the basis of the use of the word *abba* in Romans 8:15 and Galatians 4:6, we are sometimes told that the apostle Paul encouraged Christians to address God as "daddy." Through Christ we enjoy an unparalleled intimacy with God that is summed up in the word *abba*: "Because you are sons, God has sent the Spirit of his Son into our hearts, the Spirit who calls out, *abba*" (Gal 4:6).

It is true that in the Jewish Talmud and other Jewish documents we find statements such as, "When a child experiences the taste of wheat (i.e., when it is weaned), it learns to say *'abbā* and *'immā* (= our "dada" and "mama")" (*Berakot* 40a in the Babylonian Talmud). However, even if the term *abba* began as a childish babbling sound (and this is far from clear), at the time of Jesus it was a regular adult word meaning "father" or "my father" (as terms of address) or "the father" or "my father" (as terms of reference).

That is, *abba* was not a *childish* term of the nursery comparable to "daddy." It was a polite and serious term, yet also colloquial and familiar, regularly used by adult sons and daughters when addressing their father. Ideas of simplicity, intimacy, security, and affection attach to this household word of *childlike* trust and obedience. So to bring out the sense of warm and trusting intimacy that belongs to the word, we could appropriately paraphrase it as "dear father." Further, if Paul had wanted to convey the sense of "daddy," he could have used a Greek word he undoubtedly would have known—*papas* or *pappas*, which means "papa" or "daddy," a child's word for "father."

157

There are four further reasons it is inappropriate to translate *abba* by "daddy." First, in all three NT passages where the word *abba* occurs (Mark 14:36; Rom 8:15; Gal 4:6), it is immediately translated by the term "Father" (the Greek articular nominative, *ho patēr,* used in a vocative sense). Second, Jesus himself directed his followers to address God as "our Father," *pater hēmōn* (Matt 6:9). Third, each of the seventeen prayers of Jesus (not counting parallels) recorded in the Gospels begins with "Father," presumably *Abba* in each case. Fourth, for Christians, young or old, to address God as "daddy" would be inappropriate, for in English usage the term is too casual and flippant and unassuming to be used in addressing the Lord God Almighty, the Creator and Sustainer of all things, not to mention the fact that "daddy" is often abbreviated to "dad."

It may be that an improper sense of familiarity with God on the part of some Christians prompted Peter to say, "If you address as 'Father' the One who judges each person's work impartially, live in reverent fear of him during the time of your exile on earth" (1 Pet 1:17). That is, to address God as "our Father in heaven" in the Lord's Prayer is to remember he is the all-knowing and impartial Supreme Judge of every person. Therefore, we must approach him with reverential awe, not as though he were simply another "daddy."

33: REVELING IN NEWFOUND FREEDOM
(Gal 5:1)

The book of Galatians has often and rightly been called "Paul's charter of Christian freedom." Indeed, the authors of two of the standard textbooks on the life and teaching of Paul go one step further and have linked the apostle with freedom in the very titles of their books: *Paul: Apostle of the Free Spirit* (1977) by F. F. Bruce (titled *Paul: Apostle of the Heart Set Free* in the American edition), and *Paul: Apostle of Freedom* (1964; 2nd rev. ed. 2015) by Richard N. Longenecker.

Nowhere in Galatians is the theme of "liberty in Christ" more in evidence than in the section 4:21–5:1, where Paul interprets the Hagar/Sarah story found in Genesis 16:1–16; 21:1–21 to illustrate his point that Christian believers are emancipated from all spiritual slavery. Paul introduces a series of contrasts:

Hagar, a slave woman	Sarah, a free woman
Ishmael, born in the course of nature	Isaac, born as the result of a promise
The present city of Jerusalem (= Judaism)	The Jerusalem above (= the church)
The children of the present Jerusalem (= legalists)	The children of the Jerusalem above (= Christians)
Righteousness by law-keeping	Righteousness by faith

The legalists in Galatia were claiming that observing the law of Moses, and the rite of circumcision in particular, was necessary for salvation (Gal 2:16; 5:4; 6:12; cf. Acts 15:1, 5). Not surprisingly, many of Paul's recent Galatian converts were thrown into confusion by the alternative gospel of these agitators (Gal 1:7; 5:10). In response, the apostle insists that all believers are totally free from law-keeping as an imagined way to gain divine approval. True freedom comes through total reliance on the sufficiency of the death of Christ to secure a right and permanent relationship with God.

So then, "It is for freedom that Christ has set us free" (Gal 5:1). While this word-for-word translation is accurate, it seems to make Paul simply state the obvious. But more than this was probably intended. In Greek, the dative case (here "for freedom") can denote a disadvantage or an advantage. Thus, "for freedom" may be appropriately expanded to "for the enjoyment of freedom."

Relishing their release from bondage to self-effort—"a yoke of slavery" as Paul puts it (Gal 5:1)—Christians should revel in the spiritual emancipation they have gained through God's grace and the crucified body of Christ (see Rom 7:4).

34: FREEDOM FOR SLAVERY
(Gal 5:13)

The West idolizes three freedoms—freedom of religion, freedom of speech, and freedom of movement. What is more, people generally regard freedom and slavery as mutually exclusive opposites.

The apostle Paul, on the other hand, develops a remarkable paradox—that the aim of spiritual freedom is to become enslaved. For Paul, conversion to Christ brought freedom on several fronts:

- freedom from spiritual death (Col 2:13)

- freedom from slavery to sin (Rom 6:14–23; cf. John 8:34, 36)

- freedom from bondage to the Mosaic law (Rom 7:4, 6)

- freedom from people-pleasing (Gal 1:10)

- freedom from "self-pleasing" (2 Cor 5:15)

But to be truly free *is* to be enslaved. The emancipated slave is not left without a master to whom allegiance may be given. Slavery *from* leads to slavery *for*.

Romans 6:15–23 contrast two types of slavery: slavery to the ruthless despot, Sin (also called "impurity" or "wickedness"), and slavery to the generous sovereign, Righteousness (also called "grace," "obedience," "the pattern of teaching," and "God"). What is stunning about Paul's depiction of the human situation here is that there are only two masters, not more, and that allegiance to either is portrayed as slavery. Emancipation from slavery to sin leads to a willing servitude to righteousness.: "Just as you used to offer your bodily members in slavery to impurity and ever-increasing wickedness, so now offer them in slavery to righteousness" (Rom 6:19). "Now you have been set free from sin and have been enslaved to God" (Rom 6:22).

The exquisite attractiveness of the new slavery becomes evident when Paul contrasts the outcome or "fruit" of the two slaveries. For those on the payroll of sin, the wages are "death" (Rom 6:23), what

Paul elsewhere depicts as "eternal ruin and exclusion from the presence of the Lord" (2 Thess 1:8). On the other hand, those who are God's slaves will receive as a gracious gift "eternal life," the direct participation in the eternal divine life that will exclude both physical and spiritual death (see part 2, ch. 60).

And it is not only Paul who champions the *for* after the *from*. Peter expresses the same sentiment: "Live as free people, but do not use your freedom as a pretext for evil. Rather, live as God's slaves" (1 Pet 2:16).

The final paradox is that freedom *for* slavery leads to freedom *in* slavery. People who choose to express their freedom by becoming Christ's or God's slave gain a fresh freedom—the opportunity to restrict their freedom by embracing a worthy goal. So Paul could say: "Though I am free and belong to no one, I have made myself a slave to everyone, in order to win as many converts as possible. ... I have become all things to all people so that by all possible means I might save some of them" (1 Cor 9:19, 22).

EPHESIANS

35: THE HOLY SPIRIT AS BOTH DOWN PAYMENT AND PLEDGE (Eph 1:13–14)

Some Greek words pulsate with so much meaning that it is impossible to find an adequate single-word equivalent in English. In such cases, the translator is compelled to indulge in a paraphrase or to use two expressions. *Arrabōn* is such a word.

In the fields of commerce and law, *arrabōn* had two basic meanings. It was the first installment of a purchase, a *down payment*, a deposit that gave a person a legal claim to the goods that had been purchased but that legally required further payments. The size of the initial partial payment varied widely. Sometimes it was a large portion of the total cost, but sometimes it was a mere token. So a meager two drachmas (an ancient Greek silver coin) could be a deposit on an item costing three hundred drachmas.

In its other basic sense, *arrabōn* was a *pledge* that payment would be made in the future. In this case, the pledge was not part of the actual payment for the goods in question, but it did guarantee that full payment would ultimately be made. So a silver bracelet could be accepted as a pledge that a debt of three hundred drachmas would be repaid. A classic Old Testament instance of this sense is found in Genesis 38:15–20, where Judah gives Tamar his seal and its cord along with his staff as a pledge (*arrabōn* in the LXX) that he would fulfill his promise and give her a young goat from his flock.

But we might well ask: "Of what could the Holy Spirit be a mere down payment?" It should be observed, first of all, that in this metaphorical use of the term *arrabōn*, the down payment need not be an inferior part of the full payment, although it is a part of a larger whole. God's gift of his Holy Spirit is the first part of believers' ultimate inheritance as God's sons and daughters. That larger whole includes being completely conformed to the image of Christ (Rom 8:29; 1 Cor 15:49), being completely responsive to the Spirit as possessors of a "spiritual body" (1 Cor 15:42–44), and participating in the eternal and corporate worship and service of God in a renewed universe (2 Pet 3:13; Rev 5:11–13).

There is no need, however, to choose between the two meanings of *arrabōn*. The Spirit of God is the "first installment and pledge" (Barclay) or "a deposit, guaranteeing our inheritance" (NIV). That is, the deposit is also the guarantee. In the new life that the Spirit imparts, God gives believers a foretaste of their full inheritance and at the same time a promise that this complete inheritance will be received.

36: A NORMATIVE PATTERN: "TO — THROUGH — BY" (Eph 2:18)

Ephesians 2:14–18 portrays Christ as the reconciler and peacemaker who by his death on the cross has destroyed the hostility that separated God and humans and also Jews and Gentiles. He has created in his own person a single new humanity out of the two ethnic groups (cf. Gal 3:28; Col 3:11), thereby enabling both groups to have equal and unhindered access to God's immediate presence. Verse 18 affords evidence ("for," *hoti*) of the proclamation (and acceptance) of the good news of peace (v. 17) and of the creation of the one new humanity (v. 15): "For through him (Christ) we both have access (*prosagōgē*) to the Father in the one Spirit."

All three NT uses of this term *prosagōgē* are found in Paul's letters. The word alludes to the granting of the privilege of admission into the presence of a potentate. Having obtained access (Rom 5:2), believers now permanently enjoy ("we have" is present tense) this right to enter God's throne room (Eph 2:18). We have this access "with boldness and confidence, being in union with Christ and having faith in him" (Eph 3:12).

There are four characteristics of this access mentioned in Ephesians 2:18:

1. It is enjoyed by Jews, "those who were near" (v. 17), but also by Gentiles, "those who were far away" (vv. 13, 17). "Both" implies "without distinction on the basis of race," and "together" in the sense that the two groups now form a single new humanity (v. 15).

2. Access is "to the Father," that is, to the sanctuary of God's immediate presence (cf. Heb 10:19) or to the enclosure of God's favor (Rom 5:2). In the formal prayer reports in the NT, the addressee is invariably God the Father (e.g., Eph 3:14–15; Phil 1:3–4).

3. Access is made possible "through him (Christ)," that is, "through his cross" (v. 16) = "through his blood shed on the cross" (Col 1:20; cf. Col 3:17).

4. Access is experienced "by the one Spirit," that is, "enabled/ empowered by the one Spirit." But *en heni pneumati* may mean "in the one Spirit," that is, "united in one and the same Spirit."

If this "to—through—by" is the normative pattern for believers' access to God—to the Father, through the Son, by the Spirit—there are two exceptions. First, *prayer* is sometimes addressed directly to the Lord Jesus by an individual believer (e.g., Acts 7:59–60; 9:10–17; 22:16, 19; 2 Cor 12:8) or by a group of believers (Acts 1:24; 9:21; 1 Cor 1:2; 16:22; Rev 22:20). Second, the Lord Jesus, along with God the Father, is a legitimate object of *worship* (e.g., Matt 14:33; 28:9, 17; Luke 24:52; John 9:38; 20:28; Acts 13:2; Phil 2:9–11; 2 Pet 3:18; Rev 5:12–14).

37: EVIDENCES OF THE SPIRIT'S FILLING
(Eph 5:18–21)

How can believers know they are filled with the Spirit? Paul has anticipated and answered this question toward the end of Ephesians 5: "Do not get intoxicated—that leads to sensual indulgence—but always be filled with the Spirit" (Eph 5:18).

In Greek, Ephesians 5:18–21 is a single sentence. The main verb is *plērousthe* ("be filled"), which is the second-person plural present passive imperative of *plēroō*, "fill." Each of these elements is important:

- Second-person *plural*: "*You (all)* are to be filled." The Spirit's filling is not a privilege reserved for the few; all believers are involved.

- *Present* tense: "*Always* be filled." A continuous appropriation of the Spirit is necessary; it is not an isolated, single experience.

- *Passive* voice: "*Be* filled." Active yielding to the Spirit's sway is implied.

- *Imperative* mood: "You *must* be filled." This is a divine directive to be obeyed.

Following this main or finite verb ("be filled") are five participles (see below). By their nature, participles are undefined in their relation to the main verb; the context defines the relationship. They often express cause ("because") or means ("by"), but in the present case they depict circumstances that accompany the "filling," and so they describe the evidence or result of that "filling."

The first participle is "*Speaking* to one another with psalms, hymns, and spiritual songs" (v. 19a). This "speaking to one another" is explained in Colossians 3:16 as "teaching and admonishing one another." The "psalms" refer to OT psalms or songs; "hymns" will be hymns about Christ (such as Phil 2:5–11 or Col 1:15–20) or Christian canticles in general; while "spiritual songs" are songs inspired by the Spirit or spontaneous hymnody.

The second and third participles are "*Singing* and *making music* in your hearts to the Lord" (v. 19b). If verse 19a points to the horizontal dimension of Christian worship, verse 19b describes the vertical aspect. All music, whatever its source, should emanate from the whole inner person and prompt the worship of Christ as supreme Lord.

The fourth is "always *giving thanks* to God the Father for everything, in the name of our Lord Jesus Christ" (v. 20). As normally in the NT, prayer is addressed to the Father through the Son (Eph 2:18; see part 2, ch. 36).

Finally, "*submitting* to one another out of reverence for Christ" (v. 21). Since the subordination is mutual, no inferiority or superiority is implied.

These, then, are unmistakable evidences of being filled with the Spirit as exhibited in interpersonal relationships: mutual edification, heartfelt worship, constant thanksgiving, and mutual submission. There are, of course, other evidences found elsewhere in the NT, such as the character traits listed in Galatians 5:22–23.

PHILIPPIANS

38: THE SELF-EMPTYING OF CHRIST
(Phil 2:7)

There have been times when a small innocuous biblical phrase has generated a mountain of controversy. Such has been the case with the phrase *ekenōsen heauton*, "he (Christ) emptied himself" in Philippians 2:7. It has prompted what is called *kenotic theory*, the *kenosis*, and *kenoticism*, all of which seek to answer the natural question, "Of what did Christ empty himself when he entered human history?"

The problem is not one of translation. In a literal sense, the verb *kenoō* means "empty out" or "drain." When used figuratively, as here, it means "empty" in the sense "divest of status or prestige or privilege." Here are some of the answers that have been given to the natural question mentioned above. Christ emptied himself of:

- the riches of his heavenly existence (2 Cor 8:9), the glory of his deity
- the "form of God" (Phil 2:6), his divine or heavenly form of existence
- the attributes that relate to creation—omniscience, omnipotence, and omnipresence
- the independent or full exercise of his divine power

While the question "Of what did Christ empty himself?" is both inevitable and proper, the context of our phrase answers a different question: "How did Christ empty himself?" Paul's answer is "by taking the form of a slave." Paradoxically, Christ emptied himself by taking on the external appearance of a slave—unattractiveness, lack of distinction, and submission.

There is grammatical justification for this understanding. When a finite verb such as "he emptied" is followed by an aorist participle (here *labōn*, "taking"), that participle can define the means or mode by which the finite verb is carried out: "he emptied by taking." Another example of this construction is found in the next verse. "He humbled himself by becoming (*genomenos*) obedient to the point of death—even death on a cross."

God the Father's grand reversal of Christ's self-emptying and self-humbling is announced in verses 9–11: the elevation of Christ to universal dominion as supreme Lord. See further part 2, ch. 8.

39: CONTENTMENT WITH CIRCUMSTANCES
(Phil 4:12–13)

"A text taken out of context can become a pretext" for virtually any view. This old saying remains true and is well illustrated by the common misuse of Paul's testimony in Philippians 4:13: "I can do all things through Him (Christ) who strengthens me" (NASB). There is the temptation to apply the statement personally and define the "all things" by one's individual situation or need and then claim Christ's power to achieve that goal, whether it be financial success, academic achievement, or sporting performance. But the immediate context of the verse restricts the "all things" in a surprising way.

In Philippians 4:10–20, Paul is expressing to the church at Philippi his gratitude for their monetary gift brought to him by Epaphroditus (v. 18). He assures them that he appreciates this expression of their ongoing concern for him (v. 10), yet he comments, "I have learned to be content in whatever state I find myself. I know what it is to have little and I know what it is to have plenty. In any and every circumstance I have learned the secret of being content, whether well-fed or hungry, whether having plenty or being in need" (vv. 11b–12).

So when Paul says he can do "all things" through Christ's strength, he is not claiming to be omnicompetent but is pointing to his contentment in all situations—having more than enough or having less than enough, being in poverty or being affluent. That is, in this context, "all things" means "all this" (NIV).

When Paul says "I have learned the secret," he is using a technical term (*mueō*) common in the contemporary mystery religions to express initiation in the secrets of a particular cult. As Paul uses the verb, there is no idea of initiation. Rather, he is suggesting that contentment is a secret to be discovered, not an automatic possession of all believers. And, as he observes in 1 Timothy 6:6, "Godliness combined with contentment yields immense profit." We may define contentment as a relaxed acceptance of all the circumstances of our lives that we cannot ultimately control (such as health, age, others' reactions, weather) as being providentially arranged or permitted by God for our good.

What, then, is Paul's point? Whatever our circumstances may be, our ability to cope and our contentment are dependent on the constant empowering of the risen Christ. His power is needed as much to cope with affluence as with poverty, although that strength will be felt in different ways. Significantly, the tense of "who strengthens me" is present continuous. Our situations that require his strength may change, but his enabling power remains constant.

COLOSSIANS

40: JESUS — FIRST IN TIME AND RANK
(Col 1:15)

A pun is a play on words that is often humorous and involves words of the same or similar sound. For example, someone may say "That is *pain*ful to see" when a dust-laden shower muddies a freshly cleaned window*pane*. But there are also plays on words that are not puns but simply reflect a designed ambiguity in the use of one word—an intended double meaning. Colossians 1:17 affords a splendid example of this.

Colossians 1:15–20 is a hymnic passage that has two main themes and is marked by parallelism ("the firstborn," "and he himself") and chiasmus (A-B-B-A):

(1) The supremacy of Christ in creation (vv. 15–17)

"*the firstborn* over all creation" (v. 15)   A

"*and he himself* is before all things" (v. 17)   B

(2) The supremacy of Christ in redemption (vv. 18–20)

"*and he himself* is the head of the body,
    the church" (v. 18a)   B

"*the firstborn* from among the dead" (v. 18b)   A

The Greek word *pro* ("before") used in verse 17, like the English word "before," can refer to precedence in time ("before winter," 2 Tim 4:21) or precedence in importance ("before all things" = "above all," 1 Pet 4:8). Which is the meaning in Colossians 1:17? Or could

Paul be thinking of both meanings, as in James Moffatt's rendering, "he is prior to all," or the New English Bible, "he exists before everything"?

Several facts suggest that here *pro* refers to priority in time ("he himself exists before all things were created") *and also* priority in status ("he himself is supreme over all things").

- The term "firstborn" in verses 15 and 18 and the expression "have first place" or "be preeminent" in verse 18 point to Christ's unique rank.

- Preexistence ("before all things (in time)," v. 17) implies superiority in status ("preeminent over all things").

- Verse 17 marks the transition from the theme of the supremacy of Christ in creation to his supremacy in redemption, so that a reference to both ideas would be appropriate.

Among the supernatural powers itemized in verse 16, Jesus has no rival. He—and no one else—is before everything in *both* time and rank.

41: "GOD IN ALL HIS FULLNESS"
(Col 1:19; 2:9)

Literally, Colossians 1:19 reads, "For all the fullness (*pan to plērōma*) was pleased to dwell in him." But Paul is not referring to some impersonal entity ("the fullness") that has personal characteristics ("was pleased to dwell ... and to reconcile to himself ... by making peace"). Although the abstract neuter form "all the fullness" is technically the subject, the apostle is clearly thinking in personal categories—the participle "by making peace" in verse 20 is in fact masculine singular in form! Moreover, the close parallel in Colossians 2:9, "all the fullness of the Godhead" = "the Godhead in all its fullness" (TCNT, REB) or "the entire Fulness of deity" (Moffatt), fully justifies the rendering "God in all his fullness" (REB, NLT) in 1:19.

In both verses, "all the fullness" refers to the sum total of divine attributes and powers, with no aspect of the fullness excepted (this is the import of *pan to*). Also, both verses employ the verb "dwell" (*katoikeō*). In 1:19 this verb is a timeless aorist (simply "to dwell"), with the temporal parameters of the residence left undefined, although it would certainly include the incarnation and risen life of Christ. But in 2:9 the verb is a timeless present: the fullness "permanently dwells in him," "continues to indwell him."

What is special about 2:9 is its use of the adverb *sōmatikōs*, "in bodily form" (so most EVV), a word never found elsewhere in the NT. The surprising separation of the two Greek words rendered "dwells" and "in bodily form" suggests that two distinct affirmations are being made: (1) that the total plenitude of the Godhead dwells in Christ eternally; and (2) that this fullness now permanently resides in Christ in bodily form. It is true that before the incarnation the fullness did not reside in Christ "in bodily form"; it is not true that before the incarnation the fullness did not reside in him at all. Thus Paul implies both the eternal deity and the permanent humanity of Christ.

Comparable unequivocal assertions of the deity of Christ may be found in at least three other places in Paul's letters. There are, of course, the two occasions where he applies the term *theos* ("God") to Christ—Romans 9:5 (see part 2, ch. 6) and Titus 2:13 (see part 2, ch. 50). But 2 Corinthians 5:19 is also relevant: "God was in Christ, reconciling the world to himself" (NLT; KJV "unto himself"). This rendering is preferred by a wide variety of commentators, such as Windisch, Hughes, de Boor, Carrez, Lang, and Hofius, and I have defended it with detailed arguments in *The Second Epistle to the Corinthians* (Grand Rapids: Eerdmans, 2005), 442–43. Several versions that have this rendering introduce ambiguity by omitting the comma after "Christ" (RV, RSV, NASB, NEB, REB, NJB).

On the traditional interpretation (with the comma), "God was in Christ" refers to the entire life of Christ on earth in which God was personally present and through which he revealed himself. It

was only because there dwelled embodied in Christ the total plenitude of deity (Col 2:9) that reconciliation was accomplished. God
was in Christ and therefore acted through Christ (cf. John 14:10b,
"it is the Father, living in me, who is doing his work"). A functional
Christology presupposes and finds its ultimate basis in an ontolog-
ical Christology.

42: WHAT IS LACKING IN CHRIST'S AFFLICTIONS? (Col 1:24)

In Colossians 1:24 Paul makes the remarkable statement, "As things
stand, I am filling up in my own person what is lacking with regard
to the afflictions of Christ." Did Paul really believe that Christ's own
sufferings were in any sense deficient, needing supplementation?

Certainly not! With all NT authors, he shared an assurance that
the redemptive work of Christ on the cross was complete, never to
be repeated, and fully sufficient for our salvation. Jesus' triumphant
cry "It is finished" (John 19:30; see part 1, ch. 46) points not only to
the completion of his life on earth but also, and more importantly,
to the completion of his work on earth in providing salvation for
humans. As the author of Hebrews puts it, Christ "offered a sacrifice for the sins of the people, *once for all*, when he offered himself"
(Heb 7:27; similarly 9:12, 28; 10:10).

But what, then, are "the afflictions of Christ"? On occasion
Paul could use the term "Christ" to refer to the whole company
of Christian believers. For example, "Just as the body, though one,
has many parts, but all its many parts form one body, so it is with
Christ" (1 Cor 12:12). The genitive case "of Christ" probably denotes
possession: "(the afflictions) belonging to or destined for Messiah's
people." As for the "afflictions" or "sufferings," they clearly cannot
refer to physical ailments or woes. As in 2 Corinthians 1:5, the expression "Christ's sufferings" refers to any and all suffering endured as
the result of being the followers of Christ, suffering that is experienced while being engaged in his service and that benefits his church.
They were the distinctive sufferings felt by the person "in Christ"

(2 Cor 5:17) who was living "for Christ" (2 Cor 5:15) by being "always given over to death for Jesus' sake" (2 Cor 4:11).

"Filling up ... what is lacking (in the afflictions of Christ)" suggests a specified and fixed amount of suffering, a deficiency that can be measured. It seems God has appointed a quota of sufferings to be patiently endured by the messianic community of believers before the end comes. One thinks of the reminder given by Paul and Barnabas to the recently established churches of Asia Minor: "We must go through many hardships to enter the kingdom of God" (Acts 14:22). Believers are destined for trials (1 Thess 3:3).

Paul prefaces our verse with the words, "I rejoice now in the midst of my sufferings for your sake." He of all people could rightly claim to be suffering for the sake of Christ and his church. Consider the breathtaking list of his afflictions found in 2 Corinthians 6:4–10 and 11:23–28. So he could appropriately claim to be making his own distinctive contribution to the filling up of the God-ordained quota of sufferings allocated to the Christian community; "I am filling up in my own person" means "I am doing my share in meeting the deficiency."

But Paul knew that other believers also make special contributions in reducing the undefined deficiency: "We—all of us—must go through many hardships" (Acts 14:22). He also spoke of the Corinthians' "patient endurance of the same sufferings we suffer" (2 Cor 1:6). The suffering of believers, be it from physical persecution or social ostracism or verbal abuse occasioned by allegiance to Christ, is fully incorporated within God's all-encompassing will.

43: A CANCELED IOU
(Col 2:14)

"IOU" is one of many abbreviations, like IQ or IRS or ISBN, that have become part of the English language. The *Concise Oxford Dictionary* defines IOU as a "signed document bearing these letters followed by specified sum, constituting formal acknowledgement of debt." The Greek equivalent is the term *cheirographon*, which by derivation means "something written (*graphon*) by the hand (*cheiro-*)"—a hand-written document or note of any description. In particular, it was a signed certificate of indebtedness in which the signature legalized the debt. The word is not found in the Greek Old Testament and only once in the NT (Col 2:14).

In his Letter to Philemon, Paul has provided us with a perfect example of an IOU. In the course of interceding with Philemon on behalf of his runaway slave Onesimus, Paul makes a specific request. He asks Philemon to charge to his account any debts that Onesimus may have incurred (Phlm 18). He continues, "I, Paul, am writing this guarantee (= this IOU) with my own hand: I myself will repay you" (v. 19). This is Paul's signed promissory note by which he formally and legally assumes all the indebtedness of Onesimus toward Philemon.

Here in Colossians 2:14, the *cheirographon* or IOU referred to is our failed obligation to keep God's law, a debt to God acknowledged by our conscience (see Rom 2:14–15; 3:23). About this IOU "with its legal demands," the apostle makes four affirmations.

First, it "stood against us." That is, it was made out against us and stood to our debit, binding us legally.

Second, "It was hostile to us." That is, it was an ominous threat to us, for it placed us under an obligation that we could not meet. If the first affirmation highlights the brute fact of our indebtedness, this one emphasizes the direct and active opposition of the signed statement of debt. Not only was the *cheirographon* an accusation of guilt; it also constituted a threat of penalty because of our human inability to discharge the debt.

Third, God "totally erased" this IOU. The vivid verb *exaleiphō* means "cancel out" or "wipe away," with the prefix *ex* (= *ek*) pointing to the thoroughness or totality of the cancellation. Our acknowledged indebtedness to God was completely eradicated by the death of Jesus.

Fourth, God "has taken it away from our midst" (the literal sense). That is, he has set it aside or has done away with it completely. In the third affirmation Paul uses the aorist tense, emphasizing the pastness of the erasure, but here the perfect tense is used, indicating our present and permanent freedom from indebtedness.

Closely attached to this statement is the phrase "nailing it to the cross." It describes, in a remarkable paradox, the means by which God has carried out the total removal: "He has set it aside by nailing it to the cross." It is as if the superscription above Jesus' head on the cross was our IOU!

44: LOVE-IN-ACTION AS THE CROWNING VIRTUE (Col 3:14)

"Who," "which," and "that" are the three English relative pronouns, with "who" referring back to people, and the other two usually referring back to things. Greek, too, has three relative pronouns: one is masculine in grammatical gender, one is feminine, and the other is neuter. But in Greek, these pronouns must agree with their antecedent in number (singular or plural), gender, and case.

Sometimes, however, Greek can use a neuter relative pronoun to refer back, not to a neuter noun, but to a general idea found in the preceding statement. Colossians 3:14 is a case in point.

In Colossians 3, Paul has already dealt with "putting off"—or ridding oneself of—various vices (vv. 5–11). Now he turns to the opposite obligation: "putting on" various virtues (vv. 12–17). Christians are to wear moral garments that are appropriate to their calling and status: heartfelt compassion, kindness, humility, gentleness, patience, and forgiveness (vv. 12–13). Then, in a way that is reminiscent of the conclusion to the "love chapter" (1 Cor 13), Paul highlights the supremacy of love: "In addition to all these virtues, clothe yourselves with love, which is the bond that perfects them all."

"Love" (*agapē*) is a feminine noun in Greek, so the relative pronoun (here "which") should also be feminine in gender—but it is neuter! Is Paul here guilty of a grammatical blunder? Hardly! He is referring back, not merely to "love," but to the general concept of love-put-on, the putting on of love, love-in-action. Strong support for this interpretation is found in the fact that the word *agapē* here has the definite article. It is not love as an abstract notion but concrete expressions of love—love dramatized—that Paul has in mind.

A literal translation of the last clause of the verse would be "(love), which is the bond of perfection." In other words, when the final, outer garment of love-in-action is put on, it binds together and perfects all the other virtues.

1 THESSALONIANS

45: ARE DECEASED CHRISTIANS "ASLEEP"?
(1 Thess 4:13–15)

Is it not true that after someone falls asleep, they are asleep? Paul spoke of certain Christians who had "fallen asleep" (1 Thess 4:14–15; 1 Cor 15:6, 18, 20). Are they then "asleep"—in suspended animation until they are awakened at the resurrection?

The relevant verb, *koimaomai*, is more than a polite expression for death ("pass away") borrowed from conventional usage, since it is applied solely to Christians. In the present tense, this verb can refer to physical sleep: "be asleep" (Matt 28:13; Luke 22;45; Acts 12:6). But in Paul's letters in reference to death, it bears a "point" or punctiliar sense: "fall asleep" (1 Thess 4:13–15; 1 Cor 7:39; 11:30; 15:6, 18, 20, 51), even when it is used in the present tense: "those who have fallen asleep" or "those who, from time to time, fall asleep" (1 Thess 4:13), "a number have fallen asleep" or "a few are, from time to time, falling asleep" (1 Cor 11:30).

So the verb depicts entrance into the state of death without implying that the state of death is one of suspended animation or loss of consciousness. Christians who die "fall asleep" to the present world; they are no longer active in *our* earthly world of time and space. Yet they are fully alert to *their* new environment, for they are not only resting from their labors in joyful satisfaction (Heb 4:10; Rev 14:13) and safe in God's hands (Luke 23:46; cf. Acts 7:59); they are "alive to God" (Luke 20:38) and "live spiritually, as God does" (1 Pet 4:6). They are in the presence of Christ in enriched fellowship with him (2 Cor 5:8; Phil 1:23; see part 2, ch. 61).

If the "intermediate state" between death and resurrection were one of unconsciousness, how are we to explain Paul's preference (2 Cor 5:8) or desire (Phil 1:23) to depart to Christ's presence? Even with all its frustrations, an active conscious life on earth in communion with Christ would undoubtedly have seemed to him to be preferable to a post-mortem state of unconsciousness and total inactivity.

It is also possible that this verb ("fall asleep") may allude to the peaceful manner of the death of Christians, whatever the mode of their death. How apt is it that we learn that Stephen "fell asleep" (Acts 7:59–60), even though he died under a hail of stones!

46: STIFLING THE SPIRIT
(1 Thess 5:19)

The Greek verb *sbennumi,* used only six times in the NT, has two basic senses. Describing a fire or light, it may refer to literal or figurative eradication and means "extinguish," "quench," or "go out":

- "He (the Servant of the Lord) will not break a bruised reed, or *extinguish* a smoldering wick" (Matt 12:20).

- "The foolish virgins said to the wise, 'Give us some of your oil, for our lamps *are going out*'" (Matt 25:8).

- "hell, where the fire never *goes out*" (Mark 9:43, 48).

- "the shield of faith, with which you will be able to *quench* all the flaming arrows of the evil one" (Eph 6:16).

- "(the heroes of faith) *quenched* the fury of the flames" (Heb 11:34).

But it is the one other use—in 1 Thessalonians 5:19—that is distinctive and of special interest. Here, describing a function that was being hindered or compromised, this verb means "stifle" or "suppress."

In 1 Thessalonians 5:12–22, Paul spells out responsibilities within the church that illustrate his clarion call for mutual edification (v. 11). At verse 19 he moves from personal obligations (vv. 16–18) to communal responsibilities (vv. 19–22): "Do not stifle (*mē sbennute*) the Spirit." But it is certainly permissible to give the verb its metaphorical meaning here in reference to fire: "Do not put out the Spirit's fire" (NIV 1984).

Because this prohibition is in the present tense, it may be a command to cease an action, "Stop stifling the Spirit," or a general timeless admonition, "Do not ever stifle the Spirit." If the former meaning is preferred, the next verse may indicate one way the Spirit's operation was being suppressed at Thessalonica: "Do not treat prophecies with contempt" or "Do not despise the words of prophets" (v. 20 NRSV). That is, prophecies prompted by the Spirit were apparently being ignored or spurned by some people. Or if some church members at Thessalonica were abusing the gift of prophecy, just as some at Corinth were abusing the gift of speaking in tongues (1 Cor 14:1–40), the church leaders at Thessalonica may have overreacted and unwisely repressed the exercise of the Spirit's gifts, calling for the apostle's admonition.

Whatever the specific background of Paul's injunction, this prohibition has a wide application. At the corporate church level, the exercise of the Spirit's gifts should never be suppressed, provided everything is done in a fitting and orderly way (1 Cor 14:40). At an individual level, believers should never resist or stifle the Spirit's warning to avoid sin or his urging to pursue a particular God-honoring course of action. But the negative command, "Do not ever stifle the Spirit," implies a positive directive, "Obey the Spirit's promptings," as Philip the evangelist did when the Spirit told him to go up to the Ethiopian eunuch's chariot and stay near it (Acts 8:29–31).

The ultimate result of Philip's obedience to the Spirit was the passing of the gospel from the Middle East into Africa. Or recall Paul's obedience to the Spirit, when the Spirit did not allow him and his companions to enter Bithynia, so that they went down to Troas and then over to Macedonia (Acts 16:7–12). In this case, the ultimate result was the passing of the gospel from Asia into Europe. Obeying the Spirit's promptings pays handsome dividends!

1 TIMOTHY

47: IS TRADITION OUTDATED?
(1 Tim 6:20)

All too often, young people believe older folks are wedded to the past and to the status quo, while older people think the younger generation is wedded to the future and to innovation. The issue might seem to be enthusiasm versus experience, or change versus tradition, or the future versus the past. But are these mutually exclusive? Cannot both elements be embraced and complement one another?

When Paul says he is forgetting what lies behind (Phil 3:13), he is not rejecting everything that is past, all tradition. Rather, he is referring to past progress toward his goal of winning the prize—the prize of being conformed to Christ's death (Phil 3:10) or the prize of gaining eternal life (Gal 6:8; Titus 1:2; 3:7). In a four-lap race such as the 1500 meters, a runner is not preoccupied with the successful completion of the first three laps; rather, he puts all his energy into reaching the finish line first and so receiving the prize (see Phil 3:14).

Twice in his letters to Timothy, Paul instructs him to "guard the *deposit* (*diathēkē*)" (1 Tim 6:20; 2 Tim 1:14), that is, what had been entrusted to him for safekeeping, the totality of Christian truth enshrined in the gospel. This "guarding" involved protecting the deposit from any corruption or compromise that would come through heretical teaching (1 Tim 6:20b).

But we must remind ourselves of the grim possibility of a zeal for tradition that is misguided. In his pre-Christian days, Paul violently persecuted the infant church out of an extreme zeal for Jewish tradition (Gal 1:13–14). He tried to force Christian believers to blaspheme

(Acts 26:11), perhaps attempting to get them to recite the words "Jesus be cursed" (see 1 Cor 12:3). But later, with great embarrassment, he realized that this persecution arose from a zeal that was "not based on knowledge" (Rom 10:2).

Alongside Paul's enthusiasm for tradition, rightly understood, was his enthusiasm for change. First of all, there was the desire for advance in his own spiritual life. For him, sanctification was Christification—becoming like Christ (2 Cor 3:18; see part 2, ch. 11). This was his daily aim and also his final destiny (Rom 8:29; 1 Cor 15:49). But equally, he was preoccupied with promoting change in others. For example, he addresses the fickle Galatians as "my dear children, for whom I am again in the pain of childbirth until Christ is formed in you" (Gal 4:19). And he assured the Colossians that he constantly toiled to "present everyone mature in Christ" (Col 1:28–29).

So then, we should always occupy a strategic vantage point, looking back as well as looking forward, carefully preserving the best of the past while enthusiastically embracing the present and future with all their potential—guarding the deposit (1 Tim 6:20) as well as "straining forward to what lies ahead" (Phil 3:13). Maintaining this delicate balance between past and present applies, for example, to Christian worship. Contemporary songs and music that reflect present trends need to be balanced by our rich heritage of timeless hymns that represent the faith of previous generations of believers.

2 TIMOTHY

48: "SALVATION IN CHRIST JESUS"
(2 Tim 2:10)

In the short paragraph 2 Timothy 2:8–10, Paul indicates that his gospel ("my gospel" = "the gospel I proclaim") has two essential ingredients—the resurrection of the Davidic Messiah, Jesus Christ, and "the salvation that is found in Christ Jesus." For the sake of the beneficiaries ("the elect," God's chosen ones) of that gospel, he was willing to endure any indignity, such as "being chained like a criminal."

If one were asked to state the unifying theme of the OT, "God's salvation in Israel" would be a satisfactory answer, given Jeremiah 3:23: "In the LORD our God is the salvation of Israel." As for the coordinating motif of Paul's theology and the NT in general, there would be no better statement of the center than "God the Father's salvation in Christ." Each of these elements deserves further treatment (see also part 2, ch. 57).

Whereas explicit references or allusions to the fatherhood of God in the OT are not numerous, teaching about God as Father is a distinctive and common feature throughout the NT. Jesus himself was accused of an improper familiarity with God by regularly addressing him as "Abba," "Dear Father" (John 5:17–18; see part 2, ch. 32). Whenever the term "God" (*theos*) is used in the NT, it is appropriate to assume that the trinitarian Father is the referent, unless the context makes this sense of *theos* impossible (e.g., John 1:18b; 20:28). Accordingly, the compound form, "God the Father," is common (e.g., Gal 1:1; Phil 2:11). And it is this Father who is linked with salvation: "The Father has sent his Son to be the Savior of the world" (1 John 4:14).

The essence of each Testament is the announcement that salvation has been provided by God: in one case, at the exodus (Deut 6:21–23), which brought about physical deliverance; in the other case, at the cross (Col 1:19–20), which brought about spiritual emancipation. Whereas before it could be said that God "bring(s) salvation upon the earth" (Ps 74:12), now it can be said that "salvation belongs to our God who is seated on the throne, and to the Lamb" (Rev 7:10; cf. 1 Thess 5:9; 2 Tim 2;10). Jesus Christ, the Lamb of God (John 1:29), appeared on earth to bring salvation (Titus 2:11), that is, "to save sinners" (1 Tim 1:15), "to seek and to save the lost" (Luke 19:10). As "the author of their salvation" (Heb 2:10), he is the Savior (Matt 1:21; Luke 2:11) in whom people must believe if they are to be saved (John 14:6; Acts 4:12). The title "our Savior" is used in each chapter of Titus, first in reference to God (Titus 1:3; 2:10; 3:4), then, shortly after, in reference to Jesus (Titus 1:4; 2:13; 3:6).

This salvation provided by God the Father encompasses the past, the present, and the future. Once the benefits of the sacrifice of Christ have been personally appropriated, salvation can be spoken of as a past event: "by grace you have been saved" (Eph 2:5, 8; cf. Titus 3:4–5). But since salvation involves progress toward Christian maturity (Eph 4:13; Col 1:28), Paul can describe Christians as "those who are being saved" (2 Cor 2:15; cf. 1 Cor 1:18). The consummation of salvation lies in the future. "We were saved in hope" (Rom 8:24), having the certain expectation of "the redemption of the body" from its bondage to decay and sin, through its transformation (Rom 8:23); having the hope of the arrival of "new heavens and a new earth in which righteousness has its home" (2 Pet 3:13); and having the assurance of being delivered from God's coming wrath (Rom 5:9; 1 Thess 1:10).

This salvation is *in* Christ Jesus. The phrase "in Christ" is ubiquitous in Paul's writings—some 170 uses, if we include the phrases "in him" and "in whom" when they refer to Christ. In this phrase, the preposition "in" (*en*) expresses a wide range of ideas or relationships that can be brought out by a paraphrase:

1. Incorporation: "those who fell asleep *as members of the body of* Christ" (1 Cor 15:18)

2. Union: "the dead who are *in fellowship with the risen* Christ" (1 Thess 4:16)

3. Agency: "the redemption *accomplished by* Christ Jesus" (Rom 3:24)

4. Mode: "You are all one *by being in* Christ Jesus" (Gal 3:28)

5. Cause: "Consider yourselves dead to sin but alive to God *because of your union with* Christ Jesus" (Rom 6:11)

6. Location: "The love of God *that is focused in* Christ Jesus our Lord" (Rom 8:39)

7. Sphere of reference: "I know a *Christian* man ..." (2 Cor 12:2)

"God the Father's salvation in Christ" would be an appropriate summary of the essence of Paul's theology—and the whole NT.

49: DIVINE EXHALATION
(2 Tim 3:16)

Breathing is essential to maintain life. It is estimated that we humans breathe about 23,000 times each day, and some 630 million times over an average life span, inhaling oxygen and exhaling carbon dioxide.

God does not breathe to survive, for his life is inherent and eternal and is not supported by anything external. But scriptural writers draw on human experience to explain divine realities and qualities, using metaphorical descriptions of God in human terms. Without such metaphors, God would be altogether indescribable. So God is said to have an arm, a face, a hand, and a back; for example, "Arise, LORD! Lift up your hand, O God" (Ps 10:12); "The LORD gave me two stone tablets inscribed by the finger of God" (Deut 9:10).

There are two notable passages where reference is made to God's "breathing out" or exhalation. The first is, "Then the LORD God formed a man from the dust of the ground and breathed into his nostrils the breath of life, and the man became a living being" (Gen 2:7). God's breath infuses life.

In the other passage (2 Tim 3:16), we discover that the apostle Paul has coined an expressive adjective to describe the divine exhalation of the OT Scriptures. He is encouraging his "dear son," Timothy, to remain faithful to the truths he has learned and become convinced of, truths he has known from infancy through "the Holy Scriptures, which are able to make you wise for salvation through faith in Christ Jesus" (2 Tim 3:14–15). This colorful adjective is *theopneustos*, "breathed out" (*pneustos*, from *pneō*, "breathe out") "by God" (*theo-*). Thus it can be translated "God-breathed" or "inspired by God"; this latter rendering implies "breathing out into."

The Scriptures referred to here are the OT, but prospectively the term can include what we know as the NT, which was still being written. Significantly, Peter refers to Paul's letters as part of the authoritative Scriptures (2 Pet 3:15–16).

There are two translational issues in 2 Timothy 3:16a. When the adjective *pas* accompanies a noun without the article (as here), it normally means "every." But even in this case, *pas* can mean "all" or "the whole of," especially when the noun has a collective sense or is a proper noun. So we find "all Jerusalem" (Matt 2:3), "all the house of Israel" (Acts 2:36), "the whole building" (Eph 2:21), "the whole of Israel" (Rom 11:26). The other issue is where to insert the implied "is": before or after *theopneustos*. Given the fact that there are two adjectives—"God-breathed" and "useful"—joined by *kai* ("and"), this "is" probably belongs before "God-breathed," although it can be supplied after this adjective as well.

Thus, two main options emerge: "Every Scripture is God-inspired and is helpful" (TCNT) and "All Scripture is God-breathed and is useful" (NIV). The verse describes both the origin of Scripture (the breath of God) and its usefulness "for teaching, rebuking, correcting, and training in righteousness."

TITUS

50: JESUS CHRIST AS "OUR GREAT GOD AND SAVIOR" (Titus 2:13)

Earlier we saw that on occasion the KJV has a distinctive rendering of a verse (2 Cor 5:19a), in this case shared exactly only by NLT, that can in fact be vigorously defended on grammatical grounds (part 2, ch. 41). But in some other cases, such as our present verse, the KJV translation stands alone against almost all modern versions (NAB is an exception) where compelling contextual and grammatical considerations raise serious doubts about the rightness of its rendering. The KJV translation of Titus 2:13 is as follows: "Looking for that blessed hope, and the glorious appearing of the great God and our Savior Jesus Christ."

What are the reasons for instead preferring a translation such as "while we wait for the blessed hope, the appearing of the glory of our great God and Savior, Jesus Christ" (CSB)? There are three.

First is the "God and Savior" (*theos kai sōtēr*) formula. This was a stereotypical formula common in first-century religious terminology. It was used by Jews in Palestine and throughout the Roman Empire in referring to their one true God, Yahweh. It always denoted one deity, never two. If the name Jesus Christ did not follow the expression "God and Savior," this phrase would invariably and naturally be taken by any reader to refer to one person, yet the name Jesus Christ is simply added by way of clarification and to establish identity.

What causes us to think Paul is here borrowing and applying to Christ a formula from current speech? We can see from the immediate context that Paul uses several semitechnical terms associated with a royal arrival—"appear" (*epiphainomi*, v. 11), "appearance" (*epiphaneia*, v. 13), "favor" (*charis*, v. 11), "bringing aid" (*sōtērios*, v. 11), and "high expectation" (*elpis*, v. 13). Also, some years earlier, Paul had been personally confronted with the Demetrios riot at Ephesus when the people had chanted their *credo*, "Great is Artemis of the Ephesians!" (Acts 19:28, 34). Provoked by this pagan profession of faith, which may have awakened memories of the cult of Artemis in Paul's home city of Tarsus, he wished to mingle with the crowd, gain a hearing (Acts 19:30), and, one may suggest, speak of "our great God and Savior, Jesus Christ." It is difficult to avoid the conclusion that one impulse behind Titus 2:13 was Paul's desire to combat the extravagant titles given to human rulers such as Antiochus Epiphanes (*theos epiphanēs*, "god manifest"), Ptolemy I (*sōtēr kai theos*, "savior and god"), or Julius Caesar (*theos kai sōtēr*, "god and savior"), or his desire to claim exclusively for the Christians' Lord the divine honors freely granted to goddesses such as Aphrodite and Artemis or to gods such as Asclepius and Zeus.

Second, the term "Savior" (*sōtēros*) is without the definite article. When two nouns (here "God" and "Savior") in the same grammatical case (here the genitive) are linked by "and" (*kai*), the repetition of the Greek definite article with the second noun (here "Savior") would show that the nouns are separate items. If there is no repetition, it indicates that the nouns are being considered together, or (as in this case) they have a single referent—that is, "God" and "Savior" are the one and the same person, then defined as Jesus Christ.

The third reason is the presence of the adjective "great" (*megas*). As a description of God the Father, "great" is not used anywhere in the NT. But if "great" is a description of Christ, it could have been added to oppose the pagan applications of the "God and Savior" formula: Christians could speak of "*our great* God and Savior, Jesus Christ." Also, Christ had already proved himself to be a "great Savior," a unique bearer of God's saving grace (v. 11), by his sacrificial self-surrender to achieve the redemption and sanctification of his people (v. 14).

With confidence, therefore, we can follow the almost uniform rendering of this verse in English versions, and speak of Christ as "our superlatively great God and Savior." Other passages that explicitly apply the title "God" (*theos*) to Jesus Christ are John 1:1 (see part 1, ch. 31); John 1:18 (see part 1, ch. 36); John 20:28 (see part 1, ch. 48); Romans 9:5 (see part 2, ch. 6); Hebrews 1:8 (see part 2, ch. 53); and 2 Peter 1:1.

PHILEMON

51: PAUL AND SLAVERY
(Phlm 15–16)

Onesimus was a slave of Philemon in Colossae who had not only run away from his master (Phlm 15–16) but had also absconded with some of Philemon's money or possessions (vv. 18–19). Attracted by the anonymity and excitement of a large metropolis, he traveled furtively to Rome, where somehow he met the imprisoned Paul, who led him to faith in Christ (v. 10). Paul soon discovered him to be an able and willing helper as well as a Christian companion (vv. 11–13, 16). Other considerations apart, Paul would have liked to keep Onesimus at his side (v. 13), but he felt compelled to send him back to Colossae so that Philemon, the legal owner of Onesimus (v. 16), might himself have the opportunity of receiving him back as a Christian brother (v. 16) and of possibly releasing him for further service to Paul (vv. 14, 20–21). Accordingly, Onesimus returned to Philemon with this letter.

Although this letter is not an essay on slavery, from it we may deduce Paul's attitude to slavery. To begin with, Paul apparently accepted slavery as an inevitable part of the social, economic, and legal status quo, without questioning or trying to justify its existence. But acceptance of the status quo should not be equated with endorsement of the status quo. Toleration is not the same as approval. Paul did not object to slave ownership within Christian ranks, but he encouraged masters to reward slaves suitably for honest work, to desist from threatening them (Eph 6:8–9), and to give them just and equitable treatment (Col 4:1). He elevated the status of slaves by addressing them as persons and as moral agents who were responsible, and ought to be responsive, to their earthly masters as well as to their heavenly Lord (Eph 6:5–8; Col 3:22).

Further, when Paul emphasizes Onesimus's true identity as a dearly loved Christian brother (v. 16), he sets the master-slave relation on a new footing. "It may be that he (Onesimus) was separated from you (Philemon) for a short time precisely so that you may have him back permanently, no longer regarded as merely a slave (*hōs doulon*) but as more than a slave—as a dear brother" (vv. 15–16). Paul is undermining the discrimination that is at the heart of slavery and sounding its death knell. In this letter, Paul, a highly educated Roman citizen, is championing the cause of a destitute runaway slave whose life was potentially forfeit because of his flight and his theft (vv. 17–19).

Did Paul advocate freeing slaves? When he expresses his confidence that Philemon would obey him and accept Onesimus back and forgive him (v. 21a), he adds that he knows Philemon "will do even more than I ask" (v. 21b). That undefined additional element could well be the setting free of Onesimus for Christian service either at Colossae or at Rome with Paul. When he is discussing possible changes of status for believers (including slaves) in 1 Corinthians 7:17–24, his general advice is "remain as you were when God called you" (see 1 Cor 7:17, 20, 24). But in 1 Corinthians 7:21b, he parenthetically states an exception to the general principle: "But if you are actually able (*kai dynasai*) to gain your freedom, seize it all the more."

It is fair to conclude that by his teaching and his example, Paul was laying one of the explosive charges that would one day—although sadly, belatedly—detonate and destroy the institution of slavery.

HEBREWS

52: DIFFERENT YET SIMILAR
(Heb 1:1–2a)

The NT differs from the OT, yet it is similar. Hebrews 1:1–2a succinctly sums up those differences and similarities: "In the past God spoke to our forefathers through the prophets at various times and in various ways, but in these last days he has spoken to us by his Son." This discontinuity and continuity can be summed up by the following chart:

Discontinuity	
"In the past"	"in these last days"
"to our forefathers"	"to us"
"through the prophets"	"by his Son"
"at various times"	(at a single time)
"in various ways"	(in a single way)
Continuity	
"(the) God (of the OT) spoke	"he (the God of the NT) has spoken"

In the history of the church, there have always been those who drive a wedge between the two Testaments. One notable example was the heretic Marcion during the second century AD, who was so influential that the church father Tertullian wrote four volumes titled

Against Marcion. Marcion believed that the OT was marked by law and justice, the NT by grace and salvation. For Marcion, the God of the OT, the Creator, is altogether different from the God of the NT, the Father of Jesus Christ. And indeed, there are clear contrasts between the Testaments with regard to:

- the time of God's speaking (= his self-revelation);
- the recipients of his revelation;
- the agents of his revelation;
- the timing of the revelation;
- the variety in the modes of revelation.

In spite of these contrasts, however, the emphasis in this verse falls on the identity of the person who speaks ("God ... he"), and the fact that in both eras it was the same one "speaking" ("spoke ... has spoken"). The same Greek verb, *laleō* ("speak"), is used in each case, emphasizing the unbroken continuity between the two eras. Both *lalēsas* ("having spoken," "spoke") and *elalēsen* ("spoke," "has spoken") are in the aorist tense, summing up in a single, comprehensive glance, first a multitude of times when God revealed himself during the OT era, then the whole life and teaching of Jesus of Nazareth as God's final and full self-revelation. It was one and the same person, "the God of Abraham" (Exod 3:6; Matt 22:32) and "the God of our Lord Jesus Christ" (Eph 1:17), who spoke in the two eras.

Certainly, there are profound differences between the two Testaments—one is "the Old" or "the Older," and the other "the New" or "the Newer"—but the speaker is the same in each case. There is progression in the revelation, but the person revealed is the same. We recognize the discontinuity, but rejoice in the continuity (see part 2, ch. 57).

53: THE ETERNALITY OF CHRIST
(Heb 1:8–9)

The Epistle to the Hebrews is a "word of exhortation" (Heb 13:22) addressed to a group of Hellenistic Jewish Christians, probably in Rome, who were facing a crisis of loyalty during the rising tide of Jewish nationalism before the revolt of AD 66. The author responds to this pastoral need first by a doctrinal exposition (1:1–10:39) that establishes the superiority and finality of Christ and Christianity, and then by sustained practical application (11:1–13:25) that issues a clarion call to the pilgrim's life of faith and endurance. Hebrews 1:4 introduces the theme of the superiority of Christ to angels, an idea immediately developed in 1:5–2:4 (as Son of God, Christ is superior to the angels in his deity) and then in 2:5–18 (as Son of Man, Christ is superior to the angels even in his humanity).

Citing Psalm 44:7 (LXX) in Hebrews 1:8, the author demonstrates that Jesus is vastly superior to angels in dignity and status when he affirms that God the Father addresses his Son as "God" at his resurrection-exaltation ("Your throne, O God, will last forever and ever"), just as in verse 10 (citing Ps 101:26 LXX) he addresses the Son as "Lord," and in verse 13 (citing Ps 109:1 LXX) he issues him an invitation to share his throne. Over against the variability of angels' function (v. 7), the author sets the stability of the Son's rule (v. 8a) and the constancy of his justice (v. 7b). "Your throne ... will last forever and ever" means "the throne from which you rule is eternal," which implies "you will rule eternally." In its original setting, Psalm 45:7 (EVV) is a poet's address to the king at the royal wedding. In Hebrews, the eternality of the throne no longer denotes the perpetuity of David's line but the endless character of Christ's dominion.

There are three ways the NT can express "forever":

- *Eis ton aiōna*, literally, "for the age (to come)"/"to eternity" = "eternally"/"forever" (Heb 7:24, of Jesus' resurrected life). Sometimes *tou aiōnos* is added, "forever and ever," as in Hebrews 1:8.

- *Eis tous aiōnas*, literally, "to the ages," "to all eternity," where the plural may be generalizing (as in Rom 9:5, of the blessedness or praiseworthiness of Christ as God).

- *Eis tous aiōnas tōn aiōnōn,* literally, "to the ages of ages," "forever and ever," "forevermore." The two plurals side by side suggest that from one perspective eternity may be considered an interminable accumulation of endless "ages."

No NT letter speaks more often of the eternality of Christ than Hebrews, and the phrase *eis ton aiōna* (and parallels) sums up this prominent feature of the letter. Apart from Hebrews 1:8, we have the following instances of this theme:

- Three times the author cites the "forever" of Psalm 110:4 (109:4 LXX) in reference to the eternality of the Melchizedekian order of priesthood (Heb 5:6; 6:20; 7:17). Jesus himself is a priest "forever" in the succession of Melchizedek (6:20; 7:11, 17, 21).

- "You are the same and your years will never end" (1:12).

- "One (Jesus) who has become a priest ... on the basis of the power arising from an indestructible life" (7:16).

- "Jesus lives forever ... he has the power for all time to bring salvation to those who approach God through him, since he is always alive to plead on their behalf" (7:24–25).

- "Jesus Christ is the same yesterday, today—yes, and for eternity." (13:8).

54: THREE CRUCIAL APPEARANCES
(Heb 9:23–28)

As part of the overall purpose of Hebrews to demonstrate the finality and superiority of Christ and Christianity, in 9:23–28 the author
speaks of Christ's entering heaven with his once-for-all sacrifice that
achieved the annulment of sin and final salvation for his people. At
the heart of this passage are references to three "appearances":

> But as it is, he (Christ) has *appeared* once for all at the end of
> the ages to remove sin by the sacrifice of himself. (Heb 9:26b)

> He (Christ) entered into heaven itself, now to *appear* in the
> presence of God on our behalf. (Heb 9:24b)

> To those who are eagerly awaiting him (Christ), he will *appear*
> a second time, not to deal with sin, but to bring them sal-
> vation. (Heb 9:28b)

Strangely, although these three appearances are expressed by three
different Greek verbs (*phaneroō, emphanizō,* and *horaō,* respectively—
all in the passive voice), they are appropriately translated by a single
English word, "appear," referring to Christ's incarnation, his advocacy, and his second advent. The purpose of each appearance is
stated: to remove sin, to represent his people, to bring salvation.
The first and third appearances take place on earth; the second in
heaven. The first and third are single, unrepeatable appearances;
the second is ongoing.

1. Christ's incarnation. The principal purpose of Christ's appearance on earth "at the end of the ages" (or, in Paul's words, "when
the set time had fully come," Gal 4:4) was to bring about the total
setting aside (*athetēsis*) of sin, or "to deal with sin" (Heb 9:28b; see
below and Rom 8:3; 1 Cor 15:3). And whereas under the old covenant
animal sacrifices were repeated and animals were unwilling victims,
Christ offered himself in sacrifice on a single occasion: "He entered
the most holy place once for all by his own blood" (Heb 9:12; cf. 9:25).
This once-for-all-ness of Christ's sacrifice is a recurrent theme in the

letter (Heb 7:27; 9:12, 26, 28; 10:10, 12) and reflects the "once-ness" of death and judgment for humans (Heb 9:27–28: "Just as …, so …").

2. *Christ's advocacy.* Having offered a single, unrepeatable sacrifice for sin on earth, Jesus as our heavenly high priest has no need to offer sacrifices in heaven. His role is to represent us in the heavenly court as our advocate (cf. Heb 7:25; Rom 8:34; 1 John 2:1), our defense attorney. In fact, by his very presence at God's right hand (1:3; 8:1–2) he effectively pleads our cause on the basis of his completed and acceptable sacrifice.

3. *Christ's second advent.* "Apart from sin" (*chōris hamartias*, v. 28) has been taken as a reference to Christ's sinlessness ("without sin," KJV) or to the total abolition of sin ("sin being no more," NJB), but more probably means "not to deal with sin" (RSV, NRSV, GNT, ESV), in stark contrast with the purpose of Christ's first advent (Heb 9:28a). "To bring salvation" refers to the consummation of salvation on the "day" (Heb 1:14; 2:10; 10:25; 1 Pet 1:5), that is, deliverance from adverse divine judgment (Heb 9:27; 12:23) and receipt of the promised eternal inheritance (Heb 9:15). Elsewhere in the NT, this third "appearance" is described by the terms "coming" (*parousia*; e.g., 1 Cor 15:23), "appearance" (*epiphaneia*; e.g., 1 Tim 6:14), and "revelation" (*apokalypsis*; e.g., 1 Pet 1:13). The recipients of this final salvation are described as those showing eager anticipation for Christ's arrival.

55: PAIN INSTEAD OF JOY
(Heb 12:2)

Many translations render the first part of Hebrews 12:2 like this: "Looking to Jesus … who for the sake of the joy that was set before him endured the cross" (NRSV). Here, "for the sake of" means "in order to obtain." That is, Jesus was motivated to endure the cross and its shame by the joy that would be his in seeing the outcome of his patient suffering.

Such translations are certainly legitimate, but they face the difficulty that the preposition rendered "for the sake of" is *anti*, which normally indicates an exchange in which A is replaced by B—so that the word regularly means "instead of" or "in place of." On this view, Jesus chose to endure the cross and scorn its shame *instead of* having the joy of continued fellowship with God in heaven, a privilege that lay before him as a distinct possibility.

Several considerations support this view.

- In almost all NT cases where *anti* stands alone as a preposition, it expresses or points to a substitutionary exchange.

- The two major NT dictionaries give the meaning of "instead of" for *anti* in Hebrews 12:2.

- Elsewhere in Hebrews (6:18; 12:1), the verb "set before" refers to a present reality, not some future gain.

- It would seem inappropriate for Jesus' primary motive for enduring suffering to be personal advantage or future reward.

- The idea of giving up personal rights for the sake of others is a common NT theme (see, e.g., Mark 8:35; Rom 15:1–3; 2 Cor 8:9).

All this means that in Hebrews 12:2, the NRSV marginal rendering is to be preferred: "Looking to Jesus ... who instead of the joy set before him endured the cross."

JAMES

56: "NOT BY FAITH ALONE"?
(Jas 2:24)

From the vigorous theological discussions and disputes of the sixteenth and seventeenth centuries, Protestantism has identified five areas where there should be no ambiguity or uncertainty about the definitive means of salvation at all its stages. These are the five "alones" (or *solas* or *solae*, as they are usually called). The first three are expressed by the Latin ablative case, denoting means ("by"):

1. *Sola Scriptura*, "by Scripture alone," rather than church tradition or creed or teaching.

2. *Sola fide*, "by faith alone," rather than good works.

3. *Sola gratia*, "by grace alone," rather than human merit.

4. *Solus Christus*, "Christ alone," rather than any other mediator or mediatrix.

5. *Soli deo gloria*, "glory belongs to God alone," rather than to any human or angelic recipient.

Here we focus on the second one, "By faith alone." After all, did not Paul say, "We maintain that a person is justified by faith apart from the works of the law" (Rom 3:28)? But on the other hand, did not James say, "You see that a person is considered righteous by what they do and not by faith alone" (Jas 2:24)?

How are we to explain the seeming contradiction between these two writers on this crucial issue? A probable solution lies in two directions. First, the two writers are addressing *different situations*. James is responding to some Christians who mistakenly believed that good deeds were irrelevant to justification before God; they may have distorted Paul's teaching on the relation of faith and works. So James understandably insists that "faith by itself, if it is not accompanied by action, is dead" (2:17). Paul, on the other hand, is reacting to those people, whether fellow Jews or Gentiles, who imagined that following certain religious practices such as circumcision or Sabbath-keeping guaranteed a right standing before God (Gal 5:4). Accordingly, he rejects "a righteousness of my own that comes from the law," but embraces "that which is through faith in Christ—the righteousness that comes from God on the basis of faith" (Phil 3:9).

Second, the two writers were using the key terms, "faith" and "works/deeds," in *different senses*. For James, "faith" could refer to belief in the traditional sense (e.g., Jas 1:6; 2:1, 5). However, in the crucial passage, James 2:14–26, it denotes deedless or incomplete faith (2:14, 22) or mere intellectual assent to truth (2:18), while "deeds" or "actions" are evidence of genuine faith (2:18b): deeds such as relief for the poor (Jas 2:1–7) or caring for others' physical needs (Jas 2:14–16). When James asks, "Can faith save?" (2:14b), the sense is clearly, "Can *such* faith save you?" The definite article with "faith" here—*hē pistis*—is anaphoric, referring back to the deedless faith of 2:14a (see also chapter 4). For Paul, however, "faith" was always a personal trust in and commitment to God or Christ that was expressed in good deeds (Gal 5:6). Reliance on doing "the works of the law" as a way of gaining righteousness actually placed people under a curse (Gal 3:10). "A person is not justified by the works of the law, but by faith in Jesus Christ" (Gal 2:16). Nowhere does Paul express the relation between faith and works more clearly than in Ephesians 2:8–10:

> For by grace you have been saved through faith, and this is not your own doing; it is the gift of God—not the result of works, so that no one can boast. For we are God's workmanship,

created in Christ Jesus to do good works, which God prepared in advance to be our way of life.

We conclude that Paul agrees with James in believing that genuine faith is naturally and always expressed in good works—that faith and works are inseparable. "For those in Christ Jesus, neither circumcision nor uncircumcision has any value. The only thing that counts is *faith expressing itself through love*" (Gal 5:6). Elsewhere, Paul gives thanks to God as he recalls the Thessalonians' "action stemming from faith" (1 Thess 1:3), and he encourages the Philippians to "work out" or visibly demonstrate their salvation (Phil 2:12).

Another consideration perhaps justifies our effort to harmonize the views of James and Paul regarding the relationship of saving faith and good works. If we consider basic psychological and literary principles, it is unlikely that the early church would have included the book of James within their list of approved and recognized books if they thought it contradicted the repeated teaching in the multiple books by the apostle Paul on this basic issue. So the very existence of the book of James in the NT canon is an argument for the compatibility of these two authors' views.

1 PETER

57: GLORY FOLLOWS SUFFERING
(1 Pet 1:11)

In 1 Peter 1:10–12, Peter is describing the "salvation" (1:5, 9–10) accomplished by Christ, a salvation that was revealed to OT prophets and preached by NT evangelists:

> Concerning this salvation, the prophets, who prophesied about the grace destined for you, searched intently and with the greatest care. They tried to discover the time and the circumstances to which the Spirit of Christ within them was pointing when he predicted the sufferings destined for Christ and the splendors that would follow. (1 Pet 1:10–11)

There is clear parallelism between "the sufferings destined for (*eis*) Christ" and "the grace destined for (*eis*) you." In each case the preposition *eis* means "intended/destined for" and depicts destinies ordained by God. Moreover, the two expressions are related as cause and effect: Grace was destined for believers precisely because sufferings were destined for Christ. Here "grace" (*charis*) denotes the blessings or benefits of God's beneficence and is virtually equivalent to the preceding term "salvation" (*sōtēria*).

In two of the cases where the plural of *doxa* ("glory") is used in the NT, the term means "majestic beings" or "illustrious persons" (2 Pet 2:10; Jude 8). Here, in the third use, the sense is "splendors," referring to the "glorious events" or "spectacular results" that followed the sufferings divinely intended for Christ. Peter has in mind concrete instances of *doxa*, as is shown by the use of the definite article (*tas*) and the plural (*doxas*). These multiple consequences of Christ's sufferings will include his resurrection (1 Pet 1:3, 18, 21; 3:18, 21); his resurrection appearances (Jesus "presented himself alive after his suffering," Acts 1:3); his ascension, session, and universal lordship (1 Pet 3:22); and his second advent (1 Pet 1:7, 13; 5:1,4).

These three verses (1 Pet 1:10-12) point to the continuity between the Old and New Testament eras (see also part 2, ch. 52). What the OT prophets predicted and what NT evangelists proclaimed were identical — the sufferings destined for Christ and the glorious events that followed as a result. This is the golden linguistic thread that runs through verses 11 and 12 (note "the very things that have now been told you. ... Even angels long to investigate these things").

Another constant NT theme is illustrated in these verses. Glory follows suffering, or (expressed in an aphorism) "no cross, no crown." What was true in the experience of Jesus—spectacular results follow suffering—is also true in the lives of believers.

- "This inheritance is kept in heaven for you, who are being shielded by God's power through faith until the coming of the salvation that is ready to be revealed in the last time. In this you greatly rejoice, even if now for a little while you have had to suffer grief in various trials" (1 Pet 1 :4b-6).

- "Dear friends, do not be surprised at the fiery ordeal that is taking place among you to test you, as though something strange were happening to you. But rejoice inasmuch as you are sharing Christ's sufferings, so that you may rejoice and shout for joy when his glory is revealed" (1 Pet 4:12-13).

- "I consider that the sufferings of this present time are not worth comparing with the glory that will be revealed to us" (Rom 8:18).

- "If we endure, we will also reign with him" (2 Tim 2:12a).

58: JESUS AS SHEPHERD
(1 Pet 5:4)

It is a fascinating fact that in the three NT passages where Jesus is described as a shepherd, we find three different adjectival qualifiers and a reference to the three main events in his shepherding.

1. His death (John 10:11, 14). He is the *good* (*kalos*) shepherd. Jesus' goodness or nobility as *the* shepherd is seen in multiple ways: First, unlike "the worthless shepherd, who deserts the flock" (Zech 11:17), Jesus not only risks his life for his sheep but actually surrenders it in death (John 10:11, 15b, 17a, 18a). In doing so, he acts "for" (*hyper*) his sheep, where this preposition expresses both benefit ("for the sake of") and substitution ("in the place of").

- He protects his sheep from danger, whereas "the hired hand," seeing danger, abandons the sheep and runs away (John 10:12–13).

- He cares deeply for his sheep, whereas "the hired hand" cares nothing for the sheep (John 10:13).

- He knows his sheep intimately as his own possession, and his sheep know him intimately (John 10:14).

- He has other sheep (= Gentiles) who also will heed his voice, so they (Jews and Gentiles) will form a single flock with a single shepherd (John 10:16).

2. His resurrection (Heb 13:20). He is the *great* (*megas*) shepherd. Jesus' greatness as *the* shepherd is evident after his death. Not only did he surrender his life for his sheep; he came back to life as their forerunner into heaven. This magnificent resurrection was the work of "the God of peace," the author and giver of peace, and involved his bringing Jesus up and back from the realm of the dead. Only here and in Romans 10:7 is the verb *anagō* ("bring up/back") used of Jesus' resurrection. The picture may be of Jesus' coming *up* from the subterranean realm of the dead, or coming *back* into the realm of the living from the realm of the departed.

3. *His parousia (1 Pet 5:4).* He is the *chief (archi-)* shepherd. Twice in 1 Peter, Jesus is depicted as a shepherd. From 2:25 we learn that in his role as shepherd Jesus welcomes home the sheep that have wandered off and then supervises their well-being as their Overseer and Guardian (*episkopos*). In 5:4 he is not simply one of many shepherds of the flock of believers (vv. 1–3), but is the principal shepherd, or prince of pastors, to whom all undershepherds are ultimately accountable. As a generous chief shepherd, he will at his return (the parousia) reward all faithful undershepherds with a glorious crown that, unlike the winner's wreath in an athletic contest, will never lose its luster. This crown is the Christian's "inheritance that can never perish, spoil, or fade" (1:4).

2 PETER

59: SHARING THE DIVINE NATURE
(2 Pet 1:4)

At both the beginning (1:2–3, 8) and end (3:18) of his second letter, Peter draws his readers' attention to their need to advance in the knowledge of Jesus Christ. This is the primary protection he offers them against the specious arguments and ethical libertinism of the false teachers who were harassing them (2:1–22). They were to "make every effort" (1:5, 10; 3:14) to pursue a godly life (1:3), knowing the reality of the Christian hope (1:4), the expectation of a lavish welcome into the eternal kingdom of Jesus Christ (1:11): "Through these (God's glory and goodness) he has given us his magnificent and precious promises, so that through them you may become sharers in the divine nature, having escaped the corruption that is in the world because of sinful desire" (2 Pet 1:4).

Two questions arise from this verse, which has figured so prominently in the theological discussion of "deification" or "divinization."

1. What is involved in Christians' sharing in the divine nature? A distinction must be drawn between inherent participation in the divine essence, a function reserved for the three persons of the Trinity, and an unmediated participation in the very life of God, a sharing in his absolute immortality. This "sharing in the divine nature" is not an intrinsic characteristic of humans or even an acquired characteristic of believers. It is a contingent and derived immortality, a gracious gift of the divine will (cf. Rom 2:7; 6:23), involving, as God's immortality does, inviolable holiness and so freedom from all decay and death (God "alone has immortality and dwells in unapproachable light,"

1 Tim 6:16). Just as resurrected persons can be described as "like the angels" because "they can no longer die" (Luke 20:36), so also those who can be described as "participants in the divine nature" are "like God" in having become immortal but without in any sense sharing in the divine essence.

2. When does this participation in the divine nature occur? That this is a future experience for Christians seems likely for several reasons.

- "Through them" (1:4) refers back to the immediate antecedent, "promises" (*epangelmata*). These promises are about the second advent of Christ (2 Pet 3:4, 9, *epangelia* in both cases), the future day of the Lord (2 Pet 3:10), and the future day of God (3:12–13; *epangelma* in v. 13).

- The Christian hope can certainly confirm and strengthen faith and love (Col 1:4–5), and the future expectation of seeing Christ can prompt present holiness (1 John 3:2–3). But it is difficult to see how promises have the intrinsic power to enable participation in the divine nature. "Through them" must therefore mean "through these promises, when fulfilled," or "after seeing the fulfillment of these promises."

- "Escape from the corruption that is in the world" precedes the participation ("having escaped" is an aorist participle). But neither conversion nor Christian experience could produce such a dramatic and total escape, so the participation must lie in the future, beyond death.

All this means that what Christians eagerly anticipate is not total absorption into the divine being, with the consequent loss of personal identity, but direct participation in God's infinite life and holiness (cf. Col 1:22). We will enter into eternal union with God, with a consequent enhancement of individual identity; or as Paul would express it, we will permanently bear the image of the heavenly man, the exalted Christ Jesus (1 Cor 15:49). See also part 2, ch. 20.

60: DEATH AS DEPARTURE AND ARRIVAL
(2 Pet 1:11, 14–15)

Anyone visiting an airport is soon confronted by a large noticeboard that announces departures and arrivals. In the NT, the metaphor of traveling from one place to another is used to describe the nature of physical death for the Christian.

1. Departure. To fill out the general idea of death as "movement from one geographical area to another" (*exodos*, Luke 9:31; Heb 11:22; 2 Pet 1:15), Paul uses three picturesque metaphors.

First, death can be regarded as the weighing of anchor. As Paul wrestles with the options of death by martyrdom and continuance of service among the Philippians, he confesses, "I am torn between the two: I desire to *depart* and be with Christ, which is better by far, but ... " (Phil 1:23). The verb here is *analuō*, "loosen up (for departure)," used of horses and ships (also in 2 Tim 4:6). Paul is contemplating the possibility of having his bark "weigh anchor."

Second, death can be seen as the dismantling of a tent. "If our earthly tent-dwelling is *destroyed*, we have a building from God" (2 Cor 5:1). Here the verb is *kataluō*, "demolish," used elsewhere of the detachment of stones from buildings (Matt 24:2). But Paul the tentmaker (Acts 18:2–3) is here speaking of his mortal body as (literally) "our earthly house that is a tent," a tent that could at any time be dismantled.

Third, death can be viewed as leaving a residence. Aware of the frustrations of being "at home in the body" and so "away from the Lord" (2 Cor 5:4, 6), Paul expresses his preference to end his temporary exile from the Lord, to *"leave the body* and take up residence with the Lord" (2 Cor 5:8). In this case, the verb is *ekdēmeō*, "leave one's home," used elsewhere of departing from one's country.

2. Arrival. The opposite of *exodos*, "departure," is *eisodos*, "entry," the act of arriving at a destination. A departure implies a destination as well as an evacuation, a "to" as well as a "from." In 2 Peter 1:10–11, Peter affirms that if his readers "make every effort" to confirm their calling and election, they will never stumble and will be richly provided with an *entry* (*eisodos*) into the eternal kingdom of our Lord and Savior Jesus Christ. We saw above that it was Paul's preference to "leave the body and *take up residence* with the Lord" (2 Cor 5:8). The verb used here (in the aorist tense) is *endēmeō*, "be at home." He wanted to "go home," to arrive in the presence of his Master (see also part 1, ch. 28; and part 2, ch. 17).

Paul's train of thought in 2 Corinthians 5:6–8 makes it clear that the moment of departure is also the moment of arrival. To be at home in the body is, at the same time, to be absent from the Lord (v. 6). Similarly, to depart from the body is, at the same time, to arrive in the Lord's presence (v. 8). There is no interval separating departure and arrival.

1 JOHN

61: NO SINLESS PERFECTION — YET!
(1 John 2:1; 3:6, 9; 5:18)

It is a fundamental principle when evaluating texts, whether they be secular or religious, that the writers will not knowingly contradict themselves. We should always assume that they are free of contradictions—they are innocent until proven guilty.

How, then, are we to harmonize the following apparently conflicting statements of the apostle John in one of his letters (in the NRSV)?

- "My little children, I am writing these things to you *so that you may not sin*. But *if anyone does sin*, we have an advocate with the Father, Jesus Christ the righteous" (1 John 2:1).

- "*No one who abides in him sins*; *no one who sins* has either seen him or known him. ... *Those who have been born of God do not sin*, because God's seed abides in them; *they cannot sin*, because they have been born of God" (1 John 3:6, 9).

- "We know that *those born of God do not sin*" (1 John 5:18).

In each case, the same verb is used—*hamartanō*, "commit a sin"—although in 3:9a an equivalent phrase is found (*hamartian poieō*, "commit a sin"). So the solution to the apparent discrepancy does not lie in the verbs used.

The answer does lie, however, in the Greek tenses used. In 2:1, we twice find the Greek aorist tense (*hamartēte ... hamartē*) that here refers to a single action, not repeated action. "My dear children, I am writing this to you *so that you will avoid sinning. But if anyone does commit a sin,* we have an advocate with the Father, Jesus Christ, the Righteous One." Sinning is recognized to be a possibility, although it should always be avoided. But in the event that sin is committed, despair must not ensue, for situated in the Father's immediate presence we have a "friend at court," Jesus Christ, who himself is without sin, as he has always been. Of him John had earlier written, "If we confess our sins, he is faithful and just and will forgive us our sins and purify us from all unrighteousness" (1 John 1:9). Significantly, the plural "sins" is used in each case, implying that committing sins is a possibility for believers.

In the other four examples, the Greek present tense is employed, here indicating action that is repeated. The NIV has caught the significance of these present tenses:

- "No one who lives in him *keeps on sinning.* No one who *continues to sin* has either seen him or known him. ... No one who is born of God *will continue to sin*, because God's seed remains in them; *they cannot go on sinning*, because they have been born of God" (1 John 3:6, 9).

- "We know that anyone born of God *does not continue to sin*" (1 John 5:18).

Even if believers do not reach sinless perfection during the present life, a time is coming when sin will be totally and permanently foreign to our experience, as we worship and serve God (Rev 4:11; 5:10; 22:3) in the perfection of the consummated city of God, where "nothing impure will ever enter" (Rev 21:27).

62: NO TEACHERS NEEDED?
(1 John 2:27)

Of crucial importance for the right understanding of this strange verse is the preceding sentence: "I am writing these things to you about those who are trying to lead you astray" (1 John 2:26). Then he goes on: "But as for you, the anointing you received from him remains in you, and so you do not need anyone to teach you. Rather, since his anointing teaches you about everything, and since that anointing is real and not counterfeit, keep in union with him, just as it taught you."

In verse 27, John develops themes already stated in verses 20 and 24, namely, that as recipients of the anointing given by the Holy One, all Christians know the truth (v. 20); and that the original Christian truth they once heard and embraced must remain the regulative standard for their belief (v. 24). This is apparently against the counterfeit claims of the secessionists (cf. 1 John 2:19) that they have fresh truth for the initiated.

Given the references in the Fourth Gospel to the Holy Spirit as (1) the Paraclete sent by Christ (John 15:26), and (2) the one who will guide believers to all the truth (John 16:13) and teach them all things (John 14:26), it is likely that the "anointing" (*to chrisma*) in 1 John 2:27 is the gift of the Spirit as the depository of Christian truth, the true gospel. Regarding this "anointing," John makes several affirmations:

- It is given by Christ ("from him ... his anointing"; cf. 2:20).

- Received at conversion, it now permanently remains within believers ("remains in you," cf. John 14:17).

- It affords instruction about everything (cf. John 14:16), not all that can be known but all that needs to be known. This instruction is *comprehensive*, is never superseded, and does not need supplementation; it is *real*, not counterfeit or illusory; and it is *traditional* ("as it taught you"), not of recent origin. Anything at variance with orthodox tradition is not true.

- Receipt of the "anointing" calls for a practical response: "Keep in union with Christ" (cf. John 15:4–7).

When John rejects the need for new teachers, he is alluding to those who were trying to mislead his readers (1 John 2:26). He is not, of course, denigrating authoritative teaching within the church (cf. Matt 28:20; Rom 12:7; 1 Cor 12:28–29; 1 Tim 4:11). Similarly, when he affirms that the "anointing" provided by Christ instructs believers "about everything," he is not rejecting the ability of all human teachers to communicate knowledge in general or of Christian knowledge in particular; what "everything" refers to is clearly restricted by the context. By it he means "everything" that prevents someone from being led astray from the truth (1 John 2:26); or, to express the point positively and to borrow a phrase from Peter, "everything that promotes true life and godliness" (2 Pet 1:3).

63: "A SIN THAT LEADS TO DEATH"
(1 John 5:16–17)

As we consider the meaning of this enigmatic phrase, unique in the NT, we must remember that the short paragraph 1 John 5:16–17 is not primarily about two types of sin—one that leads to death and one that does not—but about prayer, and in particular which prayer requests are praiseworthy and which are unnecessary:

> If anyone sees his brother or sister committing a sin that does not lead to death, you should pray and God will give them life. This relates only to those whose sinning does not lead to death. There is, however, a sin that leads to death. I do not suggest you should make a request about that. Every wrong action is sin, and there is a sin that does not lead to death.

Several specific issues deserve clarification before the overall sense is summarized.

1. The two verbal references to sinning in verse 16 ("committing a sin ... sinning") are in the present tense, pointing to repeated or perpetual sin—sin that was observable ("If anyone sees ...").

2. A sin "to death" (*pros thanaton*) and a sin "not to death" (*mē/ou pros thanaton*) are rightly rendered by almost all EVV as "that leads to death" and "that does not lead to death" (cf. John 11:4). This is the consecutive use of the preposition *pros* ("resulting in").

3. The prayer recommended ("you should pray") is presumably a request for the repentance of the sinning fellow believer.

4. The "life" given in answer to prayer and as a response to repentance will be ongoing physical life and revitalized spiritual life. The "death" that can result from sin could be exclusion from the Christian community (= excommunication; cf. Num 15:30–31), but it is better understood as physical death, regarded as a penalty administered by God (as in 1 Cor 11:30–32; cf. Acts 5:1–10).

As for the "sin that leads to death," it could be the open and deliberate rejection of Christ, involving the denial of his incarnation or messiahship (1 John 2:22; 4:2–3; 2 John 7) and the promulgation of heresy (1 John 2:18–27); or blasphemy against the Holy Spirit, the deliberate rejection of known truth, so that repentance is never sought (see part 1, ch. 15); or deliberate sin (cf. Heb 10:26–31), sin performed "defiantly" (Num 15:30–31).

In 1 John 5:16–17, the apostle is applying his general statements about prayer requests made in accordance with God's will (vv. 14–15) to a specific case involving intercession for a brother or sister who persists in a particular (unnamed) sin. If this observable continuing sin has not led to physical death, intercessory prayer for the sinner's repentance accords with God's will, and in response God will grant such a repentant person the boon of further physical life and renewed spiritual life. But if divine judgment has already fallen on this person in the form of physical death, requests relating to that situation are unnecessary; prayer for the dead would be contrary to God's will.

JUDE

64: AN UNPARALLELED DOXOLOGY
(Jude 25)

A doxology is a brief ascription of praise to God or Christ. In the NT, doxologies normally include four elements. First, the recipient is usually indicated by the dative case: "to him ..." (e.g., Rom 11:36) or "to the only wise God ..." (Rom 16:27). But sometimes the recipient stands in the nominative ("Blessed be the God and Father of our Lord Jesus Christ," 2 Cor 1:3) or a relative clause follows the named recipient ("the Creator, who is forever praised," Rom 1:25). Second, the nature of the praise offered is then stated—often "glory" (*doxa*, Gal 1:5), but sometimes "honor" (*timē*, 1 Tim 1:17) or "sovereignty" (*kratos*, 1 Tim 6:16). Third, some temporal indicator is given: "forever" (1 Pet 5:11) or "forever and ever" (2 Tim 4:18; on these expressions, see part 2, ch. 53). Fourth, the word "amen" (*amēn*) often ends a doxology, indicating wholehearted agreement with the sentiments or truths expressed ("Indeed, it is so") or the ardent desire that the wishes expressed be fulfilled ("May it be so").

Jude 25 includes these four elements: "To the only God, our Savior, be glory, majesty, power, and authority, through Jesus Christ our Lord, before all time, and now, and forever and ever. Amen." To avoid the conceptually awkward "be glory ... before all time," we could render the doxology: "To the only God, our Savior, be ascribed through Jesus Christ our Lord, glory, majesty, power, and authority, as it was before all time, is now, and shall be forever and ever."

This doxology is unique in three respects. First, Jude's inclusion of past, present, and future is unique among Jewish and early Christian doxologies, although threefold temporal descriptions of Christ (Heb 13:8) and God (Rev 1:4; 4:8) are found outside doxologies.

1. "Before all time" (*pro pantos tou aiōnos*) could also be rendered "before time began," that is, in eternity past.

2. *Eis pantas tous aiōnas*, literally "to all the ages," can be translated "forever and ever" or "to all eternity."

Second, Jude's doxology includes more items for praise than any other NT letter writer: "glory, majesty, power, authority" (but cf. Rev 5:13; 7:12).

Third, Jude's affirmation of the eternal mediatorial role of Jesus Christ in ascribing this fourfold praise to God is without parallel. This implies Christ's preexistence and his deity.

REVELATION

65: COMMENDABLE INTOLERANCE
(Rev 2:20)

We live in an age where tolerance is the watchword—tolerance of every viewpoint and any lifestyle. In support of this approach to life, appeal is sometimes (wrongly) made to Jesus' words in Matthew 7:1: "Do not judge, or you too will be judged."

But in his message to the Christians in Thyatira, the risen Jesus condemns the misguided tolerance of some of the believers there. In spite of their love shown in service, and faithfulness shown in patient endurance—evidence of genuine spiritual progress—he says, "I have this against you: you tolerate that woman Jezebel, who calls herself a prophet" (Rev 2:20a). He proceeds to give reasons why this ongoing toleration on the part of some (see v. 24) is reprehensible. First, Jezebel was misleading some believers (Jezebel's "children," v. 23) who embraced her teaching that sexual immorality and association with idolatry were permissible (v. 20b). Second, she was apparently encouraging initiation into "Satan's so-called deep secrets" (v. 24), special inside information reserved for the initiated.

We do not know whether Jezebel was her real name or simply an appropriate name for the woman's resolute refusal to repent of her sexual immorality or (possibly) spiritual adultery (see v. 21). The Jezebel of OT infamy was the Phoenician wife of Israel's king Ahab who encouraged the idolatrous worship of Baal and witchcraft (1 Kgs 16:31–33; 18:19; 2 Kgs 9:22). The imminent danger at Thyatira was that this woman's erroneous teaching would infect still others in the church.

Yet the risen Lord focuses not on the teaching itself but on her unwillingness to change her teaching and her ways (Rev 2:21). As a result of her blatant refusal to repent, Christ would hurl her onto a bed of suffering, and would cause her offspring to suffer intensely unless they turned from following her (vv. 22, 23a). Christ instructs the enlightened minority at Thyatira who rejected Jezebel to persist in their rejection and maintain their loyalty to Christ ("Hold on to what you have until I come," v. 25). This would be commendable intolerance!

So then, there is a place for the relentless intolerance of evil teaching and evil practice—teaching and practice that does not accord with Scripture. Paul, too, shared this praiseworthy intolerance. When he heard that a man within the Corinthian church was having sexual relations with his widowed stepmother (1 Cor 5:1), he directed the church to meet and hand this person over to Satan "for the destruction of the flesh" (1 Cor 5:4–5) and to expel him from their congregation (1 Cor 5:13). The same Paul exhorted the believers in Rome to keep well away from teachers who deviated from apostolic teaching, using smooth talk and flattery to deceive the minds of naive believers (Rom 16:17–18). Such teachers are under a divine curse (Gal 1:9).

66: THE CENTRALITY OF THE LAMB IN HEAVEN (Rev 7:17)

Precisely where in heaven is Jesus the Lamb of God located? It is a fascinating detective exercise to try to plot the position of heavenly beings in relation to the central throne, using the various hints in the book of Revelation.

The first thing to observe is that while there is only one divine throne, there are two occupants—the Lord God and the Lamb (Rev 3:21; 22:1, 3)—who are both worshipped (Rev 5:13). How various beings are related to this throne is expressed by:

- prepositions (*enōpion*, "in front of," eleven times; *kyklothen*, "around," "encircling," two times)

- an adverb (*kyklō*, "in a circle," "all around," three times)

- prepositional phrases (*en mesō*, "in the middle of," "among," two times; *ana meson*, "in the center," "at the center," one time)

In the topography of heaven, then, there would seem to be three concentric circles of beings around the throne: an outer circle of a myriad of angels who "encircled the throne" (Rev 5:11); an intermediate circle of elders who "encircled" the throne (Rev 5:6); and an inner circle of four living creatures "around the throne" (Rev 4:6).

In addition, two passages are relevant as we consider the precise position of the Lamb. First, Revelation 5:6 has him standing "in the middle of the throne," which probably means "in close proximity to the throne" or "immediately adjacent to the throne" (as in Rev 4:6). But Revelation 7:17, on the other hand, speaks of the Lamb "who is at the center of the throne," reflecting the single use in Revelation of the prepositional phrase *ana meson*. If this verse points to his essential position, there are also hints that he is not stationary: "He went and took the scroll" (Rev 5:7); "He will shepherd them and will lead them to springs of living water" (Rev 7:17).

Whereas other beings surround the throne in varying degrees of proximity, the risen Jesus as the Lamb not only shares the throne equally with the Lord God Almighty but also occupies its very center. To judge by frequency of usage, the two focal points in the book of Revelation are "the throne" (forty-one times) and "the One who sits on the throne" (eleven times). But at that throne's center is the Lamb, who is one with God the Father in his being and status.

SOURCES OF SCRIPTURE QUOTATIONS

Unless otherwise noted, Scripture quotations are the author's translation.

Scripture quotations marked (Barclay) are from *The New Testament: A New Translation* (London: Collins, 1968–1969).

Scripture quotations marked (Cassirer) are from *God's New Covenant: A New Testament Translation* (Grand Rapids: Eerdmans, 1989).

Scripture quotations marked (CSB) are from the Christian Standard Bible®, copyright © 2017 by Holman Bible Publishers. Used by permission. Christian Standard Bible® and CSB® are federally registered trademarks of Holman Bible Publishers.

Scripture quotations marked (ESV) are from *ESV® Bible (The Holy Bible, English Standard Version®)*, copyright © 2001 by Crossway Bibles, a publishing ministry of Good News Publishers. Used by permission. All rights reserved.

Scripture quotations marked (GNT) are from the Good News Translation in Today's English Version—Second Edition Copyright © 1992 by American Bible Society. Used by Permission.

Scripture quotations marked (Goodspeed) are from *THE BIBLE, American Translation*, copyright © 1931 The University of Chicago Press.

Scripture quotations marked (HCSB) are from the Holman Christian Standard Bible®, Copyright © 1999, 2000, 2002, 2003, 2009 by Holman Bible Publishers. Used by permission. Holman Christian Standard Bible®, Holman CSB®, and HCSB® are federally registered trademarks of Holman Bible Publishers.

Scripture quotations marked (JB) are from The Jerusalem Bible, published and copyright © 1966, 1967 and 1968 by Darton, Longman & Todd Ltd and Doubleday, a division of Random House, Inc.

Scripture quotations marked (KJV) are from the King James Version. Public domain.

Scripture quotations marked (Moffatt) are from *The Bible: James Moffatt Translation* by James A. R. Moffatt. Copyright © 1950, 1952, 1953, 1954, by James A. R. Moffatt.

Scripture quotations marked (NAB) are from the New American Bible, revised edition, copyright © 2010, 1991, 1986, 1970 by the Confraternity of Christian Doctrine, Washington, DC, and is used by permission of the copyright owner. All rights reserved.

Scripture quotations marked (NASB) are from the New American Standard Bible®, copyright 1960, 1962, 1963, 1968, 1971, 1972, 1973, 1975, 1977, 1995 by The Lockman Foundation. Used by permission.

Scripture quotations marked (NEB) are from the New English Bible, © 1961, 1970 by the Delegates of the Oxford University Press and the Syndics of the Cambridge University Press. Reprinted by permission.

WHAT THE BIBLE REALLY SAYS
ABOUT GOD'S HEAVENLY HOST

ANGELS

MICHAEL S. HEISER

WHAT DOES THE BIBLE REALLY TELL US ABOUT THE HEAVENLY HOST?

Everyone knows that angels have wings, usually carry harps, and that each of us has our own personal guardian angel, right? What the Bible really says about angels is overlooked or filtered through popular myths. In his latest book, *Angels*, Dr. Michael Heiser reveals what the Bible really says about God's supernatural servants. *Angels* is not guided by traditions, stories, speculations, or myths about angels. Heiser's study is grounded in the terms the Bible itself uses to describe members of God's heavenly host; he examines the terms in their biblical context while drawing on insights from the wider context of the ancient Near Eastern world.

—

LexhamPress.com/Angels

PASTORS CARE FOR A SOUL IN THE WAY A DOCTOR CARES FOR A BODY.

In a time when many churches have lost sight of the real purpose of the church, *The Care of Souls* invites a new generation of pastors to form the godly habits and practical wisdom needed to minister to the hearts and souls of those committed to their care.

"Pastoral theology at its best. Every pastor, and everyone who wants to be a pastor, should read this book."
—Timothy George, Founding Dean, Beeson Divinity School, Samford University; General Editor, Reformation Commentary on Scripture

LEXHAM PRESS

For more information, visit
LexhamPress.com/Care-of-Souls